Boris Morros was a successful Hollywood
producer and a highly regarded musician
and impresario. His life had been a legen-
dary success story even in the flamboyant
annals of show business.

What chain of events in 1936 led him into
serving the interests of a Soviet spy ring?

What *even more* dramatic events brought
him into the office of the FBI in 1947 to
take on the role of a United States counterspy?

How did Morros manage to deceive Communist agents and help provide the evidence which resulted in the exposure and
conviction of the leaders of the spy ring?

This book, for the first time, unfolds the
entire drama of the ten-year ordeal of
Boris Morros.

My Ten Years
As a Counterspy

BY BORIS MORROS

as told to Charles Samuels

A DELL BOOK

Published by
DELL PUBLISHING CO., INC.
750 Third Avenue
New York 17, N.Y.

Reprinted by arrangement with
The Viking Press, Inc.
New York, N.Y.

Designed and produced by
Western Printing & Lithographing Company

TO MARION

First Dell printing—November, 1959

Printed in U.S.A.

By Way of Explanation

The publication of this book is one of the most important events of my life. In February 1957, the United States Justice Department revealed for the first time that for ten years, while posing as a Russian espionage agent, I had actually been working as a counterspy for the FBI. Since that time I have been repeatedly denounced by a certain section of the American press as everything from a twenty-three-karat phony to a traitor.

I wish to emphasize that these attacks appeared in a very small part of the press. For the most part the newspapers in this, my adopted country, hailed me as a man who for years had been the victim of unjust suspicions on the part of his former Hollywood friends and business associates.

Paul W. Williams, then United States Attorney for the Southern District of New York, was so distressed by some of the published attacks on my character that he pronounced me "a loyal citizen who acted at all times for the interests of the United States government." Mr. Williams, with his aide, Thomas B. Gilchrist, Jr., had by that time prepared the government's case against Jack Soble, the head of the Russian spy ring I helped the FBI break up, as well as the cases against Soble's wife, Myra, and Jacob Albam. They, together with other Justice Department officials, had gone over the evidence I had gathered against this trio, and the other men and women subsequently indicted for espionage, with a fine-toothed comb.

It seems to me that the words of the United States Attorney, who was in a better position to appraise fairly and approve (or disapprove) of my services in helping to wreck a vicious spy ring, should have stilled my critics. But the words of Prosecutor Williams only seemed to increase the number of violent attacks on me.

As any man would, I now welcome the opportunity to tell to my fellow Americans the complete inside story of my weird adventures as a Russian spy and an American counterspy. Let those who read this book constitute themselves judge and jury of my actions and of my character. In these pages they will be able to see what my life was like when I was hounded by the Communists and was at the same time hunting them under instructions by the FBI.

I have never been a traitor. If I did wrong, in the years before I offered my services to the United States government, I did it unthinkingly. For whatever mistakes I made I have atoned in full measure.

Every word I have set down in this book about the fabulous experiences and the danger I survived as a double spy is true. The results of that work most people know. The Sobles and Albam pleaded guilty and are today in federal prison. Martha Dodd Stern and Alfred K. Stern, rather than face a jury on the espionage charges for which they were indicted in New York, fled behind the Iron Curtain. Jane Foster Zlatovski and her husband, George, preferred to remain in Paris rather than come home and clear themselves of the charge that they had betrayed their country.

But the full results of my work as an FBI counterspy may not be revealed for years to come. For Soble, his wife, and Albam have much still to tell the Justice Department. A whole string of arrests may come if they reveal the whole ghastly story of the plotting of Soviet secret agents against the security of the United States of America.

CHAPTER 1

The Day the FBI Started Asking Questions

In view of all the globe-trotting I have done, it is ironic indeed that the most memorable and hair-raising journey of my life should have been one of less than a dozen miles. It began at my Hollywood film studio and ended at the Los Angeles office of the Federal Bureau of Investigation.

The day I finally decided to call the FBI was July 14, 1947, Bastille Day, that great day for freedom in France and throughout the world. I tried to draw some comfort out of the idea that the coincidence would prove a good omen and bring me freedom from worry and guilt. That is what I *hoped*. What I knew was that I could no longer go on tormenting myself for even another day. I just had to know, no matter what the consequences. But even after I told myself that, I spent half an hour or so in my office staring moodily at the phone.

Before I found the courage to pick it up, I had to remind myself that it was America I was living in. And that in America there was always a good chance that the authorities would give you consideration if you helped them, told everything you knew.

Perspiring, I reached for the phone and called the FBI.

"I am Boris Morros, the Hollywood film producer," I told the man who answered. "I would very much like to talk to some important person in your organization."

"Come right down, Mr. Morros," he said, and gave me a name. "I will be waiting for you." He sounded like a young man, and his voice was pleasant enough.

Pleasant, though, was not quite the right word. He was casual.

Tell all? I wanted to, with all my heart. I had no intention whatever of denying that I had been rash and foolish enough to get tangled up with a spy ring. I had my chauffeur bring my car to the door of my studio and instructed him to take me to downtown Los Angeles. It seemed ironic that this ride of less than a dozen miles should suddenly seem the most important I had ever taken.

But the irony occurred to me only later on. I was glad that it was my chauffeur, not I, who was driving. For that day I had arrived at a state bordering on mental chaos. The truth is that I had not the slightest idea of whether I was headed for freedom or prison.

Then an extraordinary thing happened. In the midst of all my terror and bewilderment, my mind somersaulted back down the years, back to a beautiful legend I had heard, or perhaps read, as a little boy in St. Petersburg.

In this (as I remembered it after more than forty years), a Russian priest was traveling down the Volga River when the steamer he was on broke down. The name of the river town where the little vessel put in for repairs reminded the priest that a monastery, of which he had heard very strange stories, was in the vicinity.

When the captain assured him it would be some time before the steamer could leave, the priest hired a carriage to take him to the monastery. It was quite a way off, and as he rode toward it the priest was consumed with curiosity. Could it be true that the monks in this retreat lived in as primitive a fashion as he had been told, with their only clothing animal skins which they had sewed together themselves? Could it be true that they were completely ignorant, and could not read or write? He hardly liked to think of the other story he had heard about them: that they knew no prayers, and consequently had to make up their own. To the pious man it seemed blasphemous, almost a heresy.

But he reminded himself that it had been many years since he heard the story of the monastery. And he hoped, with all his good heart, that conditions had changed.

On entering the monastery, though, he found that nothing had changed. The monks were unshaven, dirty, dressed in the skins of animals.

It was also true that they were illiterate. Their visitor was horrified. He thought it was a terrible thing.

"None of you here can read the Bible?" he asked.

"No, Father," said the oldest of the monks, hanging his head.

"Not even the Lord's Prayer."

"No, Father," said the aged monk, and he and the other monks began to weep as though their hearts were breaking. They explained that it was not their fault. No one had ever come to the monastery who could teach them to read and write. They meant no offense to their Lord. They had made up their own prayers only because they felt He would rather have them say something to Him each day than nothing.

The priest shook his head, deeply touched by the ignorant monks' humility and piety. So he taught them the Lord's Prayer, making them say the words after him over and over again.

Then it was time for him to go. The monks were so happy to be taught the Lord's Prayer, the real one, that they fell on their knees and kissed the edge of his robe. He left convinced they would never forget it.

The steamer was waiting for him when he got down

to the river. But as it headed out into the middle of the Volga, the priest heard voices calling from the shore. "Father! Father!"

He hurried to the stern of the little ship. It was the monks from the monastery. They now cried in despair, "Father! Father! What shall we do? We forgot some of the words, Father. This time God will never forgive us."

And looking at them, the priest smiled.

"He will forgive you, my children," he told them. "He will not care that you have forgotten some of the words."

And the priest spoke truly. For the faith of the ignorant monks had lifted them up so that they were walking on the water as they followed him in their eagerness.

This was the beautiful allegory that came back to me out of my faraway childhood. It comforted me in that moment of mounting terror. I felt much less bedeviled. For I realized that I needed only the same faith that had exalted the monks.

But still trembling I entered the office building on Spring Street, went up by elevator to the FBI offices, and asked for the man who had told me to come right down. But there were two FBI men, not one, waiting for me. They were sitting behind desks in the small office the receptionist brought me to. "Have you fellows been following me?" I blurted out.

The older of the two agents laughed. He was about thirty-five; the other man looked no more than thirty.

"Don't ask questions, Mr. Morros," the younger one told me. "Just tell us what happened." When I seemed hesitant, he said, "We have been waiting for you a long time, Boris. You should have come down here at least a year ago."

The older agent seemed to realize how that made

me feel. "Yes," he agreed, "we have been waiting for you a long time. But it's not too late."

Then I told them. I told them everything. And it was like having a ton of woe lifted from my shoulders as I told that story.

CHAPTER 2

Mother Russia's Long Arms Reach Out for Me

The Russia of the Romanovs into which I was born on New Year's Day, 1895, was as much like a walled-in dungeon as today's Russia of the Communists—for all except a lucky few.

Because we were a family of teachers, philosophers, and musicians, we were among that lucky few. The authorities even forgave us for being Jews, and permitted us to live in St. Petersburg, then the capital, so that we could sell the aristocrats our learning and our talent for entertaining. Even so, we were never unaware that there were pogroms of less fortunate Jews going on all the time in other parts of the vast empire. I don't know how I knew that as a boy; I can't imagine my parents discussing it with us.

My father was a teacher, my mother a singer; she was fragilely, delicately beautiful, and her hair remained blond until the day she died. I, the oldest of their nine children, was a boy prodigy—a concert cellist at eight, an orchestra leader in my teens. My father saw that we all obtained the best education possible. A man with a gay, lively mind and a passion for culture, Papa treasured learning above everything else in the world. That is why our being privileged to live in St. Petersburg, where the best schools in the Russian Empire were in those days, meant so much to him. He sent me to the gymnasium—the equivalent of high school in America—the Imperial Academy of Music, and the Academy of Oriental Languages.

Each summer, beginning with the year when I was eight, I made concert appearances in cities as far away as Odessa and Sevastopol. I was presented as a *Wunderkind* wherever I played my quarter-size cello, on bandstands in the public parks as well as in concert halls. Later I played before the Czar's court, where, like everyone else, I was both fascinated and frightened by the hypnotic eyes of Rasputin, the Mad Monk. During and after the Revolution I had many bizarre and thrilling experiences. I left the country in 1922 because from everything I had heard of the Soviet leaders I had become convinced they might not feel kindly toward a musician who had performed at the Winter Palace of Czar Nicholas.

After coming here I kept meeting persons who scoffed at my tales about my fabulous childhood and early manhood, but none of my stories amused them so much as my assertion that I had been the first private teacher of Gregor Piatigorsky, who is now generally recognized as the world's greatest living cellist excepting only Pablo Casals. Here is how that happened:

One day I arrived at my music school just as a crying boy and a dejected-looking man in the uniform of a military bandmaster came down the steps. I asked the boy, who was carrying a cello, what the trouble was. "My teacher has just refused to give me any more lessons," he sobbed.

"Why should he do that?" I asked.

The youngster took his hands out of his pockets and showed them to me. They were blue. He had got his fingers frozen. The teacher had been furious, as the vibrations of the heavy cello strings quickly rip the fingertips of a cold-stiffened hand to ribbons.

"How much could you pay for lessons?" I asked.

The boy looked at his father, who said, "Only twenty-five kopeks."

"I will give him lessons for twenty-five kopeks each," I told the man. "Three lessons a week."

Throughout the remainder of that winter I gave that boy, who was Gregor Piatigorsky, three lessons weekly. I had to go to his home by trolley car. The trip each way cost two kopeks. After paying the trolley fares, I had sixty-three kopeks a week clear profit. I also taught my protégé the new method for playing the scales which Klengel had just devised.

Well, that was my tale and, as they say on Broadway, I appeared to be stuck with it. Nobody would believe it. Even William LeBaron, who co-produced *Carnegie Hall* with me, tormented me about that story. "Boris," he said one day, "I've believed all your other wild yarns, but this is too much."

Well, there came the day when Piatigorsky gave a concert at Hollywood Bowl. Bill LeBaron, his wife, Mrs. Morros, myself and Dick, my son, attended it together.

"I always wanted to meet Piatigorsky," LeBaron kept saying. "I don't suppose he could have forgotten his first teacher. Do you, Boris?"

Just before the concert ended I sent Dick racing to the great cellist's dressing room. "Ask him," I said, "who was his first teacher."

A few minutes later, while Bill LeBaron was having more fun teasing me about my unusual shyness in approaching my famous pupil, I saw Dick. He waved encouragingly. And I said, "Oh, I guess we may as well go back, after all." And Gregor, bless him, embraced me and kissed me on both cheeks.

LeBaron never again questioned my veracity, although I do not deny there have been times when he might have quite justly. I am not a man to quarrel with the Broadway adage, "A little embellishment never ruined a good story." I also subscribe to the theory, "If you are in show business, truth employed indiscriminately can turn into the shovel you are using to dig your own grave."

Yet most of the tales I've told about my flamboyant early life are true. Even my claim of having performed in the Czar's Winter Palace was recently confirmed by the last authority I ever expected to bear me out in anything—a Soviet newspaper. The paper was *Literaturnay Gazeta* which, according to the New York *Times* of November 15, 1957, told of "Boris Morros, the movie producer who served as an American counterspy and testified last summer about alleged Soviet spy rings. The literary paper called him the newest American provocateur and said he began his career as a bootlicker at the court of Nicholas and as a friend of Rasputin, and finally sank as low as an FBI agent."

I admit I mistook this for abuse until a friend of mine said, "Consider the source, and you will see it is both an accolade and a confirmation of the most widely doubted tale about your early life. For heaven's sake, Boris, if the Communists have not been able to find out what went on in the Czar's palace, who can?"

I found success in America almost from the day I landed. I was a fine cellist, a fair pianist, and an accomplished orchestra conductor. But the world, then as now, was loaded with good musicians. Though I did not speak English well, and had few friends here, yet almost immediately I got a job as organ soloist in a Boston theater where I also furnished piano accompaniment to the silent films. After I became associated with the national chain of Paramount theaters, I was offered a series of opportunities such as a foreigner finds nowhere else in the world.

From Boston I came to New York as successor to Dr. Hugo Reisenfeld, conductor of the orchestra of the Rivoli Theatre on Broadway. I was music advisor to John Murray Anderson, who was then putting on the Rivoli's stage shows. Subsequently, as Paramount Publix's traveling orchestra leader, I worked in the company's theaters in such cities as Memphis, Atlanta, New Orleans, Dallas, San Antonio, and Des Moines.

It seems to me that the impact of these luxurious film theaters on the culture of America has never been properly emphasized. In one of our marble movie temples every tired scrub-lady could feel like a queen —for fifty cents—and every bootblack like a king as they lounged back in more comfortable chairs than monarchs ever enjoyed. Being a musician, I was impressed most, of course, by the ever-growing popularity of the so-called good music the large symphony orchestras in these theaters played at each performance. From the day they opened they had thrilled audiences of ordinary people (who were supposed to have appreciation only for ragtime and sentimental ballads) with first-rate renditions of standard offerings from Johann Strauss and Victor Herbert, as well as Bach, Wagner, and Grieg.

In 1929 I was appointed regional director of all Paramount theaters in the South. The next year I was brought to New York to be director of music for the Paramount theaters in Brooklyn and New York, and shortly afterward I became music director of the sixty-two de luxe theaters in the chain. Before long I had the added duties of supervising the music for the stage shows and selecting the talent. That meant, among other duties, auditioning scores of acts a week, from fire eaters, dog acts, and acrobats to comics and coloratura sopranos, not to mention

Wagnerian tenors.

It is difficult to imagine an ordeal that is more cruel and exhausting than the mass audition. Few, including the biggest stars, ever forget it. Those weekly sessions were toughest on the comedians—including Jack Benny and George Burns and Gracie Allen, who quivered and writhed and maybe prayed a little as they went on. Of all the funny men, the three Ritz Brothers and Milton Berle were the most relaxed. I must say, however, that the young Bob Hope was just as brash then, when he was in danger of going hungry, as he is now.

But whatever the act, there we were—I, my staff, and seven or eight bookers, all tired, distracted by a hundred and one other problems, some of us seemingly not paying any attention, smoking cigars, slumped in our seats, arms folded over our chests.

"Okay, kid, you're on! Your agent says you'll kill us. Well, we don't even bruise easily. But it's your show, young fellow. Make us laugh." Some of them froze up—you'd be surprised how many of the greatest ones of today did. One could hardly blame them, because it was like asking them to get belly laughs in Sing Sing's death house. Singers, as always, were a dime a dozen. If the auditions were easy on anyone, it was on the physical acts. Professional jugglers, acrobats, and dancers put in so many hours a day practicing their routines that their muscles work for them with almost automatic split-second timing.

Unless you are a great star it is always a buyers' market in show business. But never was this more true than in the years of the early thirties. And what talent came our way—some of it out of that weekly audition hopper! Most of our big box-office attractions were, of course, the established stars of stage, screen, and radio: Maurice Chevalier, Mary Pickford,

Gloria Swanson, Gary Cooper, Mae West, Frank Fay, Paul Draper, George Olsen with his band and his wife, Ethel Shutta, Burns and Allen, Will Rogers. Stage bands were all the rage; as often as not we would have the regular house orchestra working in the pit, and on the stage aggregations led by the likes of Guy Lombardo, Tommy Dorsey, Buddy Rogers, or Fred Waring, whom Henry Ford was so eager to sponsor that he came to our ninth-floor auditorium to catch the band's audition. After listening to Waring's men play a few sentimental, old-fashioned numbers, billionaire Ford spoke to Fred's comic drummer. "I like your antics," he said. Waring had the Ford Motor Company as its sponsor for years after that. I imagine Henry's favorite drummer got quite a few raises in that period.

But the performers I recall with most pride are those who weren't stars yet and whom I was in a position to help. I mention only a couple of them here. And I'll start with the biggest of them all, a gentleman named Harry Lillis Crosby.

Bing first appeared at the Paramount with Paul Whiteman's band. He was then one of the three Rhythm Boys, and the least important man in the singing trio. Whiteman had him playing the cymbals between singing numbers. Now I have known cymbal-players who were happy all their lives; slamming those two pieces of brass together every so often was all the self-expression they wanted. But to Bing, a brilliant and sensitive man, the idea of standing in the back of the band platform waiting five or ten minutes, sometimes half an hour, to clang his cymbals, was depressing and humiliating. It made him so shy he couldn't even face the audience when the stagehands rolled the piano onstage and he was given the chance to throw out those spine-tingling baritone notes of which he was already the master. Nevertheless he was a sensation with his "boo-boo-boo" style.

When it became obvious that Crosby had the makings of a top-ranking star there remained the problem of how to get him to look an audience in the eye. I solved it finally by sitting Der Bingle on a rose-covered moving platform that swung over the heads of the people in the audience. Producers had used this device for years with girls who threw at the bald-headed row their garters, stockings, and as much of the remainder of their apparel as the police allowed. But I think I was the first impresario to try it with a male performer.

Rudy Vallee and his megaphone were all the rage at the Brooklyn Paramount, so our publicity department steamed up a "Battle of the Crooners." Crosby's salary jumped from peanuts to $1000 a week. We held him at the New York Paramount for sixty-four weeks. "This child of the microphone," as I called him, was so outstanding a screen possibility that I sent memo after memo to our Hollywood studio recommending him for a screen test. They were ignored; most of them were not even acknowledged.

As I was writing this book, Ginger Rogers told a Broadway columnist that I was the man who discovered her and sent her on her way up. That happened while I was down in Houston, supervising final preparations for opening the new Paramount Theatre there. The last three days of this were my most hectic on that job. I don't recall when I slept or ate during those seventy-two hours. Finally one of my staff men insisted on driving me out to a roadhouse on the fringe of town which he claimed served the best steaks in Texas. There was a "sister" act there. When it came on I had been eating steak and snoring simultaneously. My aide nudged me. I opened one eye.

"That's a great act," he said. "The real reason I brought you out here."

Two beautiful blondes were doing a song-and-dance turn featuring the Charleston, which was all the rage. "The one on the left," I said. "Sign her up." The one on the left was Ginger Rogers, the one on the right her mother.

A few weeks later I was in Dallas to audition acts. One of them was Ginger. The house manager, after seeing her, told her, "I'm sorry, you won't do."

I told her to wait a minute, and talked to the local man. "She'll do," I said. "If you won't have her, I won't have you."

A few weeks later Ginger won a national Charleston contest and we booked her into two Paramount Theatres in the same week, the one on Broadway and the one in Brooklyn. To make sure she didn't miss the shows at either theater, we hired an ambulance to rush her over the bridge and back again. Mayor Walker, always obliging, got us a brace of his hard-riding motorcycle policemen as escorts.

I paid Ginger $75 a week, and at a party thrown for her recently at the Harwyn Club in New York, I asked her to forgive me. "Forgive you?" she exclaimed, and kissed me.

But my smartest bit of showmanship in that job, I think, was coaxing America's Sweetheart, Mary Pickford, to sign a contract for twenty weeks of personal appearances in Paramount theaters across the country.

Mary had just split up with Douglas Fairbanks and was heartbroken. It was difficult to talk Mary into returning to the stage, where she had made her last appearance as a child. She had made millions as a movie star, had her own company, and was a partner in United Artists. "What could it mean to me, Mr. Morros?" she kept saying to all my pleas. "I have all of the money I'll ever need. I'm one of the richest women in Hollywood."

It was a long time before I thought of the telling answer. I looked at that face, which everyone in the world had loved for years. And I remembered that, next to being proud of being Mrs. Douglas Fairbanks, Mary gloried in being called "America's Sweetheart."

"You might forget a lot of your trouble," I said, "if you found out that millions of your fans still love you better than all the rest of the stars in Hollywood put together. All of them, the young and the old, the women stars and the men stars. That sobriquet, 'America's Sweetheart,' belongs to you, and you only. They'll never call any other actress that in the next thousand years."

I sent for Paramount's lawyer, she for hers. I stayed in the room with Mary, the lawyers, and their stenographers, until I had her signature to the $400,000 contract. She made a fortune for us, of course.

One distressing feature of the job, to me, was the character of the small-time booking agents we sometimes had to do business with. They all looked alike, those hungry-eyed, fast-talking, small-time flesh peddlers. It always astonished me how they managed to get so many good-looking young girls to sleep with them in the belief that they could get them a job on Broadway. They also got these kids to lend them money—when the girls got some from home: Bellingham, Washington, or Chillicothe, Ohio, or Roanoke in old Virginny. Wherever it was, they couldn't go back —until they made good. And there wasn't one in ten thousand who would manage it.

All I recall now about a small-time agent who offered me Leon Trotsky, exiled co-father of the Russian Revolution, as a Paramount theater stage attraction, is that he had previously brought me Bobby

Breen, the boy singer, who quickly became a sensation. Thirty years or so before, as I well knew, the first Oscar Hammerstein had become the Barnum of his era by presenting freak attractions such as Evelyn Nesbit, the two girls who shot the millionaire, W. E. D. Stokes, and other front-page personalities. But I couldn't see Trotsky, fulminating on our stage against Stalin and his other persecutors in the Kremlin, as much of an attraction. However, to shut up the agent I promised to think about it.

Though this was 1933, President Roosevelt had not as yet recognized Russia. That happened later in the year, on November 16. Because no diplomatic or official economic relations existed between the two nations, I had been having considerable trouble getting food and clothing parcels to my parents and other relatives in Russia. One day I learned that my friend Sol Hurok, the opera and ballet impresario, was planning a trip to Russia. I asked him to look up my relatives and gave him their addresses. I was anxious about them, not having seen any of them for many years and having received only occasional letters.

On his return to New York, Hurok told me that he had seen two of my brothers, Serge and Saveli. "They are engineers but both of them were shabbily dressed," he told me. "They are either shy or very proud men. I told them you had asked me to give them anything they needed. They seemed pleased, but when I opened my trunks and laid out ties, warm clothing, and pipes on the bed, they shook their heads. They were hungry for news of you, Boris. They were overjoyed to learn you are doing so well. But when I asked them about your parents and the rest of the family, I could learn nothing. Perhaps like everyone else in that terror-filled world they are too fright-

ened to say anything—or even to think. They look
healthy enough, though. . . . No, they did not complain of anything."

Hurok advised me to look up a man named M. B.
Horton, who ran a travel company, Union Tours, and
had been quite successful in getting food and clothing
parcels to Russia for other friends of his. I took his
advice and had Horton send packages for me each
month.

One day, not long after I was offered Leon Trotsky
as a stage attraction, a Mr. Gregory Melamed, an
ugly, stocky, bespectacled man, began calling my office. He told Jeanette Mendelssohn, my secretary, that
he was a Russian commercial representative. I made
an appointment to lunch with him at the Hunting
Room of the Hotel Astor. As I had assumed, he was
with Amtorg, the commercial trading corporation that
the Soviet government had established here. Melamed
asked me the names and addresses of my relatives in
Russia, and wrote down the information. When I
came to the names of two of my brothers—Isaac and
Alexander—he shook his head. He said it was a pity
that they were on bad terms with the government, as
both were such capable men.

I could understand why this might be true of Isaac,
a Social Democrat. But the other one, Alexander, I
remembered, had had no interest in politics.

Next Melamed asked if he could do anything to
facilitate the packages. For a moment I was tempted
to ask him to help me get American currency through
to my parents. All my efforts to do this had failed.
The customs men at the frontier exchanged my dollars for rubles at the official government rate—and
rubles at the time were almost worthless.

Instead I told Melamed I would appreciate it if he
could get me receipts for the parcels. "Then," I said,

"at least I'll know whether my people are getting what I send them."

During this first conversation, Melamed mentioned —doing his best to seem casual about it—that he had heard I was interested in booking Trotsky.

I just smiled and shrugged. For then and there it suddenly struck me that the Stalinist Reds who had driven Leon Trotsky into exile might be extremely interested in keeping him out of any such forum as the stage of the great Paramount Theatre on Broadway would provide. So I did not tell him that I considered such a booking into a family theater as ridiculous, saying instead, "It would make a sensation, you know."

"We can be very useful to one another, my friend," he said very earnestly.

"All right," I told him. "If you don't want Trotsky booked into the Paramount, I can promise you he will never appear there as long as I am in charge of the stage shows there."

"That is done then," he said. "Now, isn't there something else I can do for you besides this small matter of seeing that your parcels get through? Wouldn't you like me to get your parents sent here?"

I could hardly reply for a moment or two. Then I told him that having my parents with me was something I wanted more than anything in the world. In the succeeding months I got very excited letters from Leningrad, where my parents were then living with one of my sisters. The last of these said that, though my mother was unfortunately too ill to attempt the trip, father was already on his way.

He got here in December 1933, an old man with a beard like the one in the pictures of Tolstoi during that writer's "peasant period." Papa cried when he saw me on the dock, and so did I.

Although he was worried from the moment he landed about whether he could get back in time to avoid punishment for overstaying his six months' visa, I think my father had a good time on that trip. I took him to Florida for a couple of weeks. His main occupation when we returned to New York was delivering letters that friends in the old country had entrusted to him for their relatives here. He had arrived with a satchel full.

But he would talk to no one—not to me, his son, not to the grateful people to whom he delivered the letters—about political conditions or living conditions back home in Russia. "When I get back there," he invariably said, "I'll tell them how you live here."

Of all the wonders he saw in New York he admired most the George Washington Bridge. What he disliked most was the rising platform that carried the Paramount's orchestra from the cellar to the level of the floor. "The machinery that lifts it makes terrible noises," he said (the hydraulic motors we used were noisy in those days). "How can anyone enjoy beautiful music after listening to that racket?" He also objected violently to the flashy way in which the orchestra was presented—for instance, the way the spotlight played first on one soloist, then on another. He hated our muted trumpets and singing trombones. Papa wanted music played exactly the way he had been hearing it all his life.

In May of the following year he started on the long trip home. He cried, saying he feared he would never see me again. I was cherishing hopes that I might be able to bring him and my mother over—this time for good—but I did not mention that, not wishing to arouse any false dreams.

Less than a year later I got a letter from him saying my mother was dying. I went to the Russian consulate to see Melamed, who had been appointed vice-consul since our government's recognition of the Soviet Union. He got me a passport. He also assured me that, though my two brothers were still in disfavor, I would be unharmed while in Soviet territory. I thanked him for the credentials but not for the guarantee of safe conduct, something one did not need except in totalitarian countries.

I sailed from New York with eleven trunks filled with everything I thought my family lacked—food, clothing, safety razors, even aspirin tablets. I also brought along about eight new records that I thought might interest my father. Among them were Paul Whiteman records, which showed the magnificent use to which he was putting harmonics in his jazz, and Cab Calloway records in all their wild and primitive splendor. But it was only with the greatest difficulty that I talked the Russian customs men into letting me bring them in. At that time the Soviets were making a propaganda issue of the superiority of their proletarian music over our capitalistic music. Apparently they were afraid that Calloway, particularly, would violate the virginal purity of the Soviet ears that listened to the new Communistic music. They warned me not to leave the records in their country, to make no mistake about taking them away with me when I left. They also wrote in my passport that I had those eight records and should not be permitted to depart without them. I did not worry about this after I noticed that the customs officials had not even identified them as American records. Any records, even their own, would enable me to depart.

Though practically everyone else from America who visited Russia complained of being followed, I was not conscious of being spied on during that trip, and in my eleven days there I visited three cities, Kharkov,

Moscow, and Leningrad. The only explanation I can
offer is that high-ranking Soviet officials gave orders
to let me alone because they felt I had rendered
them an immensely important service in keeping Leon
Trotsky off the Broadway stage.

The rulers of the Kremlin in those days feared
Trotsky's followers—who comprised a hard core of
zealots—almost as much as they feared any other hostile element in the world. Along with Lenin, Trotsky,
his co-creator of the Revolution, had been portrayed
in the early years of Communist rule as a saint. What
worried the Stalinists, who had driven Trotsky out
of the countrty and purged the leaders who were devoted to his theories and personality, was that he
still had millions of followers inside Russia.

So, for the service I didn't do, I was rewarded by
not being followed, night or day. Whatever free time
I had I spent trying to mingle with the people. I
wished to find out, if possible, what they were thinking about the regime that had enslaved them in the
name of freedom. But that was attempting the impossible. There was not a corner in that dark, fear-filled
desert that Russia had become where people felt safe
to talk of what was in their hearts.

The great thrill of the trip was finding my mother,
sick and old as she was, still as blond and with as
youthful a face as when I had last seen her. And I
thought of how that dear face had glowed with love
and pride the day I played my first melody on my
little quarter-size cello.

She must also have remembered that, because she
hummed that piece, the Brahms "Lullaby," this day,
after we had embraced one another.

"You think about that, Mama?" I said.

"I think about that, my darling, every day of my
life," she said, adding, "and often in the middle of

the night as well. Boris, do you know what I have hung on the wall of my bedroom directly over the head of my bed?"

When I did not answer, she said, "Your quarter-cello, Boris. The first one Papa bought for you. Sometimes at night, my son, fear wakes me up. Then I reach up and touch the strings, gently. And hearing those sounds in the night comforts me."

She, my sister, her husband, and their children all kept asking me questions about the fabulous country in which I lived. Out of habit, though no strangers were within earshot, they whispered. Could it be true, they wanted to know, that even workmen in the United States owned their own homes, had new, shining expensive cars, always were warmly dressed, and had enough to eat? Did their wives all have vacuum cleaners, electric washing machines, and electric stoves? Did they go away weekends with the family in the car on picnics?

But there was not a member of my family who cared to talk about their own lives, their own country. When I asked them about my two brothers, Alexander and Isaac, I got no satisfaction. I accidentally met a relative of Alexander's wife one day. When she saw me she shrieked, "Go away! Go *away!*" I hoped it was only my imagination playing tricks that made me think Alexander must have been killed and that this woman feared I would mention his name to her and be overheard.

During my first two days in Moscow, I purposely refused to speak Russian in any public place. But I overheard nothing worth listening to because people were not voicing opinions about the United States or anything else, even to one another.

Perhaps the most revealing experience I had on that visit happened one night when I was dining with my parents at a hotel restaurant in Kharkov. Suddenly all the lights blew out. Feeling it was safe in the dark, the musicians, one by one, crept up to the table to ask me questions. And I dropped my own voice so that they would not be frightened away. They were interested mainly in two things: the salaries and working conditions of musicians in America and an explanation of jazz music, popular music.

From their questions I could see that they had had the moral lesson behind the collapse of the Wall Street stock market hammered into them. What good are the big salaries that musicians get there, they kept asking, if their savings go into stocks and bonds that prove worthless?

That was too complicated to explain to them in the few minutes we had. Describing jazz and popular music in a few well-chosen words was almost as difficult. The only thing I could think of was to compare jazz songs to their gypsy music, street songs, or, in the inelegant Russian words, "gutter music." But trying to show them that popular was merely a term that was used as an antonym to classical was beyond me.

There were four of them in that little band, a violin, cello, clarinet, and piano. "Play your own songs," I kept telling them, because I remembered suddenly that every Russian musician is also a composer who carries around copies of his best pieces in his pocket. And that night they played their own songs while the lights were out and kept it up after they were turned on. The evening ended with my taking over the cello and playing Glazunov's "The Song of the Minstrel."

It was a most successful evening—but principally because the lights in the hotel had gone out.

I've always been glad that I was able to spend so much time with my mother on that trip, for it was the last time I ever saw her. She died a few years later.

The last thing that happened to me in Moscow convinced me that the whole Soviet system must collapse soon, because of inefficiency, if nothing else— an over-optimistic guess if ever I made one.

In all the excitement of seeing my family again, I forgot the admonition of the customs guard to bring the Whiteman and Calloway records out of the country with me. I remembered it only when I reached Moscow airport where my plane—a one-engine job— was scheduled to take off in forty minutes. That gave me too little time to get to a record shop in the city, buy substitute platters, and rush back again. When I inquired where the customs man was, a one-armed man with a sailor's walk and a sailor's hat on his head was pointed out to me. I approached him to explain my difficulty but he ignored me, though there were no other passengers waiting for the Paris plane. That was lucky for me; it gave me a chance to study my passport and discover that the Russian visa was on one page and the notation about the records was on the opposite page.

I put a blotter over the incriminating page, and handed it to the one-armed customs man. I was trembling so much that I was afraid my nervousness would arouse his suspicions. I went to the plane and got aboard. As they started the propeller revolving, I was wondering what I would do in Paris without a passport. But just before take-off the official came running out on the field and handed over the precious book all stamped and approved. He had not lifted the blotter to see what was underneath it.

I had, by the way, no luggage for him to check. I had given everything I brought along to my family, including the eleven trunks and my own clothes.

CHAPTER 3

How I Came to Lie Down with the Soviet Bear

I came home depressed over my family's tragic situation. To me they had all seemed like hopeless people in a frozen prison. Awaiting me in New York was a surprise that failed to cheer me up. Adolph Zukor, founding father and president of Paramount, wished me to become general music director of our Hollywood studio.

Though the move was described as a promotion, I said I would be happy to remain where I was. Mr. Zukor was always the sort of charming boss a man enjoys pleasing, perhaps because he always made an order sound like a personal favor he was asking of you.

In 1935 Paramount was still in financial difficulties. Mr. Zukor reminded me of the figures. In 1930 the corporation's profits had been $18,000,000. In 1931, the profits dropped to $6,000,000 and during 1932 we lost $21,000,000. Those disastrous depression years of the early thirties had sent us through various phases of receivership and bankruptcy. The pictures the studio had turned out were so poor that the company's slogan, "If it's at the Paramount, it's the best show in town," had inspired a paraphrase by the trade's Addisons and Steeles: "If it's at the Paramount, it *better* be the best stage show in town."

Mr. Zukor agreed that it had been my stage shows that pulled patrons into our theaters. But now, with the improvement of sound equipment, music was every day becoming more important to the company's film product.

Ernst Lubitsch, the director famous for his Viennese touch, was about to be placed in charge of all production. Ernst, an old friend of mine, had said that all Paramount's music department needed was my creative ability and showmanship. When he came to New York that fall I explained that I wanted to produce my own pictures. That was no news to him. Every executive in the industry had the same ambition, as producing is where most of the money is, and most of the fun. Ernst insisted that running the studio's music department was the biggest step I could take toward that dream.

In October 1935, I headed for Hollywood. Mr. Zukor did me the unusual honor of seeing me off at the station. He seemed to have no doubt that in a short time I would be producing my own pictures for Paramount. As a very special concession I was allowed to take along my secretary, Miss Mendelssohn, with me. One inexplicable thing about Hollywood in those days was that a producer could spend $100,000 to transport a thousand Ubangi savages from the African jungle without protest. But if he asked the company to pay his secretary's railway fare across the country the head of the accounting department acted as though he had been held up and stabbed.

At the studio new stars, youngsters such as Crosby, Hope, Fred MacMurray, Ray Milland, Jack Oakie, and Cary Grant were beginning to score heavily. Our established name players—Marlene Dietrich, Claudette Colbert, Gary Cooper, Sylvia Sidney, Charles Laughton, W. C. Fields, Maurice Chevalier—also were doing wonderfully well. Paramount Studios was as friendly a place to work in, moreover, as the home office had been. If I missed the constant hurly-burly excitement of organizing the stage shows, here I had the thrill of supervising the work of men who wrote great song hits—Ralph Ranger, Leo Robin, Hoagy Carmichael,

Johnny Mercer, and Frederick Hollander, among others.

Surprising things were forever happening. One morning a young fellow approached me on the lot, and said, "Mr. Morros, let's not beat around the bush. I am a genius. Wanna hire me as a song writer?"

Laughing, I said, "Sure."

As he skipped off toward the two-story wooden building that housed my department, I called after him, "Hey, what's your name?"

"Frank Loesser," he yelled over his shoulder.

Not long afterward Frank was turning out such song hits with Hoagy Carmichael as "Two Sleepy People."

I think now, as I look back, that the best part of the studio job was the sense it gave me at all times of being wanted. "Boris," a voice on the phone would say, "hurry on down to sound stage eleven. That number the boys wrote just isn't right. We'll need a substitute song whipped out by tomorrow."

Everybody needed me. Everybody wanted my advice. Even Bing Crosby, that box-office champion of champions, who had always known instinctively what he was doing and had by now acquired the confidence to go ahead and do it, would come to my office to discuss his new songs. I think he had learned to trust my judgment back in the days when he was singing with the Rhythm Boys and clanging those detestable cymbals.

Not that Crosby always took my advice. But one reason he later became the greatest popular singer in the history of entertainment is that he listened to anyone he thought might offer a valuable suggestion, before making up his own mind. And he still listens to such people because, with all the honest humility of a true performer, he has never got close enough to perfection to satisfy himself.

Another exciting thing about working in Hollywood in those days was that color film had just come in. I remember working on the first good color feature ever made, *The Trail of the Lonesome Pine*. But we were making so many pictures—fifty or so a year—that I wouldn't know how to start listing them in order of their importance. They were all important. I loved my busy life, and I enjoyed almost as much the social life. For years Hollywood had been drawing from all over the world more creative artists and gifted craftsmen than ever were gathered in one small place before. Almost as many distinguished musicians were guests in my Beverly Hills home as appeared on the stage of Carnegie Hall each season.

Yet the plight of my relatives in Russia, particularly of my father, was like a perpetual cloud lurking in the back of my mind. I wanted to, had to, do something for them, and I never stopped trying. But I was again having difficulties in getting my food and clothing parcels to them. More often than not I got no word at all of whether they had been received.

One day Miss Mendelssohn told me that a man with a thick Russian accent had been trying for a week to get me on the telephone. She had not mentioned these calls until then, she said, because he refused to give his name.

"But today he said he was Edward Herbert," she went on. "Mr. Melamed, the Russian vice-consul in New York, sent him out here to see you."

"Where is this Edward Herbert now?" I asked.

When she said he was waiting out at the gate, I had him brought in immediately. Edward Herbert, as he was then calling himself, was a thick-set man with powerful shoulders. He had red hair, and, despite the heavy accent Miss Mendelssohn had mentioned, spoke French, English, and German fairly well. He asked whether I had had trouble lately in sending parcels to Russia.

"Plenty," I told him.

"I have very good connections with the Soviet vice-consul here," he said. "I can get him to send your parcels directly from their office. They will get special attention."

He volunteered to come to my house to help me wrap and address the parcels, then to take them to the office of the Russian consulate for me. When I tried to thank him, he offered me a Leica camera as a gift.

"We've never forgotten the favor you did us a few years ago," he told me, earnestly. "Keeping Trotsky off the stage of your Broadway theater is something we'll always be grateful for." He came once or twice more to my home and took the parcels to the consulate for me.

The packages were received, just as he had predicted. In due time I got word of that.

One afternoon Edward Herbert again came to my office. I was very busy scoring a picture and told him I had little time to chat with him. He quickly got the point.

"You *are* against the Nazis, aren't you?" he asked.

I told him of course I was and that everything Hitler stood for was an abomination in my opinion. Then he said he lived in Germany and was organizing the underground anti-Nazi work there for the Soviet government.

"Isn't that dangerous?" I asked, thinking of his Russian accent.

"Very," he said. "But you could help make it less so."

"I can?" I said, in astonishment. "How?"

"To fight the Nazis effectively," he said, "I should have some sort of occupation that makes it legitimate for me to move around freely."

I could see his point but couldn't imagine what he wanted of me. "I should have some sort of trade or profession," he kept saying, and then, "Don't you want to help me? Don't you want to help a man who is devoting his whole life to fighting the Nazis?"

"Of course I do. But what are you getting at?"

"Haven't you talent scouts looking for musical talent all over the world?"

I nodded.

"Make me your talent scout in Germany."

I hesitated, even though, like everyone else with any decency, I was appalled by Hitler's pogroms and his threats to plunge Europe into war. The pogroms were particularly horrible to a Jew like myself who had grown up in a country where such massacres were tolerated almost as a sport of the Cossacks.

I thought over the matter for a few moments. That was in the mid-thirties, by the way, when Germany was producing all sorts of interesting musical turns, and novelties with trick instruments. Like other studio executives, I couldn't have too many talent scouts. I seldom met anyone about to travel abroad to whom I didn't say, as a matter of course, "If you see any interesting performers, find out what their price is and everything else about them, and send me the full details."

"If you help me in this," he promised, "I will see that your family will be helped—and not only by getting the packages you send them. Your two brothers are still in trouble with the government. But they will not be prosecuted if you help me now." And he went on, "What possible wrong can you be doing to your company, your country, or anything else by helping me? We are all in this war against the Nazis together. So all you will be doing is to help a comrade fight the worst enemy mankind ever had." He paused for a moment, and added, "You will also, I need not point out, be helping your family."

In my own handwriting that day, and on the stationery of Paramount Studios of Hollywood, California, I wrote the letter he wanted, certifying that he, Edward Herbert, was authorized to act in Germany as talent scout for my department. I signed it, "Boris Morros, General Music Director."

In fairness to myself, I must call attention to the political climate in America at that time, 1936. We all—except for Hitler's admirers over here—saw the Nazi movement as the monster it was. But most Americans did not recognize Communism as the same sort of menace. Many felt, as I did, that any work against Hitler was good work.

What we have since learned, of course, is that merely being against something is never enough, and that in fighting one evil we must be careful not to ally ourselves with evil-doers just as insidious and destructive as those we are trying to destroy.

When I signed Herbert's certification as a Paramount talent scout, I felt that I had paid in full for the favor he had done me. What was embarrassing was that he had left some money with me that he expected me to send him in $50 monthly payments to prove he was working for an American company.

I did this, but answered few of the letters he sent. I kept hoping that he would become discouraged and seek someone else in the entertainment business to cover for him. As the Nazi terror in Europe mounted it became obvious that no one in Hollywood would dream of bringing over talent from Hitler's Germany. And if anyone at the studio found out about my arrangement with Herbert, I would become the laughing stock of the industry. The idea that I, a Jew, would employ a talent scout in Berlin would make me seem stupid and ridiculous. The sooner Edward Herbert and I forgot about each other the better.

During the summer of 1937, the Soviet Union enjoyed its first success at impressing the world with a scientific achievement. Three of their small planes attempted flights to the United States by way of the North Pole. One of the planes was lost but the other two made it all the way to the West Coast, setting a new record of 6262 miles for nonstop flights. The Russian flyers were still being feted the day I was notified by the police guard at the Paramount Studio gate that Edward Herbert was outside waiting to see me. I had him brought to my office.

But the man ushered in that day was not Edward Herbert. He was younger, slimmer, and far better dressed. He crisply explained, as soon as we were alone, that he was Samuel Shumovsky, one of Herbert's aides. He said he had used his chief's name only to be sure of getting in to see me.

Shumovsky, who had lost an eye in an accident, also said that he was registered as a "flying mechanic" at the Soviet embassy in Washington. He was on the coast on two errands. One was to give back to one of the aviators a shirt which the flyer had entrusted to him—for good luck—when plans for the polar flight were first being made. The other was to find out why I was falling down on my assignment to write regularly to Herbert in Germany.

What shocked me was Shumovsky's manner. He berated me in savage language for not writing often enough to Herbert. "That endangers his life," he said. "He writes you two or three letters for every one you send him. You must keep the agreement you made with him."

I told him I was going to all the trouble I cared to. I said that if some prying executive or employee discovered that I was corresponding with a talent scout in Germany, especially a man with no experience in show business, I would have some embarrassing explaining to do. And what about Miss Mendelssohn, who typed the letters I had written to Herbert? Suppose she started wondering what I was doing with a talent scout in Nazi Germany?

Shumovsky said it would be unnecessary for me to send any more money. That reminded him that I still had more than $100 of Herbert's money. I took the correct sum out of my wallet and handed it to him. He pocketed it with smug satisfaction. I have noticed a hundred times since that, despite anything they preach publicly, most Reds have a deep craving for even small amounts of money. In this instance, actually getting that cash seemed to soften Shumovsky. But before leaving, he warned me once more not to fail to write Edward Herbert at the Berlin address he had given me.

I did not write Herbert again. I heard nothing more from Shumovsky—who, the FBI later informed me, was an active Soviet spy here for many years—and I started to breathe easily again.

I had no idea, even then, that under the pressure of threats to those in Russia dear to me I was going to be forced to give more and more cooperation to Soviet undercover workers during the next ten years —to become, in fact, a trusted member of a spy ring whose job it was to carry secret and confidential information to the highest Soviet intelligence agency, the NKVD. The delusion that I was still a free man, however, was not to be exploded for a long time.

After the visit of Shumovsky I was not troubled

again for almost two years. Without the Russian vice-consul's help I had the same old difficulties getting parcels to my family. When I thought of the matter at all, I supposed optimistically that the Russians had forgotten the whole thing. Nothing would have pleased me more. But early in 1939 I was shaken out of this mistaken notion when I was approached by another Russian emissary from Mr. Herbert. This chap complained bitterly that he had had to wait at the gate for days before seeing me. The guard there refused even to phone my office. I could well understand that. As all movie fans who have been in Hollywood know, the movie studios are almost as hard to crash as the Kremlin itself. But this man was so unprepossessing that he would have had difficulty getting past the receptionist of any business establishment. I was on my way to lunch and did not invite him inside the studio.

He was very short—only about five-three—weighed no more than 110, and was what I call a long-coat-and-short-pants man, meaning that his clothes were old, shabby, and of a style no longer acceptable even in the more remote parts of the Balkans. When he started to berate me there on the street in front of the studio, I stared at him in astonishment. He spoke broken English, fractured French, and goulashed German, but cursed eloquently in all three, not to mention swearing impeccably in Russian.

I started to walk away. But he followed me, denouncing me for endangering Herbert's life by not writing to him. I had an appointment at Lucey's Restaurant, only a block or two from our lot, and he kept haranguing me right up to the door.

I walked into Lucey's garden, knowing he would not dare to follow me. He stood there on the street, peering into the garden, where a few stars and company executives were seated at tables. That was the last I ever saw of this ragged, noisy little Russian. But years later I was told that, in his report of our meeting, he had described how graciously I had greeted him in my office, shown him around the lot, and then lunched with him in Lucey's elegant garden.

After that I had two years more of being left alone. Meanwhile, the Russians had been doing very well without assistance from me, though their nonaggression pact with the Nazis had gone the way of all pacts made with Hitler.

As for myself, I had been doing all right. At the end of 1939 I had resigned from Paramount to become an independent producer. I had produced *Flying Deuces,* a Laurel and Hardy pictrue, which cost about $300,000 to make, has since grossed more than $2,000,000, and is still being shown on television screens. The following year my own company, Boris Morros Productions, had produced *Second Chorus* with Fred Astaire, Paulette Goddard, Artie Shaw's band, and other stars. I was preparing the expensive episodic film that was eventually called *Tales of Manhattan* when suddenly the spy ring posed a nightmarish threat to my career—to my whole way of life, in fact. Incidentally, I had entertained at dinner visiting Russians, including two movie executives, Antonov and Kalatosov, and a Mr. Irsky who was a sound expert of great renown in the Soviet Union.

It all began at a cocktail party given at the home of a neighbor of mine. There were several Russians there when I arrived.

"Oh, now we have a Russian translator," said the host on seeing me. He introduced me to the few guests I did not know.

One stout fellow in the Russian contingent smiled quizzically at me on being introduced, but I could place neither him nor his name. In a few moments, however, he came over and took my arm. "Don't you know me?" he whispered. "After all, you should. You saved my life, you know." He led me out to the garden so we could talk in private.

Now it is always embarrassing for a producer, who sees dozens of actors and other motion-picture workers every day, to be taken at a disadvantage in this way. But this brutal-looking, fat, bespectacled man resembled no actor, song writer, lyricist, or director I had ever known.

It was not until we reached the garden that it dawned on me who he was. The reason I had not recognized him was that he had got so fat and bloated-looking. "Why, you're Edward Herbert, aren't you?" I said, doing my best to appear pleased to see him.

"You could have done better, you know. You should have written me more often while I was in Germany."

I thought a jocular tone might help. "What could I do," I said, "when all you recommend to me was acrobats? Japanese acrobats are bad enough, but German acrobats, Nazi German acrobats at that . . ."

He ignored the feeble joke.

"Forget that I was ever Edward Herbert," he said. "I am now with the Soviet Embassy. My name now is Zubilin, Vassili Mikhailovich Zubilin."

After he identified himself I saw there was another reason I hadn't recognized him. Beside the physical coarsening, he was better dressed, and seemed more aggressive and self-assured than I remembered his being at our other meetings. The fact that he was talking very good English also gave me something to think about. Just a few minutes before he had pretended to be having great difficulty with the language.

When he asked about my family I told him my mother was dead. The Red Cross had notified me of that some time before.

"And your father?" he asked.

"Well, Papa, of course, is very lonely," I told him.

He thought about that for a moment, then said, "Maybe you would like me to get your father over here for you. This time for good."

"Could you do that?" I asked.

He nodded, and added, "In the meanwhile I suggest you attend no more parties like this where you meet other Russians. Or give dinners to visitors like Antonov and Kalatosov.

I suppose that should have given me pause. But the idea of having my father with me made everything else seem unimportant. Getting him out of that cold, dreary, godless country—why, it would be the greatest thing I ever could do. Standing there with Mr. Edward Herbert, alias Zubilin, I could see Papa sitting in my yard in the sun, talking philosophy, playing chess with those other patriarchs, the fathers of my friends.

There is one aphorism stemming from the capitalistic credo that the Communists subscribe to without reservation: "Get a good price for everything, even for what you pretend to be giving away."

I got an idea of what the price of my father's passport might be a few weeks later when I obtained the stage scenery at a Russian War Relief Benefit at Los Angeles in March 1942. That evening I dropped backstage to make sure that some drops and drapes I had talked a theatrical house into supplying for the affair would be returned to the company's warehouse next morning.

Right after talking about this to the men in charge of the props I ran into Zubilin. He had obviously been drinking and did not conceal his rage at finding me there. Ignoring the danger that someone backstage might hear him, he shouted in Russian, "What happened to your memory, my good Boris? Didn't I tell you not to be seen with Russians at affairs like this one? Do you want the whole world to know that your sympathies are with us?"

He seized me by the coat lapels and slammed me against a wall. Then he shoved a gun that he had in his pocket against my stomach. I didn't have a chance to explain what I was doing there. He didn't care. He was drunk and in a rage. "If you want me to do you favors, you gotta do what I say. You are not to mix with any Russians. You will be of no use to me, you fool, if you become known as a man who openly associates with Russians."

I was scared out of my wits. I promised to do my best. I would have promised anything to get away from him that night.

The next month—April—I got a call from him at the studio. He said he would like to drop in at my house and get a bundle of clothes to send my family. During this visit he said he was keeping his promise about having my father brought over.

"You can really do that?" I asked once again.

"I can do anything."

By this time, my son Dick was at the Severn School, the preparatory school for Annapolis. During a trip I took in May to see Dick I stopped off in Washington to ask Zubilin how he was getting along with his effort to bring my father to this country.

I was utterly bewildered when the embassy's receptionist assured me there was no such person on the staff. Zubilin had been introducing himself all over Hollywood as an embassy attaché. It made so little sense that I asked to see Maxim Litvinov, who was then Russian ambassador. I had met him in 1934 in

New York at the banquet given at the Waldorf-Astoria for the American engineer Hugh Cooper, to celebrate his completion of the great dam on the Dnieper River. But Litvinov was out of town. At least that is what I was told.

I left. But I had hardly got outside when the girl receptionist rushed after me. She pushed into my hand a little slip of paper with a telephone numuber written on it. "Call that number," she said, "and you may be able to get in touch with Zubilin after all." I returned to the Willard Hotel, where I had checked in overnight, and called the number from my room.

Zubilin answered the phone himself and exploded with anger because I had called at the embassy. "What did you expect me to do?" I asked. "That was where you told me I'd find you whenever I came East."

That calmed him down, and he told me to meet him on a street in Washington which has so many movie-company distribution offices that it is nicknamed "Film Row."

Zubilin got there shortly after I did. When he hailed a taxi he whispered the address to the driver in so low a voice I could not hear it.

I still do not know the location of the flat to which he took me on that day. But it had the sparsely furnished, un-lived-in look of many of the places where I met Soviet agents later on. These were all places the Zubilins and other spies could abandon on a minute's notice, leaving no evidence that they had been there.

This one was on the first floor of a row of adjoining houses in one of Washington's poorer neighborhoods. Zubilin's wife, a frail, pretty, middle-aged woman with an aristocratic manner, was there, and also their seven-year-old son, Peter. As I shook hands with Mrs. Zubilin she told the little boy, who was just going out to the back yard to play, not to stray too far from the house. "Your dinner will soon be ready," she told him. But I saw no food in the house. She remained in the kitchen, but she cooked nothing, and I heard no plates being put on the table. When I reflected about that it seemed to me that the Zubilins were not living in that flat at all, but used it solely for meeting such newcomers as myself whom they did not trust.

In view of what I later learned about Elizabeth Zubilin—sometimes also called Helen, sometimes Liza, the diminutive for Elizabeth usually used by Russians —I think she might have been there to look me over and give her bully-boy of a husband an opinion of me as material for their espionage organization in America. Later on I often heard other Communist women talking of Elizabeth Zubilin as though she were a sort of Red Joan of Arc, a saint whose faith in the Soviet was pure and bottomless. They also had great respect for her intellect and judgment. Often I heard these wives of other spies say, while in the midst of a dispute over some matter of strategy, "Well, what did *she* say about it?" or "Let's ask Liza," or "Don't argue, Helen said so!" as though Madame Zubilin had the last word. She was generally acknowledged to be the real brain behind whatever shrewd moves her blustering husband made. The other women also told me that Zubilin occasionally beat his wife, and that she took these thrashings with saintly resignation.

Of course I heard all this about her in later years. That day all I noticed about this Joan of Arc of the Soviet Union were her aristocratic features and manner.

The conversation that followed was similar to the torture I had undergone backstage at the Russian War Relief Benefit in Hollywood.

"As I understand it," he said, folding his huge arms across his chest, "it means a great deal to you to bring your father over here."

"I thought you knew that."

"I do," he said, jutting out his jaw at me. "Now you must understand something; for such favors I must be paid."

"When are you going to bring my father here?"

"Very soon now," he said.

"You can do that?" I asked, as I had twice before in Hollywood.

"I can do that. I can do a great deal more. One thing I do best is collect for favors like this one you want me to do for you. And you might as well know who I am, while we're at it. I am head of the NKVD in this country, and I feel as free here to do exactly as I want as anywhere else in the world."

He beat his chest, flexed his arms. I felt that his bulging eyes were almost boring holes through me. "You *have* to do what I say! There is no way out for you! For I have long arms, long enough to reach anywhere in this country. You know I am strong. I play tennis every day. I play four hours, seven hours, ten hours. But you"—he slapped one of my arms—"you have no muscles—you're flabby."

I wanted only one thing—out! I regretted that I had got in touch with him and I swore to myself that if I got out of that place alive I would never see him again. For I had no way of foreseeing that day when he really could bring my father to America for me.

"How could you bring my father to America?" I asked. "How could you get him through the German lines? Would you fly him over the war zones?"

He laughed impatiently. "You are a fool, little Boris. I will have him brought here by way of the Pacific.

"You will bring my father here by way of the Pacific?"

"You will see. I told you I could do *anything*. I will bring him by way of Vladivostok on a ship that will land on the West Coast."

There was no question of his determination to force me to work for him. The one purpose of that meeting was to impress that upon me.

I got out that day, but I remained shaken for hours afterward. And I began wondering what in God's name he would expect me to do for him if he did bring my father to me.

"Never call me at the embassy again, you understand?" was the last thing Zubilin had said. He had given me the New York address of a woman named Leah Melament, and instructed me to write her in advance whenever I was coming East, saying when I would arrive in New York and where I would be staying.

"As a precaution, you will send her this information in love letters," he explained. "The information you wish her to pass on to me you are to write in the last line or two." I was to sign my letters with a double clef, he said.

That, as I say, was in May.

In July, Zubilin telephoned me at my home in California, from New York. He told me I must come east immediately to see him. I told him I was too busy with my work on *Tales of Manhattan* to leave. But he was so insistent that to end the argument I agreed to go.

But I did not go.

And I kept stalling Zubilin all that summer, whenever he telephoned. I had to go to New York in September for the première of *Tales of Manhattan*. Knowing I would be busy with last-minute details, okaying the advertising, checking the guest list, and endless conferences, I did not bother to notify Leah Melament that I was coming.

Yet Zubilin gave me quite a start by appearing at my hotel-room door a few minutes after I checked in. As in Washington, he threatened me, talking a good deal about his big muscles and long arms. After exhausting his supply of invectives, he told me that my company was to employ the men he sent me as technicians—musicians, electricians, prop men, cameramen. When he mentioned cameramen, I all but laughed in his face. Hollywood has many unions that are difficult to get into, but the cameramen have the tightest closed shop of them all. At the time, I believe, they had two hundred members, or possibly less. I tried to explain that, but he was not interested in problems. He said that only results interested him.

That day he insisted that I go with him to lunch. He laughed at my protests that I had an important business conference. "For you and me, Boris," he said, chuckling, "there is only one business that counts." He slapped me on the back, almost knocking the wind out of me.

He took me to lunch at Luchow's. Zubilin tried to be pleasant there and to behave like a host. His wife, I think, had advised him to soft-soap me along for a while. Zubilin didn't do it badly—for a while. But he was drinking vodka, alternately mixing it with vermouth and beer, and the more he drank, the tougher and nastier he became. Even for a Russian, by the way, he was an astonishing drinker. Unless he put away two or three bottles of vodka a day he considered himself practically on the wagon.

Before we left he gave me an ultimatum. Unless I wished reprisal measures started against my family I was to find from one to three jobs in my organization for his aides within ninety days. He brushed aside my pleas that I had partners and a very efficient company manager named Sam Rheiner who would object violently to acquiring unneeded help. "We call him Sam Eyes-on-the-Cost-Sheets Rheiner," I told him. "They will not only object, they will reject any such suggestion, and there is not one damn thing I can do about it."

"Ninety days," he kept saying. "That's what you have, Boris. Ninety days to come through, and you *better* come through. Here in the United States, where people think they are so safe from us, we manage to catch up with those who forget what they owe us."

I felt as though my head were splitting. It would have been bad enough at any time, but that day, with so much left to do about the première of the most important picture I ever made, I was eager, above all else, to get rid of him if only for the time being. I would have agreed to almost anything to get him out of my way until *Tales of Manhattan* was launched.

"All right," I told him. "I'll do anything I can."

"Anything is not enough. You have, as I keep telling you, just ninety days." That caused me to make one last effort to backtrack. I said, "I'll be frank with you. I just do not know how to do what you wish me to do. I would try, I assure you I would, if I did understand it."

That made him laugh. "Stop worrying. We'll supply anybody you want—technicians, electricians, prop men, or any other sort of studio worker." Now he was laughing so loud he was hardly being able to control himself. And he concluded, "So, you see, Boris, you have no problems. None whatever."

So there it was, I thought, as I took a cab up to the business conference I had had to delay. "My

God," I kept asking myself, "what have I got myself into?" There was no escape. If I wished to avoid having my family annihilated I must help the Soviets. Zubilin was blackmailing me with a threat to their lives. It was as simple as that, as horrible as that.

In December, I got an ersatz love letter from Miss Melament, the woman in New York I had never seen, reminding me that my ninety days of grace were up. In January came another. I shrugged them off.

Then came the bombshell.

A day or two after the second Melament letter arrived I got the most exciting telegram I had ever received. It was from the State Department, and it announced that my father was arriving in the country. Because of wartime security regulations they gave me no additional information. I went all but mad with anticipation and joy. It is likely that, if I had seen Zubilin at that moment, I would have kissed him.

I was on pins and needles with anticipation for days after that. On January 20 another wire came. It said that my father would be in Seattle within the next few hours. That sounded great. To meet him all I needed was a plane. But I soon found that the Armed Services had left nothing available to fly me there. I called everybody I knew in Seattle and a great many persons I didn't know, starting with the mayor and the police commissioner.

To each I described in vivid and harrowing detail the perilous journey across the Pacific my eighty-two-year-old papa was completing. "Through ice-filled seas," I kept saying, "dodging submarines below the water and Japanese bombers above."

I had been phoning for hours when it suddenly occurred to me that Frank Newman, a Kansas City theater owner, now lived in Seattle. He was running a string of theaters in the Northwest. Newman, bless him, agreed to meet my father and see that the old man was comfortably settled in the Olympic, Seattle's finest hotel.

When I got there next morning I found that Newman had slept in the room with my father just to be on hand in case he wanted anything during the night. But my father looked thin and wasted. He was five feet seven—taller than I—and normally weighed 150 pounds. It had been a terrible journey for him—sixteen days on the Trans-Siberian Railroad, then twenty-eight days aboard the *Smolny*, a Liberty Ship. The run took that long because, since it was wartime, the *Smolny* had to proceed without lights at night, and thus traveled more slowly than usual. During that long voyage my father had had practically nothing to eat but rice and barley soup. We remained for two or three days in Seattle while he regained strength from substantial foods.

In that interim I took him to a movie theater. I forget what picture was playing, but my father enjoyed it very much. I said, "That is what I do now, Father. I make pictures like this one."

"Is that all?" he asked with a shrug. "Look at your brothers. One is a professor, another an engineer, a third is a great linguist. But all you do is make movies. Do you make a lot of money doing that, Boris?"

I said, "Yes."

"Well, that's *something*," he said. And there was no misinterpreting the look he gave me. I had abandoned learning, culture, everything he had trained me for, to take up what seemed to him a frivolous and childish profession.

When we got home to Beverly Hills, I tried to get him to talk about what living under the Communists had been like, but he would tell me nothing. When I asked him about my brothers, he just shook his head sadly.

About three weeks after my father's arrival, Zubilin appeared at my Beverly Hills home, loaded down with champagne and caviar. I introduced Zubilin as the gentleman who had been instrumental in bringing him over, but Father refused to stay in the room with him for more than a few minutes. He had a drink of vodka with our caller, then left abruptly. I explained to Zubilin that the old man was not feeling very chipper, that the long trip had been a strenuous one for a man of his age.

Zubilin just shrugged and made a date to meet me at Perino's Restaurant the next day.

The moment for the pay-off had arrived, and I knew it.

CHAPTER 4

I Begin to Learn the Score

Now Zubilin had a different proposition—a better one, from his point of view. He wanted letters from me authorizing his men to act as talent scouts for my company, Boris Morros Productions.

I claimed his scheme was not possible. "You forget I am no longer with a big company like Paramount," I said. "Little companies like ours don't have talent scouts. They can't afford them."

"You can put my men on the payroll, Boris," he said, "and it won't cost you a cent."

I explained that money was not the problem, but that such a transparent cover would attract the suspicions of any official who knew how film companies were run. He then switched back to the idea of planting a Soviet cameraman, a couple of electricians, and a prop man in my company. When I repeated the arguments I had made before, he kept saying, "Boris, you *must* cooperate. You can't do this to the man who brought your father to you."

Next he offered a plea I would have laughed at, if I had dared. Zubilin said it was not fair that his agents should not have the comfort and security of a job with a legitimate firm. They worked so hard. They were such sincere revolutionists. They deserved at least that protection. I was tempted to point out that they had a hell of a nerve expecting to be protected by the capitalistic system they were doing their best to torpedo out of existence. But such logic would only have angered him.

With my father safely here, all I wanted was to get as far away from Zubilin as I possibly could. But it still seemed best—for the sake of the rest of my family in Russia—to avoid angering him, if possible, by withdrawing gradually.

Suddenly he leaned over the table, a glass of vodka in his hand, and said, "What about taking my men into your music company?"

I just stared at him.

"Don't look at me as though you didn't know what I'm talking about," he said. "You have a sheet-music company. It's at Sunset Boulevard and Vine Street. The office is on the ground floor of one of the buildings down there, and the sign on the door says 'Boris Morros Music Company.' I have spent some time checking up on the people who go in and out of that door."

"It is not mine," I told him. "I started it for my son, who's in the Army. I wanted to build it up so he'd have a nice little business started when he got out of the Service."

"Sounds like the perfect cover. We could have men around the United States and a few in South America—all on your payroll."

I interrupted. "Here, too, I have a partner. His name is Abe Frankl. He's managing the company on a salary-and-percentage basis. I also have song writers working for us on a salary-and-royalties basis. How would I explain all this to them?"

"Perfect," said Zubilin, ignoring my objections. "Just what we've been looking for. It would seem natural," he said, "for a music company to have men working in other countries, finding native songs and developing talent, making tie-ups with foreign music publishers. They'd have every excuse in the world to keep moving about."

As I studied his face and listened to him, I realized that nothing I could say or do would make him change his mind—for the moment, at least. Later it might be different. So I stalled the whole thing, saying, "Let me think this over for a while, Vasya. Let me digest it, get used to the idea that you are convinced I have a debt to you. I may be able to give you a satisfactory answer later on, after I've appraised the whole situation and decided how far I can go along with you on any such deal."

Before Zubilin left town he came to me with another suggestion that he seemed to think would make everything easier for me. This new arrangement required only the use of my name to give the project the appearance of legitimacy. His people would organize an entirely new music company and run it themselves. In this way there would be no Abe Frankl to worry about.

I had a couple of months' peace before Zubilin came to Hollywood again and we lunched at Perino's. This time he upset me greatly by revealing that he had found out my bank balance—to the penny. How he acquired this informtaion I have never learned, but someone in my bank—or worse, someone close to me—had been talking.

He knew precisely the amount of my investments in certain film properties I had bought into lately. He knew how much my home was worth, how much I had paid for it. He had found out that I was about to launch a musical stage show, *The Waltz King*, and knew the amount of financing I would need before I could open it in Los Angeles.

"I've decided," he announced after only a few glasses of vodka, "that we'll expand your music company. What more can you want, my little friend? I'll get the backing for you, and guarantee you against losses."

This time he left Hollywood believing that I had agreed to expand the music company—with whatever financial backing he would obtain for me—beginning that summer.

My various projects were taking me to New York about once a month during this period. Usually, I didn't advise Leah Melament I was coming. That is why, when making my August trip, I was shocked to get a phone call from Zubilin a few minutes after I had taken a room at the Sherry-Netherland. This was the second time he proved how close a check he was able to keep on my movements. A few minutes later he was up in the room with me. Zubilin checked the closets, the telephone, and the electric lights to find out whether the place had been "bugged." He did this almost automatically. All he wished to tell me on this short visit was that I should meet him at Leah Melament's apartment at seven that evening; he was checking the room for my sake, to inform me if there was a tapped wire in the place.

But the secretiveness of the rigamarole depressed me. At that time the American authorities worried me not at all. Let them tap my wires, ask questions. Zubilin was the one who worried me. Did he have people everywhere? In the banks I used, in the hotels I stopped at, in my own office? That evening when I started out for Melament's place—she had moved to another apartment whose address he had given me—I wondered which doorman, desk clerk, or bellman at the hotel had tipped him off that I was coming to New York.

When I got to the Melament apartment no one was there, but when I turned the knob the apartment door opened. I went in and sat down to wait. After a while Mme. Zubilin came in. She took me around the corner to the Beacon Theatre, on Broadway. We were just walking under the marquee when her husband joined us.

"Good night," she said, and left us to ourselves. This time Zubilin was sober and quite polite. And he was very excited. He told me that he had the right fiancial set-up at last, if only I would cooperate. Now he was asking me instead of ordering me to do things, but I didn't like it much better.

"All you have to do is let us use your name," he kept saying. Before he left he apologized for his abusive language at our few meetings.

I had a good excuse that fall of 1943 to stall him off. I was dickering with the Victor Herbert estate for the production rights to *Babes in Toyland,* and for several O. Henry stories. I also had a troupe of sixty people starting a tour in my stage show, *The Waltz King,* which opened in Los Angeles that September.

I was getting quite smug over the way I had been able to postpone doing anything. I kept hoping I

could keep on being resourceful; then the really critical time came.

In December, I got a long-distance call from Zubilin
that was too peremptory to ignore. He phoned me
in California from a booth in New York. I knew it
was a booth because I could hear the *"bong-bong"*
noises as he dropped the quarters into the box.

All details of the financing deal had been worked
out. I must come east without delay. Zubilin claimed
that he had found a wealthy couple who would back
me for $100,000, for $200,000, for anything I wanted.

I was in New York a few days later, having notified
Miss Melament in advance of the date, December 21,
that I would stop at the Sherry-Netherland. This time
Zubilin telephoned me to meet him on Broadway at
eight o'clock next morning. Starting at Sixtieth Street,
I was to keep walking north to Seventieth.

As I started uptown, I had to admit that many
things about the situation fascinated me. One was
the involved precautions he was taking—just in case
I had decided at the last moment to betray him to
the authorities: telephoning to me across the country
from a public phone booth; using Miss Melament as
a human mailbox; meeting me this morning in this
curious way. By having me walk for blocks he could
observe me at his leisure from a doorway or a roof,
and determine whether I was being followed before
approaching me.

Did he, or whoever did his thinking for him, have
the mind-reading gift? For the fact was that I had
been considering going to the FBI and letting them
take the problem of Mr. Zubilin off my shoulders.

It is hard to say now just why I delayed making
that move. I suppose I preferred, as almost any man
would, to get out of the mess on my own.

But there was something else. If I couldn't get out of it, I had made up my mind to go ahead with the thing, and see how far they would go. I foolishly flattered myself, and I had all along, that I could get out any time things got too hot for comfort.

I must also admit that, as a businessman, I was bedazzled by the idea that Zubilin's couple were willing to invest $100,000 or more in my $6,000 company. Where had he found people like that? Some of the great Broadway stage impresarios spent months every year trying to raise that much for their shows.

Near the end of my ten-block walk up Broadway, Zubilin stepped up to me. He led me to a two-door sedan which he had parked not far away, on the other side of the street. He drove, and I sat next to him on the front seat. He took the Henry Hudson Parkway, continuing north into Westchester County. Turning off the Cross County Parkway he followed the Merritt Parkway into Connecticut.

For a half hour or so after we started, Vasya was busy watching the cars behind us in the mirror. When satisfied that we were not being followed, he relaxed and started to talk. It was a beautiful, crisp day; snow was on the ground, and Westchester and Connecticut looked like a series of Christmas-card scenes.

Vasya's main topic of conversation was the wealth of the couple we were about to meet. He also rhapsodized—in Russian, German, French, and English—about the wife's vivacity, intelligence, and high social position. When he said that her father had been one of America's most important diplomats during the Franklin D. Roosevelt Administration, I decided he must be drunk, though it was still early in the day. To me, nothing that he was saying made sense.

After turning off into a smaller road, we went to the charming town of Ridgefield, where Vasya stopped the car and went into the Western Union office to telephone. Then he rejoined me in the car.

In about fifteen minutes a thin, lanky man with a pock-marked face drove up in a station wagon and parked near us. He was wearing a leather windbreaker and snow boots. Zubilin introduced the newcomer as "my good friend, Alfred K. Stern." We shook hands and got into Stern's car, and he drove us to his home. It was a typical old New England house, freshly painted. As we walked up the pathway, Mrs. Stern, a vivacious-looking young woman, opened the door for us.

After shaking hands with me, she threw her arms around Zubilin and kissed him on the mouth passionately. Walking arm-in-arm they led the way into the library, Stern and I following. All the furnishings were early American. It looked very expensive, all of it.

The endearments between Zubilin and our hostess continued until Stern, after glancing at me sheepishly, said, "Now, Vasya, that's enough." That made Zubilin roar with amusement. Incidentally, I had never seen him in such high spirits. He released Mrs. Stern and slapped her husband so hard on the back that the fragile man grunted.

"Now we have no more trouble about money," Vasya said, nodding at Stern. "Here is our treasury, our millionaire. All you have to do is set him up in the business and train him as a music-company executive. Soon as you get the business on a workable basis, you can step out, Boris. And then you can let our money man, this Sears Roebuck we have luckily found, handle the whole business."

It was not until later that I understood the point of his reference to the mail-order house. Stern previously had been married to Marian Rosenwald, daughter of Julius Rosenwald, who had made millions of dollars running Sears Roebuck. Stern himself had inherited several hundred thousand dollars from his father, a North Dakota banker, but proved a failure as an executive in the mail-order organization. However, he was reputed to have increased his fortune to over a million dollars by the time the former Miss Rosenwald and he were divorced.

Zubilin's first suggestion was that Stern put up $200,000. "I want no argument about *that,* Alfred!" he thundered. Stern, however, did argue about it. Turning to me, he asked my opinion.

"That is up to you two gentlemen to decide," I said. "I'll step out of the room while you make up your minds. Call me when the money part of it is settled."

Before Zubilin could object, I hurried out. I stood for a long while at the window in the living room, looking out at the snow.

Now I must make a confession right here. Ever since the news of my years as a spy for the Soviets and as a counterspy for the FBI was published, people have continued to ask me where I found the courage to do what I did. I cannot answer that for the best of reasons: I do not know. The only possible explanation that occurs to me is that the previous part of my life was lived in a world of fantasy where it is often difficult to tell what is actually happening and what is only being imagined. That started way back, of course. As a boy musician, I had learned to communicate my thoughts and emotions by musical sounds rather than by words and actual deeds. And what could be more unreal than living and working in Hollywood, where dreams for all humanity are manufactured? Every sort of dream—dreams of love, beauty, hate, revenge. In these Cinderella has a thousand faces, Romeo lives everywhere and forever. It is impossible to take part in such dream-making without losing yourself in it. Who could slip inside a dream and out of it each day on schedule?

So in that strange world where nothing is ever quite what it seems is possibly where I found the courage. And, while Zubilin had been 3000 miles away, the nightmare he was trying to trap me in seemed less real than the gangsters in the last cops-and-robbers picture made at my studio.

Perhaps that is also why I believed so naïvely that with my father safe in California and my mother dead, I would be able to break away from him whenever I wished. At that time I was not even dimly aware of the danger to our country of international Communism. Certainly at any other time I might have been more wary of dealing with such a man. But in 1943, and for some time before that, the valiant fighting Russians had been feted and hailed as heroes from one end of the country to the other. They were our friends, even conservative, native-born Americans were saying—our allies and our comrades-in-arms against the common enemy. The responsibility toward my brothers and sisters remained, but this naturally did not weigh on me nearly so heavily as had my obligation toward my parents.

And now I considered myself in the happy position of a man who feels quite safe while enjoying all the fun of playing a very dangerous game.

I had been standing at the window for quite a while when Mrs. Stern joined me. "You really do not remember me, do you?" she said, smiling.

I shook my head.

"Well, I was using my maiden name when we met that other time. So I will forgive you."

"And your maiden name, Mrs. Stern?"

"Martha Dodd."

Astonished though I was, I tried not to stare at her. Zubilin had not been drunk or crazy when he described her as the daughter of a top-ranking diplomat. Her father, Professor William E. Dodd, had been our ambassador to Germany during Hitler's years of glory.

"We met at the studio," she said. "Twentieth Century-Fox."

That other meeting of ours had been very brief. Michael Kanin at the time was writing the screen play for *The Grand Street Boys*, a picture I was preparing to produce on that lot. His wife, Fay, had come into my office with Martha and introduced us. She also explained that Miss Dodd was working at the studio on a screen adaptation of her book, *Through Embassy Eyes*.

In the library Zubilin and Stern continued discussing the financing matter for a full hour, while Martha Stern sat in this other room talking to me. She was pretty, well-educated, and imaginative, had a gift for telling phrases, and did not lack humor by any means. And I kept marveling to myself; what in God's name was this lovely young woman doing, married to a millionaire backer of a Russian spy ring?

It made no sense at all then. It makes little more sense to me today, though no one can read *Through Embassy Eyes* without understanding the wild emotional storms and inner conflicts that drove this spoiled, neurotic woman first into the arms of the Nazis, then to the other extreme. But that, of course, is only part of the story of her betrayal of everything her gentle father, Professor Dodd, a liberal himself, believed in and fought for all his life.

When we were at last summoned back to the library, we found Zubilin rubbing his hands briskly together. They had decided at last, they said. Stern was to put up $130,000, of which $100,000 was to be invested in the Boris Morros Company of Los Angeles. The remaining $30,000 would be kept by Stern in a fund in New York. I could not draw on this $30,000. They made no secret of their intention to use this for the salaries and expenses of agents posing as talent scouts. Some would be sent to South America, and others would be in various sections of the U.S.

"Don't worry about these men, Alfred," Zubilin said. "I will give you nothing but first-class"—he looked at me and winked—"first-class talent scouts. Each will be a college-bred man of high intelligence, fine appearance, and charming manners. I need not add that they will also be men I am convinced are devoted to our Cause."

While lunch was being served, some of the other details were worked out. Stern said he would deposit $80,000 within the next few days to the company's account, the balance a few months after.

Zubilin urged me to teach Stern the music business from the ground up. "I want you to train him so he will know thoroughly the entire business side of music —operatic music, concertos, popular music. In other words, the commercial side of everything from Bach and Beethoven to Gershwin."

He added that the placement of his men would be completely in Stern's hands. These could cover themselves by working as song pluggers or as scouts for popular singers and bands, by contacting foreign music publishers with the idea of buying American rights to their songs and selling Spanish and Portuguese rights to our hit numbers.

The conversation took an explosive turn when Stern mentioned that my lawyers need only wait to draw up a contract until he consulted with his financial adviser.

"Who is that?" demanded Vasya.

Stern mentioned the man's name, saying he was an official at the Chase National Bank.

"Forget him!"

Stern refused. That caused our NKVD chief to pound the table. There were not to be, he insisted repeatedly, any papers whatever, no contract, no notes.

"No notes?" Stern and I asked together.

"*No notes!* Alfred will bring the money to you in cash, Boris." He glared at Stern. "And keep away from that reactionary at the Chase National Bank!"

"I am sorry, Vasya," I told him, "but I wouldn't think of going into a partnership with anybody without consulting my attorneys."

Though finally convinced I was adamant on that point, he still would not agree that Stern should talk to his financial adviser. I suggested that Stern should receive an annual dividend—twenty-five per cent of the profits—when our music company started to make money. I also insisted that four per cent interest per annum be paid Stern on whatever money he invested in the concern.

Late that afternoon the Sterns drove us to the village, where they left their car. Then they got into Zubilin's car with us for the drive back to New York.

The final grotesque incident of the strange day was that ride home. Zubilin drove with one arm around Mrs. Stern. He had had a good deal of vodka before, during, and after lunch, and now, while driving, he bellowed in his lusty, unmelodious voice, "If the War Comes Tomorrow," and other Red Russian marching songs, with Martha joining in. She knew quite a bit of Russian even then. It was a strange feeling I had, rolling past that Connecticut countryside, so beautiful with its blanket of snow, and listening to the NKVD's bully boy howling the words that meant "down with our enemies" with his pretty admirer, the daughter of a distinguished American ambassador, joining in.

They dropped me off at my hotel and then the Sterns went on to their luxurious apartment on Central Park West.

The next day, of course, I should have visited the Federal Bureau of Investigation. If I had, I would have avoided more misery than I had known during my whole life.

CHAPTPR 5

The Millionaire Communist

The next day Stern came to breakfast with me at the Sherry-Netherland. He said he was very happy and kept repeating fervently that with my help he hoped to develop into an influential executive in the music business and through this make an important contribution to the cause of world Communism.

After breakfast he took me to his office at 30 Rockefeller Plaza. Stern had one employee there, a secretary. He explained that he needed the office to handle his investments. With a pride that seemed childish he pointed out the exact spot on the glass door where he was going to have printed "Boris Morros Music Company. New York and Hollywood." He suggested that I be president, he vice-president.

When I left him I went to the offices of my lawyer and told him to draw up a contract for the partnership. On hearing that I had found a financier who was eager to invest $130,000 in my $6,000 music company for only twenty-five per cent of the profits, he told me I was either drunk or crazy.

"Draw it up," I told him.

He agreed, but said he thought it wrong to charge me a fee. "This clown is kidding you," he said. "When the moment comes to sign the papers he will balk."

"Alfred K. Stern is a millionaire," I explained. "Crazy, but a millionaire."

"Well, he won't be a millionaire for long if he makes many more investments like this one," he said.

During the week or so I remained in New York on that visit I had almost daily conferences with Stern and Zubilin. They talked jubilantly of the recent meeting of Stalin, Roosevelt, and Churchill at Tehran.

"After letting us bleed ourselves white," Zubilin said, "Roosevelt and Churchill now agree to a second front. They want to get in on the kill, then claim all the spoils and the credit they can."

"As usual," chimed in Stern.

I hardly listened. Now that the die was cast I was perversely fascinated by the possibilities. Would Stern be silly enough to sign the papers?

They were ready on New Year's Eve. When I told my lawyer that Stern would sign that evening, he said, "I've been curious to see this rare money bird you have bagged for yourself, Boris. But I live out in the country and on the noisiest night in the year I prefer to be there rather than in town. So I'll be unable to watch your amputation operation on Mr. Stern's bankroll."

Zubilin came to my hotel room with Stern on New Year's Eve to witness the signing of the papers. After a couple of swigs of vodka Vasya started singing his favorite Soviet marching song, "Tomorrow We Go to War!" But he interrupted his singing on seeing Stern pick up a copy of the contract.

"Don't read it, you fool, you stupid sonofabitch," he roared. "Just sign it."

Sighing meekly, Stern took out his fountain pen and signed.

From the start, Alfred was pathetically eager to learn all details of the business. Vasya suggested once or twice that he could master these details far more quickly if he spent six months of the year with me in California, but Martha, who said she detested everything about Hollywood, vetoed the suggestion.

I soon realized that the circumstances of war had brought a revolutionary change to the popular-music industry. It had become impossible, for example, to make money on sheet music alone. Sales had to be stimulated continually by recordings, sung by the right singers. Because juke box and disc jockey had become essential in putting over a song, I started a recording company.

The war, of course, also had created millions of new customers. Both servicemen and stay-at-home war workers were hungry for music and entertainment, and they had the money to pay for it. But the war had also created shortages of the materials we most needed; shellac, for instance, was almost unobtainable, as was nickel, without which it was impossible to make the master records.

It took months but by the summer of 1944 we were finally beginning to roll. I had a crack engineer working in our recording studio. I had a smart sales manager in Shelby Yorke, who was on friendly terms with executives of all the juke-box manufacturing firms. I had brilliant performers signed up— Frances Langford, Bob Crosby, Hoagy Carmichael, Phil Harris.

During the first half of 1944, Stern and I got along beautifully, though he knew nothing about the music business or music itself. I had to explain what a bar of music is, a refrain, how songs were written, published, put over; how no one really knew what would catch on until the public itself let us know. But he let me run my business in Hollywood and I let him run his business, if any, in New York.

Late in March 1944, I had a telephone call from Stern. He said, "Wait a minute. A very dear person wants to talk to you." I recognized the voice of the woman he put on the phone as Mrs. Zubilin's. She said that her husband was very anxious to see me, adding, "We are leaving town soon."

Realizing that something important was happening, I got into New York two days later. Stern met me at LaGuardia Airport. He told me that the Zubilins were going home, where he was to be promoted to the rank of general for "important services he's rendered over here." Stern almost had tears in his eyes as he said, "I don't know where we'll ever find another leader to take his place."

To me, Stern's attitude was baffling. The passionate manner in which his wife and Zubilin kissed and fondled one another each time I saw them together convinced me—would have convinced anyone —that they were lovers. In fact, the way each spoke of the old days in Berlin inclined me to the idea that they had been sweethearts during the time her father was our ambassador there. I could not understand why this millionaire not only tolerated his pretty wife's intimacy with a brutish muzhik, but now was almost breaking down with emotion because the man who had seemingly made a cuckold of him was about to leave the country.

The answer, of course, lay in the character of my new partner. Stern, a weak and easily led man, worshiped both in his wife and in Zubilin the strength he lacked himself. She dominated him completely. The reason he did not object with any firmness when Zubilin let his big hands rove over Martha's curves was that he did not dare. Alfred, who never in his life had needed to think for himself or stand on his own feet, let Martha lead him around by the nose. He was inordinately proud of everything about her: her intelligence, her good looks, her position in the intellectual world as an author, her position in the social and diplomatic worlds as the daughter of ex-Ambassador William E. Dodd. The ideology of the Soviet Union must have appealed to this impressionable man because it represented strength and the determination to rock the world with the dynamite of revolution.

Zubilin telephoned me at my hotel to arrange a rendezvous on a Broadway corner near Columbus Circle. Again, instead of showing up himself, he sent his wife to meet me. She walked me to Columbus Circle. We found Vasya waiting there, near the Far East, then a well-known Chinese restaurant. It was on the second floor, and as we started up the steps Zubilin told his wife, "Say good-by to Boris here. You will not see him again." Obediently, Liza and I bade one another farewell.

The restaurant was dimly lit. Only two or three tables were occupied and Zubilin led me to a booth at the end of the room where a man was sitting alone. "This is my successor, Jack Soble," he said. "From now on he's your boss. Stern? Never mind—he'll see Stern."

The next thing Zubilin said that day in the Far East made me shudder. "Our Comrade here," and he nodded at me, "is completely devoted to the motherland, and is one of our most trusted and loyal agents." However, I have reason to think that he told Soble other things about me, that night and afterward, which convinced Soble that I might prove neither loyal nor trustworthy enough for his purposes, and had better be watched. And, as I was soon to find out, Jack Soble was a more intelligent and interesting man than either the dim-witted Stern or Zubilin, the muzhik with the mighty muscles.

I suppose if even today I could analyze Jack Soble's complicated motives, follow the twists and turns of his jackrabbit of a mind, weigh and understand his sincerity—something which went hand in hand with his deviousness—I would be able to contribute much to the free world's knowledge of how to cope with other Communists. But I am not a psychiatrist. I know little more about Soble than what happened to him. Everything beyond that—his background, his previous career as a spy, the complexities of his personality—I had to learn only after filtering through the thousand and one lies, half-truths, and contradictions he told me. But of one thing I am certain: if a man like Soble is useful to his masters in Moscow, he also is an ever-present danger to them. They have no choice; they must use men like him. And the Jack Sobles, no matter how often they are put through the Soviet's psychological meat-grinders, remain men. Like everyone else, like all people everywhere, they have their vanity and pride, their weaknesses and strengths.

Soble is a Lithuanian. He held the rank of colonel; at least he was permitted to travel as a Russian Army colonel while in Europe, which is not always the same thing. Later he told me that he had handled several millions of dollars while working as a secret agent in the Balkans, and in Spain during the Spanish Civil War. He also had worked as a newspaper reporter in Hitler's Germany, while pursuing his dangerous undercover recruiting activities in that police state. At the time I met him, Soble had given Moscow no reason to distrust him.

The clue to the strange fate that caught up with Jack Soble finally may lie in his passionate love for his son, Larry, and for his wife, Myra. In the non-Communist world this sort of devotion is accepted as the norm. In the Soviet world it is regarded with deep suspicion. If a man lets family love interfere with his duties to the state, the Kremlin considers his usefulness ended.

Myra and Jack had been married for twenty-odd years when I met them, and their son Larry, named for Lavrenti Beria, was about four. Soble himself was forty and weighed between 170 and 180 pounds. But he was over six feet tall so, unlike Vasya, he was slim. His dark hair was thinning. If I had been asked to guess his occupation I would have said he was a garment worker dressed up in his Sunday best.

From where we sat in the restaurant we could see everyone who entered the place. Someone had put dozens of nickels into the juke box—selecting the loudest numbers—and the few other patrons could not possibly hear our talk.

Though Soble was replacing Zubilin as my superior, Vasya gave me the definite impression that the newcomer was by no means taking over his whole job as NKVD chief in charge of espionage in America, and that his work was being split up among Jack and several other men. He explained, "Soble will have the responsibility of supervising your work, and it will be to me that he will report on what you are doing, regardless of where in the world I happen to be." And then he threw in a none too subtle threat. "There will be no trouble, of course, Boris. But if there is, I assure you I will be able to reach you—through him."

That was the whole thing, all I needed to know. I was to have no more contact with Zubilin, who said he was going at once to ·Moscow. Among my other orders, he said I was to forget Leah Melament as I would have no further connection with that human letterbox. As far as I know that was her only function. I never saw her or heard her name mentioned after that.

During all this, Soble said little, just smiling and acquiescing to whatever Zubilin said. He asked no questions about the company, even after Zubilin explained that I was to have charge of the musical part, Stern the political function. He had said that Stern would meet Soble at another time, and I had the feeling that Soble that evening was seeing a succession of agents and contacts. I stayed there only fifteen or twenty minutes. Before I left, Soble gave me his address in the Washington Heights section of Manhattan. He said his number was in the phone book, but that I should not call except in an emergency.

Zubilin told me, "It's getting tough here, so I'm glad to return to the motherland." I learned later that he was leaving by request of the United States government. "Even if I'm sent to the Orient," Zubilin added, "I will know, Boris, whether you are or are not carrying out the original plans we agreed upon. And, when I am in Russia, I will be able to reward your family with privileges—if you obey my dictates. And if not—I leave what will happen to them to your imagination."

Imagine my shock and horror, after listening to that speech, to be told by my father, when I returned from that trip East, that two of my brothers, to the best of his knowledge, had been killed by the Soviets. "I did not tell you before this," he said, "because there was nothing you could do about it.

But I cannot keep it from you any longer."

Papa was right. There was nothing I could do about it—unless I was willing to take the responsibility for having the rest of the family exterminated. But from that day onward the hope of revenge lay in back of my mind. It seemed to me that there must be some way out without sacrificing the others. All I regret now is that I lacked the faith and the courage to find it sooner than I did.

I have said that Stern and I got along well during the first few months of our partnership. After I had a recording studio built in Hollywood, I went back to New York and dined with him and Martha in their elegant Central Park West apartment. That night I suggested they go with me to a small night club where a woman singer I wanted to hear was appearing.

A curious thing happened as we were leaving the apartment house. One of the building employees called Stern aside and whispered to him as Martha and I got into the taxicab the doorman had summoned for us. Alfred joined us, white and shaken.

"That fellow said that there were men around here tonight asking questions about me," he said. "They said they were FBI men and even showed him their credentials."

"Oh, Sam is just drunk again, Alfred," Martha commented. "They never should have let him out of the alcoholic ward at Bellevue."

I looked at her in astonishment. Then I noticed that she was nudging Alfred with her knee. When we got out in front of the night club—a Greenwich Village spot since closed—Alfred paid the driver.

"He gave me a funny look," Alfred said after the cab was gone.

"Little cab drivers have big ears," Martha told him,

and, looking at me, she added, "and they are not the only ones." But she remained unperturbed. "Let's enjoy the show," she said. "I hope the girl's good."

The girl turned out to be a run-of-the-mine $75-a-week blues singer. But Alfred thought she was great, and wanted me to sign her up. I shook my head. That may have irritated him. But I am not sure. I do know that not long after this he began telling me how to run the music end of our business.

That summer it became known all over the music trade that I had latched on to an angel with a wide-open checkbook. I was even approached with offers to buy Muzak, the company that supplies "canned music" to restaurants and hotels all over the country. We visited ex-Senator William E. Benton of Connecticut, who was then an official of the Muzak corporation, but Stern, who was the one who would put up the money, decided that the price of $600,000 asked for the properties was too high. He would go no higher than $400,000. Today, Muzak, of course, is worth millions.

During August, Stern visited Hollywood, and I made the astonishing discovery that he already knew more about music, both artistically and commercially, than Paul Whiteman, myself, and Stravinsky.

Meanwhile, I had surmounted many of our difficulties, and records were being produced. That fall we had a hit recording by Joe Reichman's band. This was "Nobody's Home on the Range," a travesty of the song "Home on the Range," which had boomed into renewed popularity because it was President Roosevelt's favorite.

But Stern disapproved of almost everything we were doing. He disliked my office staff, including my sales manager. He wanted the man discharged, and wished me to switch control of the sales department to his office. Above all, he thought that we should concentrate on songs of a more cultural type. For example, he disapproved of "Chattanooga Choo Choo" as a vulgar title, and predicted it would never be popular. He asked a million questions such as "Why don't we sign up Bing Crosby instead of his brother Bob?" It was tiresome to have to point out that someone had had the same idea years before.

This was the man to whom I had had to explain a few months before what a bar of music was, what the refrain was, the man who asked the usual foolish question, "What is written first—the words or the music?"

All that fall Stern showered me with daily letters of five to eight pages each. On hearing that we needed record-pressing equipment, he rushed out and bought $17,000 worth of second-hand presses that were so outmoded they could not be used.

I am afraid I was not very patient with my vice-president. By this time I had three shifts working in our little plant. They were turning out thirty thousand platters a day. They had to. Our "Nobody's Home on the Range" was headed for the hit class.

Shortly after the partnership arrangement started, both Soble and Stern began pressing me to open a branch in Mexico City. They were still at it, though I had stalled *that* deal with the argument that before we could do any such thing we must have enough numbers to distribute to justify a catalogue. However, I was getting more infuriated every day with Stern's silly letters of abuse and criticism. By now he was disapproving not only of the songs but of the arrangements.

At the end of the year I decided that life was too short to bother with this money man, and so informed Soble. But it was not until March—this was in 1945—

that Jack decided he must do something to calm down both of us. He came with Stern to California to settle our differences. They arrived toward the end of the month and visited the plant.

"He is a musical ignoramus on all levels," I told Soble. "I feel it is impossible to go along with him. The only thing we can do now is to break up this ridiculous partnership."

"Artistic temperament!" clucked Jack Soble.

The next day they came back to the plant. When the angry words started to fly all over again, Soble suggested that we go to my home in Beverly Hills. I suppose he did not want our employees to hear the dispute. My visitors stayed in Hollywood about a week. Soble, trying to act as peacemaker, kept repeating that the Cause was the one thing that counted, not my petty grievances or Alfred's. We just *had* to get along.

I have never pretended to be an even-tempered man. During that stormy week I called Stern every foul name I could think of in all the languages I knew—and I know profanity as it is spoken and spluttered around the world. Stern, the Harvard man, just sat there and took it with the uncomprehending look of a hurt child.

When the week was over with the issue unresolved, Soble said he had to get back to New York. But he was sure that some way to reconcile our differences would occur to him. He asked me to go with them on their trip East so that we could have further talks while traveling. I got a compartment that connected with the drawing room they shared.

En route Soble came up with what he considered the sure-fire solution: if I would agree to continue working with Stern he would invest another $100,000 in the company.

I refused this, telling Soble, "I don't want any more of his money. In fact I would be happy to buy back his twenty-five-per-cent share of the business for what he paid for it."

"This is going to make Vasya Zubilin very, very angry," Soble said. "I'm afraid that he will be very hard on your family in Russia—unless you cooperate."

"You said you were going to investigate this whole matter," I reminded him. "You have not been impartial. What I want is a simple thing: to be left alone to do my job, unbothered by nincompoops." I glared at Stern.

On reaching New York, we had a final meeting at the Tavern-on-the-Green Restaurant. When it ended, we were as far apart as ever.

A couple of nights later Martha Dodd Stern visited me in my hotel room at the Sherry-Netherland. She was all sweetness and light. Martha blamed herself for neglecting to take a more active part in the business. "If I had, Boris," she said, "there would have been no such misunderstandings between you two tried and true Communists." She kept pounding at the point Soble had: the welfare of the Party should be our only consideration.

"Sorry, Martha, my dear," I said, "you are being very charming and sweet, wistful and feminine—but too many wrong things have been done and said."

My lawyers began drawing up the papers for dissolving the partnership in April. I paid Stern $100,-000 for his one-quarter interest in the Boris Morros Company and its record-making subsidiary, American Recording Artists.

He rendered an account of how the $30,000 allotted him had been spent. I was amazed to see that he had given Zubilin $5000 cash and charged it to the company. He had also charged petty items, including the purchase of a record player and two dozen tennis balls for Zubilin, as well as the full cost of his and Soble's trip to Hollywood.

But I was glad to get rid of him. I thought I was also extricating myself from Jack Soble's spy ring. To put it mildly, I was being naïvely optimistic.

I had been willing to pay a high price for the privilege of disassociating myself. To raise the $100,-000 in cash to pay off Stern, I was forced to sell my share of a film property. But they still wished me to engage in a new venture with Alfred K. Stern.

Jack Soble kept coming to see me. "What *can* I do, Boris?" he said. "You have put me in the difficult position of having to write a bad report on you to Moscow. I am holding it back. I am afraid that Zubilin will be unable to control himself when he hears that you have split up with Alfred. I'd hate to feel responsible for the extermination of your relatives in Russia. Wouldn't you?"

As I look back now, it amazes me that during the next two years, though I continued to see and hear from Jack Soble frequently, the truth that he was already thinking of defecting from the Communist cause never dawned on me.

The only explanation is that I was a newcomer to the underworld of the espionage agent. Having had no occasion to study any others at close range, I assumed that they all talked and behaved like Jack. Otherwise, I think I would have recognized the fact that he wanted to run away from his career of spy and recruiting agent for Moscow. He was pulled both ways. He believed with all his heart in "the Communist ideal." At the same time he wished to take his wife and son out of the ever-present danger that was an integral part of his role as a secret agent operating in a foreign country. The two dreams he nourished were dragging him in opposite directions.

Just a few months after I met him, Jack had started complaining of the humiliation the NKVD had imposed on him when it ordered him to run a grocery store. He sometimes referred to it as a cafeteria. However, he always stuck to his story that it was on the outskirts of New York. And it was years later that I learned, from another source, that his business was actually a cafeteria but in the west Thirties, which is midtown Manhattan.

Jack was very proud that Lavrenti Beria, supreme head of the Russian secret police, had personally summoned him from Germany to the Kremlin in 1940 to tell him he was being transferred to the United States. Jack blamed Zubilin for the humiliating order that he run the grocery. Incidentally, he bought this with funds supplied by Moscow. He considered it an unjustified demotion. Dozens of times he complained to me, "I have to get up to open the store at five o'clock in the morning. I stay there until late at night. But when I close up I am often given assignments that require hours of work. Sometimes I get assignments that force me to close the store in the middle of the day. What kind of work, what kind of life, is that for a man like me?"

Zubilin apparently had felt that while Jack was awaiting his United States citizenship papers, he would be mixing every day with his customers, ordinary Americans, and thus getting a good sampling of their political theories. With a better understanding of what typical Americans wanted out of life, of their morality, mores, and mental habits, he would be more efficient in converting them to Communism.

Jack, of course, could not see it that way. He grumbled that it was a great come-down after being a newspaperman for years in Germany, and having $3,-

500,000 to distribute to Spanish loyalists and Communist sympathizers in the Balkans. "Without ever asking me for an accounting," he sometimes concluded, bitterly. "And now they have me running this wretched grocery, and they watch the small sums of money they send me like so many suspicious old bookkeepers."

I had thought Zubilin's precautions on entering a hotel room were extraordinary, but they were nothing compared to the trouble Soble took each time to protect himself. Never would he talk to me in a hotel room before he had completed his painstaking search. He went through the same routine each time; he would take out each light bulb in the room, put his finger in the socket, lift each chair and other piece of furniture, go over the radiators—behind, in front, under them—move everything movable. He would snap off and on each electric light switch four or five times.

If a single lamp did not work, that would trouble him. He would take off the shade, remove the bulbs, take the whole thing apart, including the plug. He traced every wire in the room to see where it came to, looked over and shook down the drapes. He would take as long as necessary for this examination.

At first I would ask, "What in hell are you doing, Jack?"

He would hold his finger to his lips.

In the bathroom he would flush the toilet and turn on all the faucets. He would get on his knees to trace the places in the walls and floor where the pipes came in. He would go into the closet and tap the walls. He examined each article of clothing and looked under the bed. Then he would go into the kitchen of the suite and check every installation there. He would look behind pictures, behind mirrors. The telephone particularly fascinated him; he would lift the mouthpiece receiver, listen for the buzzing of a tap, and run his fingers along the length of the cord. And after all that he would caution me to lower my voice when we started our conversation. Then he would speak a multilingual sentence, using one French word, the next English, the next a word in an Oriental language. If there was a radio in the room he would turn it up as an added precaution.

I was eager to break off relations with him but did not dare to do so because of Zubilin's threats. I kept hoping that they would get tired of trying to force me to provide a business "cover" for their agents. For this reason, I thought the intelligent thing to do until that happened was to keep on seeing Jack whenever I was in New York.

I kept hoping I would be as lucky as the youthful wise man who was summoned, with the other wise men of the kingdom, to his monarch's palace. The bored old Shah had decided that if the wise men were as intelligent as they pretended to be they could teach even a donkey in his stable to talk.

"That would be most difficult, Your Majesty," said the oldest of the wise men.

The Shah flew into a rage, and said that he would have the heads of all of them cut off unless they could promise him to teach his favorite donkey to speak. The wise men all looked at one another in terror. As the Shah was about to summon his official executioner, the youngest of the wise men spoke up.

"Your Most Divine Highness," he said, "I can do as you wish. I can make the donkey speak."

"You can?" said the Shah. "I'll have the beast brought—"

"Not today, Your Majesty. It is not easy. It will take time. But I can do it—in two years."

The Shah shrugged. "But remember, if the donkey, after two years, cannot speak, I will have the heads of all of you."

After they bowed themselves out of the royal chamber, one of the older men said to the presumptuous young philosopher, "What nonsense! You cannot teach a donkey to speak in two years, or two hundred."

"I may not have to," replied the other. "Many wonderful things can happen in two years to save us all."

"What?"

"The donkey is very old. The Shah also is no longer young. So who can tell? If the Shah isn't dead after two years, the donkey will be."

And that's the way I played it with the Russians.

As time went on, it seemed to me that Soble became friendlier than he had been at first. His wife was a movie fan and I think that they were coming to think of me as a Hollywood celebrity.

So things continued on that basis all through that year. And in December Jack confided something to me that gave me hope that he would be out of my future permanently very soon. He was about to be given his final American citizenship papers, which he had applied for shortly after his arrival in this country in 1940. He pointed out that this would entitle him to an American passport, which he could use on a trip he was planning soon to take to Paris. How important this American passport was to his career as a secret agent I discovered only later on.

In June 1947, when he got his papers and passport, he recklessly traveled to Europe on a Russian ship—something that would have aroused the interest of American agents if Soble had been under observation. Yes, the same punctiliously careful and cautious man who checked all hotel rooms so thoroughly, did this rash thing. "I am traveling with a very important personage," he added, but did not reveal who the personage was.

"In Moscow," Jack said in our last talk before he sailed, "I will see the bosses, the big bosses, but I'll have to talk fast when they ask me about you. In their eyes I have failed completely with you. I hope you realize that. As I've told you, I am your friend and I will do the best I can for you. However, the fact that I badly need your business as a cover may help me persuade them to forgive you."

That, of course, crushed all hope that the Russian espionage men would tire of me, eventually, and give up the idea of using me. As I found out later, they never do tire. They have all the time in the world and they know it. They can and will wait years— just as long as they think necessary—for the right time to trap you in their net.

After that talk with Jack, I forced myself to face the fact that there was no end in sight and that there would never be one. And this was not all that was happening to keep me awake nights, half sick with fear. For some time past there had been many disturbing incidents, each unimportant in itself, that indicated the Russians might not be the only ones who had placed me under observation. On a visit I made to Chicago a short-wave radio I had just bought for my son—which was equipped to send and receive messages from abroad—had disappeared mysteriously. This happened during a press party I was giving at the Bismarck Hotel to promote *The Waltz King*. There were fifty persons at the party, including the cast. It was disquieting to learn, on making inquiries, that an unidentified, uninvited male guest had been observed walking out with the radio. Adding to my nervousness was a suspicion that Russian espionage agents had also begun to check up on me more and more carefully and with shorter intervals between the checkups. I now also recalled that the second time I lunched with Vassily Zubilin at Perino's I had observed an alert young man in the next booth. He was apparently listening with interest to the conversation we were conducting in Russian. When he saw me watching him, he winked, as though he *intended* me to know he was there to listen. Thinking of this, along with everything else, gave me a creepy feeling.

And lately, wherever I had gone, to night clubs, restaurants, theaters, even as I arrived and left my studio offices each day, I had the uneasy feeling of being followed by one side or the other, or by both.

In addition to all this, other members of my family complained to me that they felt strangers were watching them. One morning, as my son, Dick, left the house, he noticed a car parked across the street. In it were two young men who seemed to be watching our front door. Dick had never seen them before.

Dick drove away. After going a short way, he discovered that a car—he believed it the same one—was following him. He turned, and the car behind him turned. He tried it again. The car behind him turned again. When Dick drove faster, the other driver also stepped on the gas. When Dick slowed down, the car following did, too. Worried and puzzled, he stopped off at a drugstore to telephone me. After listening to him, I said, "It's nonsense. Forget it." I didn't want my war-veteran son to worry. One worrier in our family was enough.

It was right after this incident that I went to the FBI. Until that day, as you can see, I had been living for years almost like a hunted creature. The worst part had been having to keep my humiliating secret from everyone—even from my wife, Katerina. We had been married in 1924, twenty-three years before. But even if I had confided in her, understanding would have been beyond her. I'm not so sure that even now she understands what happened to me, or why. For Katerina Morros's most bitter and burning memory, today as always, is of seeing several of her brothers shot by Communist rioters and looters. The pillaging Reds took one strapping brother of Katerina's after another, ordered him to stand against the wall of her father's house in Rostov, then shot him down.

She had told me the story ten thousand times. She had told it again to every Russian she met, ending it each time with the same anguished words, "Bolsheviki! Swine! They did not even *blindfold* my brothers before shooting them down like dogs!"

It took a whole week of sessions to tell the story to the FBI men. I racked my memory to recall every detail. As I talked, each of the two men took notes independently of the other. They interrupted me occasionally, but only to ask a question or two. I think I interrupted myself just as often, always to ask: "You boys were following me, weren't you?"

They never became angry, but always gave the same answer: "We'll ask the questions, Boris, if you don't mind."

They did not deny that they had followed me, but they did not admit it either. And when I had told everything, they asked me a question that I interpreted as forgiveness and evidence of their faith.

"Would you like to cooperate with us?"

"When do I start?"

"Now. Today. We can give you your instructions now—unless you'd like to think the whole thing over for a day or two."

"I don't have to think anything over," I replied.

"If you think your life was difficult and complicated before, that is nothing to how complicated it will be once you begin working with us. Because you will have to pretend to be playing ball with them all the time. You will have to remember a thousand details that you will not dare to write down, that you will be able to pass on to us only verbally."

I shrugged.

"And it is only fair to tell you that it is dangerous," the younger one said then. "Very dangerous."

I am not a brave man, and have always known it. But I felt brave at that moment and I asked, "What are those instructions?"

The first thing impressed on me was the necessity of confiding in no one, not even members of my family, that I had become a counterspy for them.

The first thing I had to do, they said, would be to seem to yield, gradually and reluctantly, to Soble's importunities that I provide the business cover he said he so desperately needed for his ring of secret agents. "If you quit arguing with him too abruptly," I was told, "he may become suspicious of your about-face, your sudden change of heart."

I was also instructed to keep a record of every conversation, telephone call, or other message I received from the Communist secret agents.

"What about assigning an FBI man to work with me?" I asked, on hearing that. I could put him on the payroll of my film company, Federal Films, as my private secretary, I pointed out, and he would be able to keep an eye on everything that went on. They agreed, and assigned me one of their younger agents. I told my other employees that this man, whom I'll call here Bob Burton, was a nephew of Bob O'Donnell, an important film exhibitor in Texas, and that Bob had sent him to me to learn the business.

He learned the business, all right. He was so useful around the studio office that my partners complimented me on having acquired a gem of a secretary. He fully earned the $50-a-week salary I paid him. He also earned his FBI salary by listening in on every phone call I made or received, by traveling with me everywhere I went—and by protecting my life, which suddenly the FBI considered important because of the strange and perilous position I had jammed myself into.

And that Bastille Day when I went ot the FBI boys I wrote in my diary, "I don't know exactly what the two of them think of me. . . . I have not hidden anything from them. I respect them thoroughly. If they respect me half as much—I'm pleased. How can I expect more? It was a day of clearing the conscience. It had to come."

CHAPTER 6

I Start Trapping My Trappers

With Jack in Europe, the easiest way to keep in contact with him was through his wife. I telephoned her from Los Angeles a few days before each trip I made to New York during the next few months. I had her dine with me at my hotel two or three times, and one afternoon I took her and her little boy to the Music Hall.

She said she was afraid I was in trouble. Jack was trying to straighten everything out for me but she was not very sanguine about his succeeding. She told me that the Sterns had invited her and her boy to visit them at their country place, but she had refused because several recent Westbrook Pegler columns criticizing their political sympathies had recently been published. She thought the safe thing to do was to keep away from them as much as possible until it became clear whether or not the Pegler columns had alerted the United States authorities.

It was during those evenings with Myra, I think, that something dawned on me which was bound to be a great help to me in my new work as a counterspy. I had noticed how impressed Jack Soble was because I lived in luxury hotels, and because I always picked up the dinner check. Now, from Myra's talk, I became aware that he admired me tremendously as a successful businessman. She shared this admiration, particularly because I was in a glamorous profession that fascinated her more than anything in the world. In fact, Myra read nothing but the Hollywood gossip columns and the movie fan magazines; Louella Parsons and Hedda Hopper were the supreme goddesses of information to Myra. That was almost all we two talked about when we were together.

The FBI once had me strap a tiny radio transmitter around my waist. They were able to hear every word Myra Soble uttered one evening. I never asked my FBI contacts why this experiment was not repeated with Myra. My guess is that they had heard enough on that one evening of what Hedda, Lolly Parsons, Sheila Graham, and the others were saying in their columns about the wonderful, adorable, delicious performers Myra had been seeing lately in the movies.

Myra, Lithuanian like her husband, looked like a full-blooded, passionate woman. I am sure that if it had been necessary for the sake of the Cause to be unfaithful to her husband she would not have hesitated to give herself. But it would have been only as a sacrifice. She loved Jack with all her heart, despite the edicts of the Kremlin that love for each other must never interfere with love for the Party. She also helped out the family finances, sometimes by working in an office and at other times by dressmaking.

It was a curious experience, I must say, to sit with this plump housewife and listen to her ecstatic description of that look in Gregory Peck's eyes as he took Ingrid Bergman in his arms, and her speculations as to whether Clark Gable would ever be happy again, having lost Carole Lombard in that dreadful plane crash. She went to the movies every day and had all sorts of questions for me.

"What sort of wife do you think Clark would be content with?" she'd ask. Could any woman—now really—hope to hold a hunk of magnificent man against all the other glamorous women in the world? Could even the late Carole Lombard have done *that* for all her beauty, worldliness, and adaptability? Was Janet Gaynor happy in retirement? Or Norma Shearer? Could they give it all up, the glamour, the sense of being yearned for by millions of men, the excitement, the name in lights from Tacoma to Timbuktu?

Not only was Myra a movie fan but her interests and daily worries were the same as those that harassed the middle-class housewives she lived among. And I do mean that the same thoughts ran through her head: "Will we be able to afford to send junior to summer camp this year? When will we get an apartment with enough rooms and, even more important, more closet space? Is it right that the child, growing up now, should continue to sleep in our room? How do we know when he is awake, when asleep, the little rascal? When he is listening, or even watching?"

When I say that Jack Soble was more intelligent than Myra, I am not forgetting that she, long before he ever suspected me of counterspy activities, warned him against me. But that was feminine intuition, the female's gift for catching the scent of the enemy quickly and, usually, accurately.

Less intelligent or not, Myra had the stronger character and, despite what I have written above, was far more devoted to the Great Cause. She also was stirred by a deeper, more elemental allegiance to Communism. Now I do not contend that all this was clear to me at the beginning, but I do know that I began to sense, early in the game, the hints of divided loyalties in Jack, and to a lesser degree in Myra, and that I later profited from this growing awareness in ferreting out their secrets.

From time to time, I did get tidbits of information from Myra. Jack was coming home, he was in Moscow, next in Warsaw. He had cabled her that he wanted a typewriter sent to him. I was in trouble with Moscow but Jack thought he could save me. This and that. Nothing substantial. Nothing that seemed worth knowing.

When Jack came back from Europe in November 1947, I found him jubilant about the success of his trip. He said he had saved my life. But before giving me the details about this he talked at great length about a private business—a bristle factory—that he had taken over at Verberie-Oise, a village about two hours' drive from Paris. It had been his father's years before and he had owned a share of it, in partnership with his brother and brother-in-law, for some time. But now, he said, he had bought out the two of them. Among other projects he was developing was a completely new process for bleaching the bristles that he expected would make him wealthy eventually. He had sold the cafeteria.

In addition to this, he had set up a black-market deal in Paris that could not miss bringing him a fortune. The one thing he didn't like about this deal was that he would have to be separated from Myra and his kid for whole months at a time. The deal would necessitate his delivering consignments of Chinese pig bristles—the costliest kind and the most difficult to obtain—to the black-market traders over there in Paris, with the pay-off going to Myra in New York. "All in American dollars." They already had a secret cable code, he said. "Say Myra gets five thousand dollars on a shipment. She wires me, 'I have bought five dresses here.'"

I told him I thought this was immensely clever but that I was eager to hear, not unnaturally, how hard he had to work to "save my life."

"Zubilin," he said, "wanted to shoot you. He is really burned up at you. It took me a long time to calm him down. I had to whitewash you and blame all the difficulties on Stern." Soble now warned me to stay away from the Sterns forever. He was just as angry at them as Zubilin was at me. They were the ones making all the trouble, not to mention double-crossing him. Martha Stern had been so indignant about my breaking up the partnership with her husband that she had written a report to Moscow, denouncing me. But Soble had known nothing of this until he got "Home," as they called the Kremlin. She had not shown the report to him before sending it. She had used a contact at the embassy, despite orders from the higher-ups that everything must go through him, Jack Soble.

Despite her, both Vasya and he had been promoted, he confided. Vasya was now head of *Inostranni*, the foreign division of the NKVD. This meant that he was supervising all spy work throughout Europe and the United States.

Soble did not underestimate the magnitude of the important service he had done me. He stressed that Zubilin had made him write an independent report on the whole affair, and it was in this that he had whitewashed me.

He had also prevailed on Zubilin, now General Zubilin, to get his agents in the United States to improve their appearance. Too many of them dressed like long-coat-and-short-pants Europeans and would be instantly recognized as foreigners. Some of them also spoke English very poorly.

The first man sent to the United States to take over his work, Jack lamented to me, had proved unsatisfactory. His name was Studenko and he had to be recalled immediately because of his bad manners. On arriving in the United States Studenko had grilled Alfred K. Stern, abused him, and demanded complete information about his financial status. The Sterns had complained to Moscow, presumably through Martha's contact in Washington.

Martha's forte was recruiting new volunteers to the Cause. She was particularly successful in bringing women in sensitive positions into the Reds' secret service. Alfred's role was that of a financier. At all times his funds were available for the ring's use. But Moscow repaid him for whatever he laid out as quickly as was practical.

Jack told me that Stern had been assigned to another espionage ring in which the shipment of penicillin to Mexico would be the cover for his and Martha's espionage work there. This set-up later collapsed, because the doctors involved rebelled against Stern's demanding eighty per cent of the $12,000 in profits the scheme had yielded. The doctors, I was interested to learn, had no idea that the main reason for the penicillin shipments was to provide cover for the Sterns' undercover work.

The most astonishing thing to me in the report that Jack brought back from Moscow was what finally swung judgment there in my favor. It was that I had paid back the money, the $100,000, which the Kremlin (through its agent, Stern) had invested in my music company. This was an event, Jack told me, unique in the financial history of Russian espionage. He said, laughingly, "I wouldn't be surprised if it is also unique in the whole history of spying."

The men who ran the worldwide Russian espionage system may have been as bowled over by my returning Stern's money as Jack declared, but it was a long time before they came to trust me.

Meanwhile, without making too many efforts to indoctrinate me, they began to test me out first by giving me unimportant assignments, then more and more important ones. It took no particular brilliance to pass these tests. I had the greatest team of coaches any man could have asked for. Some of the best brains of the FBI were guiding my footsteps, calling the plays in advance, trying to outguess the NKVD every step of the way.

I also had one other great advantage, having Soble, a man with divided loyalties, as my judge. He was distracted by his admiration for me as a successful businessman, the kind of man Myra wanted him to be, so he was inclined to give me the benefit of many doubts that arose in his mind.

Jack seldom stopped talking for very long about his business ventures, particularly this bristle business of his. The plant was called *Etablissement Labor,* though the word was not chosen, he assured me, because of his love and respect for the horny-handed sons of toil, as they used to be called in the long, long ago. The "l" in the word *Labor* was for *le,* the French article, "a" for his brother-in-law, Arnold, and "bor" for Boris, one of his brothers.

What Soble did not reveal to me, at this time or

any other, was that Moscow had bought this factory
for him, by purchasing the interests in it held by
other members of the family. The idea was that as
an American citizen running a business in France
he could have the perfect cover for his spy work. The
Sûreté would not be asking too many questions of
an American.

Soble was inordinately proud, incidentally, of his
establishment of satisfactory "cover-up" jobs and businesses for the men working with him. The irony was
that most of these men remained more interested in
milking Moscow of its espionage funds and expense
money than in running the Soviet-financed enterprises
at a profit. At least that is the way it seemed to me.
And I was to watch that interest gradually develop
in Soble himself.

When Soble transferred his headquarters to Paris,
the FBI asked me whether it would be possible for
me to spend a good deal of the time over there. This
I arranged with no difficulty whatever. The whole
trend of movie-making just then was toward Europe,
partly because of high production costs in Hollywood,
partly because the companies when shooting films
abroad could use the large sums which were due them
for rentals of their pictures, but which had long been
"frozen" in the various countries.

"It will not only look legitimate," I said, "it will *be*
legitimate." Bob Burton, my "private secretary"
whom I could introduce as my Hollywood lawyer,
would accompany me on my trip abroad to advise
me. I was taking with me prints of several of my
pictures, but the principal property I was offering
abroad was *Carnegie Hall*.

With Bob Burton I sailed for Europe in the middle
of April 1948. A few days before we left, Myra asked
me to take along a load of stuff that Jack had asked

her to send him in Paris, where these articles were still in short supply. When she said she still had to buy them, I thought it might be amusing—and might lead to Bob's getting information from her—if he helped her shop. So he did one day, and also he helped her pack them—the typewriter, a dozen Parker 51 pens and a quantity of ink for them, also quite an extraordinary amount of salami. What information, if any, she leaked to him, as they artistically arranged the salami, canned foods, typewriter, and Parker 51s in-Jack's gift package, I never learned. But she told me he had been a great help to her and was a fine young man. She was going to Europe herself in June, and hoped to see us there, she said.

Soon after I delivered the package to Soble in Paris he revealed that he was able to operate from Paris now because of the rise of a dear old friend of his, Peter Vassilievich Fedotov, a soft-spoken intellectual, who had been Stalin's bodyguard at both Potsdam and Yalta. Fedotov was also a member of the Central Committee, a member of the Supreme Council of People's Commissars in charge of iron ore, and was connected with the Department of External Activities of the NKVD. He was very close to Beria, the boss of the entire Soviet espionage network, but was not entirely beholden to him, as Stalin would see him at any time.

Shortly after I reached Paris, Soble made a ten-day trip to Warsaw. On returning he described how he had gone on to Moscow with Fedotov. The way he met his old friend and new chief, I thought, was rather interesting, considering that Warsaw was then completely behind the Iron Curtain. He met a man at an appointed street corner and asked him for the address of a certain music store. They tipped their hats to one another, and he was taken to Fedotov.

This is what he called a "controlled rendezvous," which was one arranged in advance.

For me the best news Soble brought back was that Zubilin had fallen from grace, at last, because of his drinking. He was retired and living in Siberia. Though not banished, he was out of favor.

Soble said that Fedotov was very anxious to meet me, but being so well known in Western Europe, he would prefer to meet me behind the Iron Curtain. If my business did not permit me to make that trip, Fedotov would send a deputy to Switzerland to meet me. After getting instructions from my "Hollywood lawyer," I told Soble my business would detain me in Western Europe for quite a time.

Soble shook his head, gloomily. "I had better try to get Fedotov to come here, then. I would not like you to face Alexander Mikhailovich Korotkov."

"Who is that?" I asked.

"Korotkov is the man Fedotov has named his permanent deputy in charge of the United States and Europe, in place of Zubilin. He is a great admirer of the Sterns. I might almost say he is a fan of theirs. I had better see if Fedotov himself can't meet you in Switzerland."

I talked to the FBI men about that. I wanted to know what I should do.

"We'd like you to meet Korotkov," they told me.

"I don't know why," I said, "but this scares me."

The FBI said it was for me to decide. The reason I had refused to meet Fedotov in Soviet territory was that the FBI men could not go along with me there. But they could go to Switzerland.

"See you in Switzerland, boys," I told them, and half-heartedly tried a little joke. "I hope you'll be close enough, when I'm with Korotkov, to get there in time in case I suddenly have to send up my distress yodel." We all laughed.

But I was frightened at the very thought of meeting Korotkov. Perhaps it was because he was the first high official in Moscow's espionage machine that I had had to face in Europe. I would have been less terrified, I think, if I were meeting him in the United States. And I was really scared; I could not fool myself about that.

I spent most of that June of 1948 touring Spain as the guest of José Iturbi. By the time I returned to Paris, Myra and the child had joined Jack in Paris. Soble told me that Fedotov was occupied behind the Iron Curtain settling some difficulty Moscow was having with Tito.

But Soble assured me that Fedotov had not forgotten me. Perish the thought! Our chief had wonderful plans for my future, had decided that I should take him, Jack Soble, into my movie company, Federal Films. I hurriedly got out of that deal by pointing out that my partner, William LeBaron, would have to be consulted, and I was sure Bill would ask many embarrassing questions about the arrangement.

As an alternative, and in an attempt to carry out the FBI's orders to become as much involved as possible with Soble, I suggested that we start a television producing company. Soble was most enthusiastic. He wished to incorporate immediately and lose no time in getting started. He promised to obtain an appropriation of $250,000 from Moscow, though he frankly said he could not set a time when the money would be available.

Soble insisted on only one thing: that Jacob Albam, the man who was designated to replace him in America, should be taken into the firm. Albam had done some technical work in motion pictures in Moscow, Jack informed me, and knew a great deal about photography. He introduced me to Albam one evening at the Dominique Restaurant in Paris. Soble's successor proved to be a soft-spoken, gray-haired man of distinguished appearance.

"There isn't a passport or a document in the world," Soble said later, "that Albam cannot reproduce." Unlike Studenko, the crude chap first chosen to replace Soble, Albam had excellent manners, would never exceed his authority, and would do everything required of him for the Cause. Meanwhile a date with Korotkov had been arranged.

I passed on to the FBI all the dope that Soble was gossiping away to me. Today I have an idea they had all this in their files already. It was only later on that I was to sense their excitement—when I started bringing them the big stuff, the hot stuff, the details which fitted into the pattern they were putting together of Soviet spy strategy around the world.

It was with considerable trepidation that I drove to Geneva with Jack, his wife, and my wife, on August 22. We checked in at the Beau Rivage Hotel. Then the women went off shoping. Jack and I drove across the bridge to the other side of the lake. Jack didn't ease my tension by a series of instructions he gave me. I would be addressed as "Djon," the code name given me. I was not to let Korotkov know I knew his name. I was not to let him know that Jack had confided to me that Jake Albam was being named his successor as chief of the American spy ring. In fact I was to utter not a word about anything Soble had confided to me.

We met Korotkov in the beautiful garden of the Eaux Vives Restaurant on the far side of the lake. Korotkov, like my companion, was over six feet tall, so both of them towered over me. A stern-looking man, he had broader shoulders than Jack, but was almost as slim. Korotkov began the conversation by conveying to me the regards of Zubilin, who he said was not well, and not happy in his retirement. Korotkov said he was looking around for a new post to keep my old Comrade happy in Moscow. With these preliminaries attended to, he began to question me about my inability to cooperate with the Sterns.

When I tried to explain, he shook his head. "This is a most serious matter," he said. "There is only one important thing to consider—how much you have hurt the Cause."

Jack had assured me that after the Sterns had gone over his head to send in the critical report of me, he was completely on my side. But he had also begged me not to mention his friendliness with me, or the fact that he had allowed me to meet Albam, without first getting permission from "Home." But I had no way of knowing to what degree he was intimidated, how far he would dare to go in my defense.

After probing thoroughly into *l'affaire Stern*, the point Korotkov made was an effective one: not co-operating with the Sterns meant not cooperating with the Soviet government itself. Next, he said that my breaking off with the Sterns was an affront to Martha. Korotkov, like the other Russians I had met, felt that she was a tremendous asset to them and to the Cause. They were right. They rarely had a finer advertisement for those they were trying to win over than this woman from our highest diplomatic level. "What a little recruiter!" he exclaimed. "A thousand more like her and the battle would be won."

"This is all very well, Comrade," I interposed meekly, at the first chance I got. "But it was not Mrs. Stern I had to do business with. It was her soft-headed husband!"

Korotkov conceded that Stern might be no great

shakes as a businessman, or as a human being either. But he kept hammering on the same old argument: "Selflessness is expected of all! The Cause! The fight to save humanity from its own corrupt capitalism is much more important than such petty grievances!"

When I hung my head in mock shame, he reminded me that my two brothers, Alexander and Isaac, were still behaving badly, and now also one of my sisters.

So I sat there, hanging my head in shame at my brothers' disloyalty, knowing that they were both dead and knowing that this sonofabitch knew it. And now my sister? What of her? I still don't know if my sister is alive or dead, whether she was alive or not on that day when we had this cruel parody of an earnest conversation.

While I was talking to them at the far end of the lake, my wife and Myra Soble were shopping and dining at the Beau Rivage. Katerina once again talked of seeing her brothers lined up, blindfolded, against a wall and shot. I had often pleaded with her to forget the ghastly tragedy. But each time she met a Russian she would have an uncontrollable fit of talking and weeping. The whole scene would come alive to her again.

And Myra was a "Communist patriot." Later I found out that Myra had encouraged her when she began telling the story and denouncing the perpetrators: "Murderers! Swine! Cattle!"

CHAPTER 7

Love and Hate among the Communists

Myra Soble obeyed blindly and unquestionably the inhuman tenets handed down by the Kremlin. She believed that, now and forever, the Party, the Cause, must come first. Later, I think, she came to realize that Jack and the child had to be her prime considerations or she would go mad. But that gradual change in her thinking was still years away.

After egging on my wife that day, Myra hurried to her hotel room and wrote a report many pages long, quoting Katerina's denunciatory words precisely. This she delivered to Korotkov, knowing that, after reading it, he would pass it on to Jack's other highly-placed friend, Fedotov.

Jack and I had arranged to meet Korotkov again next day to discuss the television project. But when we met the NKVD official he was in a towering rage. *"What kind of a Communist are you?"* he demanded. "If you have a decent drop of blood in your body why don't you indoctrinate that vicious, lying bitch you're married to?"

Like everybody else, I often fail to think of the right answer when I most need it. But this was an exception. I waited till he was out of breath, then asked, "Would that be so wise, Comrade?"

He was astonished. So was Soble.

"What nonsense are you babbling now?" Korotkov demanded, waving his thick forefinger back and forth under my nose.

"What better cover could I have than a wife who denounces all my Comrades and our Cause unceasingly?" I asked.

That did it. He continued to argue the matter, but with less conviction. It was a new idea I had given him, and therefore difficult for him to cope with or even absorb quickly. Flexibility in thinking is the last thing the Kremlin wants from the people. Therefore, no matter how clever a Communist is—and Korotkov and Jack Soble were very clever—they had been trained to think along a straight line. Often you could outwit them just by saying something they didn't expect. For the time being, I had won a reprieve.

Next he asked me to disprove, if I could, certain charges that a Soviet attaché at the Washington embassy had made against me. This official's report to Moscow asserted that I had severed all ties with the old country, had come to think of myself solely as an American, even to forgetting how to speak the Russian language. Coming after the other problem, this seemed easy.

But Jack interceded for me, saying, "As I told you, Comrade Korotkov, these charges are untrue."

"I can see that for myself," Korotkov agreed. "He is talking right now to me in perfect Russian."

"If the attaché lied about that, he may have lied about the rest of it as well," Jack pointed out.

Gradually, the stern spy-gang boss relaxed. For several hours we discussed the television company. Though I was still nervous, and very much on my guard, I could not help being immensely amused to see that Jack Soble was already acting like a Hollywood executive. He claimed the whole television company idea as his inspiration, the moment he saw that the boss liked it. After considerable discussion, we agreed to hold at least one more meeting.

Just for fun, after we left Korotkov that day, I asked Jack if it was not wonderful that interest in his scheme was building up so fast in Korotkov's mind. But even when we were alone, Soble did not disclaim credit for the idea, having already progressed to the second Hollywood stage in his thinking: he now sincerely believed that he had made the original suggestion.

"Let's get back to something else," I said. "How in hell did Myra—who, like you, pretends to be my friend—write that terrible report about Katerina? It might have got me kicked out."

"What else could she do? She only did it for your own good." (This, incidentally, is a good example of the way Communist espionage workers regard friendship.)

When I reported the events of the day to my FBI "ear," he was far more interested in something else I mentioned: the fact that Jack had begun to criticize Zubilin. It was not merely a matter of that muzhik's stupidity, crudeness, and drunkenness. Vasya, he said, was a thief who had stolen $80,000 which the NKVD was still waiting for him to return or to explain.

I told my FBI man, apologetically, "All he would say about this, though, was that Zubilin was supposed to have given this money to 'a certain professor.' When I pressed him, he snarled, 'You ask too many questions, and you talk too much.'"

"This information about the eighty thousand dollars right now is less important," I was told, "than the fact that Soble is beginning to confide in you. Soon he will probably be criticizing other members of the ring. Any details he leaks may help us identify them."

A White Russian chauffeur drove us from Geneva to Lausanne, where we had another date with Korotkov. When Soble found out that this man had fled to France during the Russian Revolution, he insisted he drop us off in downtown Lausanne. We then switched to a taxi that took us to the Beau Rivage Hotel, where we got off and walked the rest of the way to the meeting place which Jack and Korotkov had arranged in advance.

General Korotkov's enthusiasm over the proposed television company had increased since our last get-together. Now he proposed that Moscow contribute $350,000, or an extra hundred thousand, to finance the new company. "Money is nothing," he declared solemnly. "When it comes to legitimate projects, our funds are unlimited." (This later gave my FBI contact and me a good belly-laugh over the difference in the Communistic conception of the word "legitimate" and ours.)

Then he went into a long harangue about the accounting methods to be used in the new company. The increased budget meant, of course, that we would be able to go along without extra partners or outside investors. The budget would be listed as an "operation account" and would require only his signature, whereas, if it were listed as a "firm account," Beria would take charge of it. This is how far the Soviet bureaucracy had come in thirty years toward donning the straitjacket of routine like that which shackles French governmental agencies one hundred and sixty-nine years after *their* Revolution.

Having held before me briefly this $350,000 plum, Korotkov brought up another source of discontent with me at Home. This time it was the fact that my file was empty. I had been expected—like all other hard-working Communist agents—to send in information regularly on whatever I imagined would be useful for the officials to know. I was not supposed to wait for assignments but to display initiative. For that matter, he pointed out, I had already been offered one assignment which I had disdained.

"That is true," I told him. "Soble asked me to get something on Mrs. Lucius Clay, wife of the United States administrator in Germany. I could have done that easily enough. I could have made something up to please you. But I would be rendering no service by making up fanciful lies. For one thing, the Clays would have found it too easy to disprove them."

"All right," Korotkov told me. "But here is an assignment you can't avoid on any such grounds."

I was bewildered when he said I was to "get the goods" on Thomas E. Dewey, governor of New York, and Earl Warren, governor of California, who were currently the Republican candidates for President and Vice-President.

The Reds had wanted to discredit Mrs. Clay because her husband, General Clay, was proving so able and popular an administrator in Germany that the Germans were naming streets after him. Unable to find any mud to throw at the distinguished Georgia soldier, they thought a juicy scandal about his wife might prove so embarrassing that the general would ask to be relieved.

Of course, they could not have found a less profitable target for scandal-mongering anywhere. And Dewey and Warren were equally impossible to smear for acts of moral or any other sort of turpitude. But I told him I would do my best on the two governors.

"You can't say you don't know Dewey," said Korotkov.

I gave him a knowing smile, although I had not then—and have not now, for that matter—ever met Governor Dewey. Only later on, when I thought the matter over, did I realize where Korotkov had got that idea. When we were shooting *Carnegie Hall* Governor Dewey, who, as a former singer, was interested in the picture, dropped in one day to watch. I was busy at the time, working out some musical ideas for the picture with Artur Rubinstein. I hadn't gone to the set that day, and thus missed meeting Dewey. Our publicity department, of course, had not overlooked the good copy the governor's visit provided. Jack Soble, reading about it in the papers, assumed that Dewey and I were friends. He had reported this erroneous idea—as he reported everything else he could learn about me—to the NKVD at Home.

It seems obvious that Korotkov had been assured—along with members of the Union League Club in New York and other Republican strongholds—that 1948 was bound to be a Republican year and that Truman, the Soviets' implacable enemy, would go down to defeat. He wanted inside stuff on the two Republican candidates for the Presidency. He also wanted answers to the questions: "Who controls the White House?" "Who are the backers of Dewey?" "Of Warren?" He also wanted the names of the chief contributors of campaign funds to the Republican Party. He wanted to know the background of John Foster Dulles, who was becoming very prominent in the State Department's handling of international affairs.

"Of course, it's Wall Street," said Soble.

Korotkov sneered, saying he wanted something new. Before we left, he made me promise to do the best I could about getting this new information.

Soble had begged him for a new, highly placed contact in Europe. Korotkov decided that the Soviet ambassador to Switzerland was the perfect choice. Soble boasted about that to me, pointing out that when they gave him a contact on the highest diplomatic level it indicated increased respect for him "at Home." Korotkov and he would meet His Excellency at public functions, in restaurants, even pass the ambassador on the streets without speaking to him, or he to them.

At our final meeting, Korotkov announced that he had stayed longer in Switzerland than he had intended to. Though Korotkov reminded us that we would have to wait for a final decision from Moscow, Soble suggested that it might be intelligent—as long as all the preliminary details were set—for us to go ahead and establish headquarters in the United

States. Korotkov agreed that this would facilitate everything, pending the okay from Home. He thought our headquarters should be in New York rather than in Hollywood.

His last word to me was to "bring Jack into higher business circles without further delay."

A most significant event occurred during another trip I made to Switzerland that summer. This time Jack and Myra let me accompany them to the Geneva branch of Credit Suisse, where he transferred $1500 in funds to a spy in Buenos Aires. I could not get close enough to see or hear the name of this man but the FBI man guarding me said it was further encouraging evidence that Soble was relaxing his suspicions of me.

Soble urged me again and again to lose no time about organizing the company when I returned to the United States in October 1948. Though Korotkov, now in Moscow, had by then sent him word that it might be some time before he could discuss the television proposition with Beria and get his okay, Jack seemed to take it for granted that approval was assured. Just before I sailed, Soble warned me to watch my step when I got home, meaning I should do my assignment of getting the "inside stuff" on Dewey and Warren. Moscow was still convinced, along with *Time* magazine and most American newspapers, that the election of the two governors was a sure thing.

I prepared a report in longhand—covering four sheets of typewriter paper—from notes furnished me by the FBI. They were innocuous biographies, of course, which the Russians could have found in the files of any American newspaper, or in any London newspaper, for that matter.

Soon after arriving in New York, I took the first step in raising the social level of the Sobles, as Korotkov had suggested, by trying to find them an apartment. I took Myra to a couple of places—after I had consulted the apartment rental list of the FBI, which made suggestions—but she found one of her own.

If she had chosen one of the FBI-recommended spots, of course, there would have been FBI men working as doormen, porters, and elevator operators in that building and serving as delivery boys in whatever stores the Sobles traded with.

But I did select a penthouse office—at $500 a month rent—for our television company. When Jack finally got back from Europe in February 1949, he regretted that he had none of the $350,000 for the backing of our firm, but he had plenty of criticism for my selection of an office. It filled him with dismay that the penthouse was the top floor of a duplex and was not shut off by doors from the floor below—where the producers of that typically American television show, "Howdy Doody," then had their headquarters.

He had another worry over which he fretted even more. Jacob Albam, the forger who was to take his place as the head of the spy ring here, had parachuted from a plane into France, then forged his own passport to the United States. What he needed was American citizenship, and at that time a foreigner married to an American citizen could get his final papers within three years instead of five.

"I not only got Albam in on the French quota," said Jack, "but Myra found a bride for him. It was a lot of trouble, but the girl, a university graduate and a nurse, is presentable anywhere. They praised me very highly in Moscow for the job I did for Albam. What bothers me is that they seem to expect me to find brides for all the other men they want to send here. Finding a wife for a smooth, pleasant gentleman like Albam is one thing. But who could find girls to marry some of the bums and roughnecks they're always sending over here?"

Later, when I became friendly enough with Albam, I asked him, "Did Moscow really order you to get married to your wife? Did Mrs. Soble find her for you?"

He nodded solemnly, but then added, "Yes, but I did all of my own courting."

That day, after seeing our penthouse office suite, Soble said that Korotkov, despite his passionate hatred for everything American, might come over shortly. Korotkov was even studying maps of the United States and taking lessons in English. Jack said it would be helpful if we had turned the television project into a going concern by the time Korotkov arrived.

I couldn't resist remarking, "It would be even more helpful if he got some of the three hundred fifty thousand dollars you're always talking about out of the conversation and into some bank."

He just sighed, and said, "Meanwhile I have other problems. I was given twenty-five thousand to buy Albam a share in an herb business that some of his relatives operate here. But Albam, though a brilliant engraver and accomplished forger, is such a poor businessman that I almost feel it might be more economical for me simply to pay his living expenses until we're ready to employ him in the television company."

In getting jobs and establishing businesses for spies all over the world, the leaders of the various Communist espionage rings were forever trying to solve that two-pronged problem of finding a business that both served as a cover for the agent and would support him.

As my association with Soble continued, I found him becoming increasingly critical of most of the other Communist agents. This one, he would tell me, was too crazy about women, or that one was too money-mad to be devoted to the Cause. Zubilin, of course, had disgraced the whole service by his shocking drunkenness and thievery. Soble confessed he did not understand why the Kremlin hadn't really punished Vasya, the great tennis player, for his misdeeds.

The only Soviet agent in the United States whom Jack wholeheartedly approved of was "Chaliapin," a man who worked in San Francisco for the United Nations. The most interesting thing Jack told me about this one trustworthy agent concerned Chaliapin's stormy relations with a former United States Army officer who Jack claimed was an official of some veterans' organization. At first, Jack identified this second man as an Irishman. Later he forgot this and said he was a Belgian. Later still the ex-Army officer became a Syrian. Whatever his nationality, the gentleman appeared to be an inveterate poker player who had the great bad luck to lose heavily whenever he sat in on a game. Chaliapin would have considered this none of his business if the Irishman-Belgian-Syrian had not maintained that these losses were all suffered for Moscow's sake. The exasperated Chaliapin finally complained that the NKVD bookkeepers were asking why his man never won at these high-stake affairs. "Well, if that isn't just like a bunch of God-damned Russians," cried the ex-Army officer in disgust. "Don't they realize that if I win the others will be in such a bad mood they won't tell me *anything?* Getting my money loosens their mouths, man, oils up their tongues!"

In early March, I saw Jack in New York. He told me to be in Geneva between April 4 and May 14, as the $350,000 appropriation for our television firm had been approved.

Jack and I were booked to sail in May. A few nights

before we left, the Sobles invited Jack's brother and me to their apartment for dinner. His brother warned Jack against going to Moscow, but Jack merely laughed at the idea that this might prove dangerous. "I'm all right," he said. "I'm in high favor at Home."

Nevertheless for Jack and Myra the evening resembled a nightmare because another invited guest, the son of the owner of one of Paris' best-known cafés, failed to appear. In the underground world of the spy, such an unexplained absence can mean catastrophe—or nothing. And, as always when such things happen, they sat waiting, tense and nervous, for the footsteps on the stairs, for the knock on the door that could mean the end.

Contributing to their anguished suspense was the fact that the newspapers for days had been carrying front-page stories about the arrest of Judith Coplon, pretty girl employee of the United States Department of Justice, and her friend, Valentin A. Gubichev, a member of the Soviet delegation to the United Nations. The American girl was accused of gathering information for him.

Soble was bitter and outspoken about Moscow's mishandling of this ill-starred adventure. He said the people "back Home" sat there with their maps, deciding what should be done in a certain city, and how it should be done, even though they had never been in the United States themselves. These maps, incidentally, are more detailed than the ones we have here ourselves.

"And no detail of the plans they make at Home," he added, "can be changed without permission." He said he would try hard to get this policy altered so that we could make our own decisions without having to have each move we made approved in advance by Moscow.

"They should know by this time," he declared, "that emergencies arise even in a checker game that one cannot foresee." And he demanded, "Were *they* in the Kremlin able to anticipate how much the Marshall Plan would accomplish, or the prestige the United States would gain with her counter-blockade of Germany? Well, you'd think they would have learned something from such surprises, wouldn't you?"

I agreed. I always agreed with Jack when I could, without committing myself to anything. Shrewd and suspicious as he was, Jack never noticed this. Like most men on both sides of the Iron Curtain, he treasured nothing so much as an attentive and respectful listener who invariably agreed with him.

On May 13, 1949, Soble and I sailed for Europe aboard the *Queen Elizabeth*. I had first-class accommodations, he second-class, but I arranged with the purser for Jack to be able to visit me whenever he wished. Also aboard was the FBI man still posing as my Hollywood attorney. I came to regret traveling on the same ship with Jack. He issued orders to me like a general with one soldier, and called me into secret conferences twice a day: promptly at eleven in the morning and at three in the afternoon.

Nothing could have been more irritating. For many years, my favorite relaxation has been bridge, and I never seem to manage to get enough of it except when traveling on the high seas. On this trip I quickly discovered three genial gentlemen to play with. We immediately adjourned to my cabin, intent on spending as many hours as possible at the card table there.

But there was Jack, bursting in unannounced, and demanding that I leave with him at once. He turned his back when I tried to introduce him to the other players. As soon as we were alone, however, he in-

sisted I furnish him with full information about them.
I finally told him, "The hell with you and your two
conferences a day. I'll meet you at dawn or at midnight but I'll not interrupt the bridge game for you
again."

We were three days out before Jack learned that
one of my fellow players was president of one of the
world's largest razor-blade companies.

"I would like to be introduced to him," he then
said, beaming. "Maybe we could arrange to sell his
blades, and shaving brushes made with my pig bristles, in a combination package deal."

"Sorry, Jack, but I can't pave the way for that," I
told him.

"Why not?"

"This razor-blade tycoon is an eccentric."

"What has that got to do with it?"

"He believes that everybody who doesn't play
bridge is insane. He refuses to do business with anyone who doesn't know the game. So unless you can
master it—"

That ended that conference. But Jack did not waste
his time on that trip. One day he introduced me to
a beautiful Viennese passenger. She was in her late
twenties, and sparkled with the vivacity and beauty
typical of that city's women. Later he told me that
during the short trip he had seduced this pretty thing
—the girl had recently acquired American citizenship
—both physically and politically.

Like Zubilin, Soble mixed sensual pleasure in this
way with his Party work whenever possible. He was
an elegant dancer, could be very ingratiating, and
knew how to please the ladies with little attentions.
Being a Communist, he never allowed considerations
of morality, or the possibility of breaking his wife's
heart, to interfere with carrying out his duty. Soon,

I was to find out that most of the women, married or single, in his spy ring were his mistresses. "It's the best way," he once told me, "to insure their allegiance to the Cause." It was the Party's established policy that most of the Communist spy-ring leaders, both men and women, should use their sexual attractiveness whenever it helped recruiting.

"We'll get off the ship separately," Jack said, just before we put in at Le Havre. I had made reservations at the Hotel Raphael in Paris. When Jack came there, before uttering a word, he made his usual personal inspection of all the good sound-conductors in my room. He had also developed a new procedure with the telephone. After inspecting the wire and connection he picked up the receiver to see if the girl on the switchboard answered properly. Then he had them ring the room to see if the receiving apparatus worked as it should. After that, he turned his attention to the usual toilet-flushings, under-the-bed searches, and so forth.

On this visit I discovered that Soble had at least one of his relatives on Moscow's spy payroll. For example, each time he called on me at the Raphael a young man, Michel, whom he introduced as his right-hand man at the bristle factory, waited outside. Soble never mentioned that Michel was his nephew or that he stationed him outside the hotel to watch out for secret police. It was a chance remark of Michel himself that gave away the fact that his mother was Jack's sister.

One evening Jack came to the Raphael and said he had two lovely ladies downstairs whom he would like me to take to dinner. Previously he had told me he was going to introduce me to one of his most important workers. "She is a lovely person," he said, "an American girl."

When he described the work she had done I could see why she would be all that from his point of view. The "lovely person" had lived in the Far East and had worked there for the Cause. She had brought in a trunkful of information, Soble said, on which the Russians had based their telling speeches on the Indonesian question. She had gathered this information in the years she lived in the Dutch East Indies with her first husband, an officer in the Dutch Foreign Service. Jack explained that she had been recruited originally back in 1938 by Martha Dodd Stern, who turned her over to Zubilin, who in turn had handed her over to him when he replaced Vasya as chief of the espionage agents in the United States. She was waiting with another woman in the lobby, he explained. Could he bring them up? I said he certainly could. A moment later I was shaking hands with Jane Foster, the "lovely person," and her friend, a Frenchwoman.

Jane, a painter of no small talent, was from California. She and her second husband, George Zlatovski, an ex-United States Army lieutenant assigned to intelligence work, were to be involved with me in my counterspy role for years, although I had no way of knowing it at the moment.

At this time Jane was forty or thereabouts and blond, and had an interesting face. The Frenchwoman was older, shorter, and slightly stouter. She worked at the French Foreign Ministry.

They had a few drinks, then we picked up Michel, who was outside, and we all drove to the Petrograd, a Russian restaurant. The small car was crowded, and Jane Foster sat on Soble's lap. They necked all the way to the Petrograd like a couple of teenagers.

A gay time was enjoyed by all that evening. Soble was having such a good time that as we were finishing dinner he left the table to phone a married couple he liked to join us for brandy and coffee. The couple brought a woman friend and invited us to their apartment for a nightcap. This turned out to be an evening particularly well spent from my point of view. For some time the American embassy in Paris had been aware that Russian secret agents seemed to know promptly each time our ambassador, David Bruce, made an appointment. On learning the names of the young couple invited by Soble to join us they got a good notion where the Soviets were getting their information. A relative of the wife was Ambassador Bruce's personal chauffeur. He was replaced and after that the NKVD had less reliable information about our ambassador's daily activities.

What Soble liked best about me, as I've said, was that he could always depend upon me to pick up the check. Then he, like any traveling salesman in the ladies' underwear line, put the cost of the dinner on his expense account. In this way he ended up with everything he wanted—the pleasure of being co-host at a lavish function, enjoying a fine meal, letting me pay the bill, and getting more out of it than the restaurant owner and the waiter combined. The restaurant owner, after all, had to pay something for the food and wines.

He and Myra were both overwhelmed each time we walked into a first-class restaurant and I was able to introduce them to people such as Artur Rubinstein and other world-famous musicians, not to mention stars, directors, and producers whom they regarded almost as living legends.

And all this, as you will see, was an important reason for whatever success I later enjoyed as an FBI counterspy. These men were less vigilant in checking up on me than they would have been if I hadn't always been their good-time Charlie, the sucker who spent and tipped lavishly. That is the reason, and I believe the only reason, they did not catch me transmitting information to my FBI contacts.

The arrest of Gubichev in the United States was preying on Jack's mind. He kept going back to the subject again and again, analyzing what had gone wrong and why. And he never stopped pounding away at *me* on the need for safety, safety, safety. He was warning the man who was happily turning in all he said and did to the FBI!

Our next rendezvous with one of our superiors was set for June 4 at Geneva, but the meeting place was changed to Vienna and postponed until later in the month. When Soble told me of these changes he said that he might ask me to carry my own and some other reports to Vienna.

I protested that a report on Dewey and Warren, seeing that they had lost the election months before, might be of little interest to Home. But he talked me out of that. "At least," he said, "it's *something* for me to send them for your dossier."

He would go on ahead, he said, but I must get to Vienna not later than June 19. The night before he left he gave me the reports of the two women. I had ten suitcases in the closet. He watched me slip the three reports in a large envelope. I then put the envelope in the top suitcase. He shook his head as though depressed at this evidence of my carelessness and stupidity. He insisted that the suitcase containing the envelope be on the bottom of the pile. I felt frustrated as we moved them all, then stacked them one on top of the other again. While we were doing this, I saw one of the FBI men I had been working with walking back and forth in front of the Unesco building, across the street from the Raphael Hotel.

I was grateful that I had accepted the first-floor room the management had reserved for me, instead of one on an upper floor. I knew that my FBI man had been watching us.

The minute Soble left I hurriedly started unpiling the luggage to get at the bottom piece. By the time I had the envelope out, the FBI man sauntered past the grilled window of my room, enabling me to hand the envelope to him.

The FBI man rushed the reports to his own room, where he photographed them. In a half hour he had them back in my hands. But I had to move all the bags one more time to replace the envelope in the lowest one—just in case Soble, changing his plans, should return and ask me for it.

This was the first real coup I had made as a counterspy. One of the reports was a comprehensive account by Jane Foster of her years of work in Indonesia. The other contained confidential information written by her friend, the Frenchwoman, extracted from the correspondence between American authorities and the French Foreign Office.

I felt I had accomplished something—at last.

CHAPTER 8

I Walk into the Kremlin's Dark Shadow

I took the Orient Express from Paris to Vienna, and had no trouble getting Soble's documents through the border controls. But it was easy to understand why he had been apprehensive about smuggling them over the frontier. Austria was still under joint occupation of the United States, Soviet Russia, France, and Great Britain. The representatives of all four gave my luggage only the most cursory of examinations.

Jack Soble met me at the station, and no one was ever happier to see me. He could hardly wait until the taxi got us to the Krantz-Ambassador Hotel in the International Zone to make sure I still had the envelope the reports were in. He picked them up the next day.

I well understood his eagerness. The report of Jane Foster alone was dynamite. It covered the past four years of her activities as a spy and recruiting agent for the Soviets. For a long time she had concentrated on extracting information from the CIA men at Salzburg, Vienna, and Berchtesgaden. She had got drunk and slept with many of these officers. Later, Soble told me that Jane had given him much valuable information on the sex lives, personal problems, and financial affairs of many of the American officers and government officials there. Every secret she had wormed out of these and other Occupation officials during the past four years was included in her report, he said.

The next day when Jack came for these reports he was bubbling over with news. He had met his new contact in Vienna and liked him. (These contacts, I was soon to find out, were continually being changed. The NKVD never trusted even its own people very far, did not believe it wise or safe to leave any secret agent in the same city for any great length of time.) Jack was going to meet this new contact that evening. When I generously offered to go along with him he said he had no right to take me.

Jack also announced that he would be going to Moscow soon, and that he would leave from an airport in the Russian Zone that the Western powers were unaware existed. He had planned to wire a query about the holding up of our $350,000, but now that he was going Home (he used *Doma,* the Russian word for it) he would have a chance to look into the matter personally.

Laughingly, he recalled how often his brother and his brother's wife had warned him about making too many trips to Moscow. What interested me was, that for all his scoffing about their fears, he was taking precautions against the possibility of some fatal "accident"—precautions that would have been ridiculously fantastic if he were going to any place but Russia. "I will be gone only a few days," he told me, "but I've asked Myra to cable you for anything she might need in case—in case I am delayed there for very long." If he found reason to communicate with me, he said, the messenger he sent would make himself known by whispering three words, each in a different language. The words were *Dritter . . . Romeo . . . Wagram.* But this *parol* (the term the Russian secret agents used for such signals of recognition) was for use only while he was on this trip. I could forget it when he came back.

Soble also mentioned that if he returned to the United States he would use his genuine American passport. He felt this was too valuable to take to Russia, where it might be picked up and confiscated. I later found out that this was the custom of the Kremlin's spies who had been lucky enough to get legitimate American passports.

Soble had expected to be gone only for four days or so. When he had not returned after more than a week I began to wonder whether I would ever hear from him again. But no cable came from Myra in New York, and no little man approached me and whispered, *"Dritter . . . Romeo . . . Wagram."*

After ten days Jack suddenly reappeared. That evening we took a walk through Vienna's streets. All but bursting with pride, he told me how he had been assigned accommodations in a nice hotel and treated like a person of considerable consequence by his superiors. His most important news for me, he said, was that Korotkov's report on the television project and on me as a Comrade to be trusted had been approved by the NKVD's top men. Korotkov himself was so delighted that he had sent me a cigarette box made of beautiful Ural Mountain stones.

All that was holding up the $350,000 now, Jack said, was finding a safe way to transfer it to New York. This problem, he said, was always the brain-twister when such large sums were involved. He suspected that the FBI and the CIA had ways of learning immediately when large deposits appeared in banks anywhere in the world.

When Jack handed me Korotkov's gift box, he said, "This will look very nice on the coffee table in the living room of your California home." Then he laughed, and added, "But don't tell any of those rabid anti-Communist friends of yours out there in Hollywood where and how you got it." My report on Dewey and Warren had been favorably received, he said. Later, when I got to Moscow myself and had to listen to blistering comments about these same perfunctory reports, I wondered why Soble told me that.

He was still fretting a good deal about the arrest of Gubichev. Again he blamed the insistence of the NKVD bosses in Moscow on arranging controlled rendezvous for secret agents thousands of miles away that couldn't be changed without permission. Jack also said that the apprehension of Judith Coplon's recruiter endangered his own position. He had met Gubichev several times and feared that the FBI had found his own name and address on Gubichev's person—or had grilled them out of him.

Early in July, Jack took me to the rendezvous with his new contact, introducing him only by his first name, Vitaly. It was not until later that I learned his last name—Tcherniavsky. The meeting was under a viaduct in the Prater, then in the Russian sector.

The Prater, like the rest of Vienna, had fallen on evil days. Once the playground of Emperor Franz Josef, his courtiers, and his royal ladies, it later became the people's amusement center with merry-go-rounds, tinkling bands playing Strauss waltzes, picnic grounds, and the sort of rides you see at our Coney Island. But its Ferris wheel now was rusty and the calliope inside the carousel groaned and wheezed like the tired old music-maker it had become.

Vitaly proved to be a handsome man, thirty or so, dark-haired, tall, cultured, and carefully dressed. Soble introduced me as Djon, and Vitaly gave the impression that he was delighted to meet me. But I was almost ignored by both of them in the conversation that followed. They spoke German and Russian. Vitaly, whose accent and appearance indicated that he was Rumanian, spoke both languages with an easy familiarity.

When they finished talking he handed Soble an envelope which I saw was filled with twenty-, fifty-, and one-hundred-dollar bills. We agreed that my next rendezvous with Vitaly would be in the same place. He then expected to have information for me about the financing of my television company. The parol he gave me was "Riabov."

We were leaving next day for Zurich and Soble came to my room in the Krantz-Ambassador to ask me a favor. He wanted me to carry the American currency to Zurich for him. It was against the law to take more American money out of the country than you brought in with you, but for some reason the customs men had made no record of the cash I had had when I arrived.

In Zurich Jack deposited most of the money at the Credit Suisse. He told me that he had to pay $1100, sending most of the rest to Jane Foster for salary and expenses. She and her husband George Zlatovski, the ex-Army officer, got $150 each per month for their services to the NKVD; Albam was paid $500 a month.

In that year, 1949, I became an intercontinental commuter, traveling frequently on business between Paris, Vienna, New York, and Hollywood, with side trips to Switzerland and Italy. But most of my work as a counterspy was done in that cradling place of the waltz and psychoanalysis, Vienna.

On my stop-overs in New York I saw Myra Soble on four separate evenings. She still yearned for the world that Clark Gable and Marlene Dietrich breathed and moved in, and kept asking me to confirm or deny various products of the ever-busy Hollywood romantic rumor mills. But she talked approvingly of George Zlatovski, whom she had entertained several times recently. She described him as an ardent worker in Jack's group and said he was going to join his wife in Europe shortly.

I said politely that would be very pleasant, as my wife was accompanying me abroad on my next trip. But I did not think anything would be less pleasant than throwing my Katerina into the society of either the Sobles or the Zlatovskis. I had found no way to stop Katerina from denouncing the Communists and I could not explain to her that I was working with them at the suggestion of the FBI, because I had promised the Bureau that I would never even hint of my double-spy function to a living soul until they gave me permission.

Myra, I had been told, was also to be employed in an executive capacity in our television concern. She was an intelligent, vital person, and I made no objection to having her as an aide.

But the weeks and the months rolled by with nothing more done about the promised $350,000. Protest to Soble was pointless. He was more eager than I to get the money out of the vaults of his beloved Kremlin. Finally, one day in Paris, he announced that he had thought of a way to transfer the money without arousing the curiosity of "the three-letter organizations," meaning of course the FBI and the CIA.

"You could sell the Russian rights to several of your pictures for three hundred fifty thousand dollars," he told me gleefully.

I shook my head. "These Russian rights have in the past brought very little, seldom more than twenty thousand or so per picture, even for Hollywood's best and biggest."

"They will *this* time, I think," said Soble, nudging me. "And when you announce the history-making price for your *Carnegie Hall, Tales of Manhattan,* and one or two others in the trade papers, Boris, you will be hailed as the financial wizard of the age. Nobody, not even Chaplin and Bernard Shaw, has siphoned so much dough out of Russia."

Soble had thought of everything—so he believed. "The first step," he said, "would be to show one or two of your pictures to the embassy staff here."

In a day or two he came back to me and said, "I have fixed it so you can call Ambassador Bogomolov and get him or his secretary on the phone without any delay. All you have to do is call and say 'This is Federal Films, Hollywood, California.' They are expecting you to call between ten and eleven tomorrow morning."

When I telephoned the embassy and identified myself, the ambassador's woman secretary was put on the wire at once. She said she regretted that His Excellency was out at the moment, but added that an appointment had been arranged for me the following day, which was September 23, 1949, at six o'clock.

On arriving at the embassy, 79 rue de Grenelle, I was escorted at once into the office of Bogomolov and was introduced to him and Nikolai Nagornov, his cultural attaché. There was a third man present to whom I was not introduced. Wherever I went in the embassy that day and on succeeding visits, this chap followed me.

That evening His Excellency spoke in praise of the pictures I produced in Hollywood, and said that Mr. Nagornov would shortly arrange for me to show them to him and some of his staff.

At this time I was involved with the late Sacha Guitry in the production of a picture, *The Miracle,* or *Le Trésor de Contenac,* as it was called in France. Six days later Nagornov phoned and arranged for me to screen *Tales of Manhattan* at a projection room in a building at 49 rue de la Faisanderie. About thirty people, including the ambassador and Mme. Bogomolov and Mrs. Morros, attended. A Russian picture was shown, then my film.

"We will let you know," were Bogomolov's last words as we shook hands after this double feature. Soble subsequently told me that Bogomolov and Nargarnov were very pleased.

I told him that the perpetual dragging out of the television deal was getting on my nerves. "I'm wasting too much time on it," I told him. "Let's call the whole thing off." But he was sure that after the ambassador saw my other picture, *Carnegie Hall,* he would recommend to the Kremlin that I be invited to Moscow in order to show my movies there.

On October 21 Jack Soble entrusted me with the sending of $2000 in cash to South America for him.

The money handed me was all in ten- and twenty-dollar bills. Jack had me send the draft to a man living on Calle Uruguay, Buenos Aires. Needless to say the FBI men were delighted when I gave them his name and address. The next day Jack told me he had sent an $8000 check drawn on a Swiss bank to his wife.

After some weeks I was invited to show *Carnegie Hall* to the ambassador. Several curious things happened at this screening. I brought my FBI man along, introducing him as my Hollywood attorney. I suppose this was one of the very few times a Soviet diplomat ever shook hands with an FBI agent.

Also, when the ambassador asked me what I was working on, I told him *Le Trésor de Contenac,* and explained its theme. One trouble with the world is that people no longer believe in miracles, I told him, and so they have stopped looking for treasures. But centuries ago, when people believed in miracles, they looked for treasures and found them. "Our story is about the little town of Contenac where people still believe in miracles and still go on treasure hunts which prove successful because of their faith."

"Faith in miracles!" the ambassador exclaimed in delight. "That's Marxism!"

But the oddest event of the evening came when they unveiled a new Russian picture in which a spy was shown operating a bristle factory as a cover for his espionage activities.

I could hardly restrain myself until the lights went on again. "How could you distribute such a picture?" I asked Bogomolov. "Did no one tell you—"

He drew me to one side so I could continue. In Russian I said, "Do you understand what you are doing, Your Excellency? Do you not know that the very gentleman who arranged for me to come here is in the bristle business?"

The ambassador's eyebrows went up. He called in the projection-booth operator and gave him orders to destroy all prints. Bogomolov, very agitated, assured me that he would see that this was done.

The ambassador's consternation was nothing, of course, to Soble's when I saw him a week later and told him of the way some brilliant scenarist had cooked up a plot that gave away his whole elaborate cover-up.

"And at the end of the picture," I said, "the spy was caught. What do you make of that, Jack? You don't suppose they made that entire picture just to warn you to watch your step?"

He shuddered. But before he could reply I asked him, "Now when is this stalling about the money going to end? I know, of course, that no one was trying to frame you in making that picture. It was pure inefficiency; but if that is how they operate we'll never get the three hundred and fifty thousand."

"There is only one way to do it," he told me. "That is for you to go to Moscow yourself with the pictures. I think Bogomolov would recommend that. Getting a visa for you would be no trouble at all."

The next time I saw the two FBI men who were working with me, I asked their opinion of Jack's suggestion. We were in the habit, by the way, of meeting in restaurants all over Paris. One FBI man preferred eating in the restaurants around Les Halles, the great Paris food market which Zola so aptly called "the belly of Paris." He found it almost impossible to believe that he was in Paris, a place he had dreamed of visiting all his life. Paris was most real to him, he said, when he sat down at a rough table, surrounded by the working people from the markets, and ate the excellent onion soup served there at all hours, *foie de veau,* and *tripes à la mode de Caen,* washed down with a bottle of *vin ordinaire.*

But this night we were eating at the Pomme d'Amour, which is off the Champs Élysées. I told them that Soble was convinced that the one way to settle the financing deal was for me to go to Moscow, that point of no return for so many. "Now, fellows, what do you think I should do?" I asked.

They looked at each other. Then one said, "Of course, we want you to go, but under no circumstances will we give you orders or instructions to go. It is up to you."

I suggested that they cable Washington or New York for inspiration. But they refused. I had to make my own decision this time. "It is dangerous," one said. "We can't protect you there. We can't go along. Our office wouldn't sanction it."

"What would you want me to find out there?"

"You used to be a musician, Boris," he told me. "You'll have to play this one by ear."

I said I would go.

One difficulty was my wife—yes, she who was forever denouncing the Bolsheviki, and declaring that she didn't care to breathe the same air as those swine, insisted on going along. "If you have to go to Moscow on this big deal of yours," Katerina said, "I'll go too."

It wasn't because she wished to see her family. She had two sisters living in Russia, one in Leningrad, one in Moscow. On a previous trip to Paris I had suggested she call them. She got one of them on the phone. The woman, when Katerina called her, refused to identify herself. "Katerina? I have no sister in Europe. You must be mistaken. I have no sister Katerina."

Soble was greatly displeased at the idea of Katerina's

going along. But strangely enough there was no more trouble about her visa than there had been about mine. I called Nagornov, the cultural attaché, and he got it in two days.

On the way to Moscow we stopped over at Vienna to spend New Year's with Willy Forst, the Sacha Guitry of Vienna. I told him about the picture, *The Miracle*. Willy said, "You make it sound wonderful. But don't you realize it will be another miracle if you and Katerina ever get back from Moscow alive? For so many innocents like you two, it has been a one-way journey."

Our first stop after Vienna was Prague. Here I was given good reason to heed Jack Soble's advice about being doubly cautious while in Soviet-dominated territory. After we checked into the Alcorn Hotel there, Katerina left to do some shopping. She could hardly have been out of the front door when a sexy blonde, with cleavage in abundant display, knocked on the door. She gave me one of those "Oh, you wonderful little man, you!" smiles, and said, "I saw by the register downstairs that you're from Hollywood. That's my life dream, to go to Hollywood and be an actress!" She stepped inside the room.

Lady Luck must have been nudging me, because I told her, unhesitatingly, "Get the hell out of here! Who are you, anyway?"

When she gave no indication of leaving, I shoved her out of the room, and slammed and locked the door. Then I picked up the telephone and called Silin, the Russian ambassador in Prague.

I told him what had happened. "Do you think I'm a child?" I asked him, and went on angrily, "If this is the way you intend to treat me—sending one of your Goddamn girl whore spies—I'm not going on to Moscow. When arrangements were made for this trip

I heard that the red carpet was going to be laid out for me—not a blonde or a brunette. Not even a red-head."

I was only guessing, of course, but it was a good guess that the beautiful girl must have been sent to test me—to get me drunk and sleep with me, if possible—just to see if I would blab anything. If so, I would be out of business. And Ambassador Silin never denied the charge I made. He said he would send an important official who "would protect me against beautiful and luscious blondes and all other dangers."

Following that incident I was given the V.I.P. treatment all the way to Moscow. The next day Silin sent his closest associate, Alexei Mikhailovich Klescho-winov, to take care of us. He arranged all the details for the rest of our trip.

At Warsaw we were met by a Russian muzhik—turned important official and well-dressed gentleman—and his Polish chauffeur. He had the Polish version of an Irish shillelagh under his arm and presented me with a similar combination walking-stick and weapon when we moved on to Brest Litovsk.

In Brest Litovsk, where we arrived at five in the morning, an Intourist girl greeted us. She was Ukranian, and so sweet and helpful that Katerina suggested she have breakfast with us. She refused, and when I pressed her, she said, quietly, "I would have to write a report on all you said while I was enjoying your hospitality, and send it home. I wouldn't want you to be embarrassed by that later on."

It was a strange sensation, believe me, to be riding through that so recently ravaged land in old first-class coaches of the International Pullman Company. The seats and bunks were hard and uncomfortable, but there was evidence that special efforts had been made to make them presentable. The service was excellent and the quality of food served on the train also surprised me—all sorts of meat, different kinds of smoked fish, plenty of butter. Caviar was much in evidence, though expensive. The favorite drink of the Russians would be enough to set a cowhand to turning somersaults all around the old corral. It was half vodka, half Polish beer, served in large beer steins and swilled down like so much water.

The two incidents of our journey that most deeply impressed me revealed the attitude of certain Russians toward the United States. The first happened on the train when I noticed a little boy who was running up and down the corridors with a toy pistol in his hand, shooting imaginary enemies.

"Are you shooting Indians?" I asked him.

"No, not Indians," he said. "Americans."

The other incident had occurred in the Brest Litovsk station. A Soviet Army general and his wife were waiting for their train for Warsaw, in the opposite direction. They were both reading through spectacles perched on the ends of their noses. He was reading a newspaper, she a novel. On looking up, she noticed I was wearing a camel's hair coat.

"American?" she asked.

"I am an American now," I told her. "But I was born in Russia."

"When you reach our Moscow you will find a beautiful city," she told me.

"I am sure I will," I agreed.

"But you have not yet seen our beautiful highways?"

I shook my head.

"They are beautiful," she said, dreamily. "Do you know who built them?"

"No."

"Germans! German prisoners of war. Too bad we

had to send them back."

"Because the highway system is not complete?"

She nodded, and took off her spectacles.

"No, but pretty soon we will have new prisoners."

"Who?"

"Americans."

The general, her husband, had appeared not to be listening. But now he took off his glasses. "You foolish woman!" he said.

"But, darling, you yourself told me that only yesterday," she replied.

It was dark when we arrived in Moscow on January 15, 1950. Here the red carpet was really out for me. No less than three dignitaries met me at the station. They were Nikolai Petrovich Ivanov, of the Ministry of Cinematography; Alexander Semenovich Trusov, representing the Soviet Television Department; and Eugeny Vassilievich Kovaliov, representing the Department of Art.

There were two cars. In one we were driven to the Metropole Hotel, accompanied by Ivanov. The other car took our luggage and the cans of film.

I was not there long before I realized that Kovaliov was the man in charge of all the arrangements for our stay. But Ivanov seemed to me the most intelligent of the three. He looked like a professor, and talked with great insight when he took me to the theaters. He seemed not only to be a knowledgeable man, but also to have a broad philosophical understanding. But I thought it interesting that when I asked him questions about his wife, children, and other relatives he evaded any discussion. When I told him that nothing would please me more than to have dinner at his home, he looked harassed. He hastily excused himself and I did not see him for two days.

In the fifteen years since I had been there the world

had done cartwheels. The collapse of Germany and the failure of the great steamroller that was the Nazi Army to crush the Russians had enhanced Soviet prestige throughout the world as nothing else possibly could. And everywhere one looked in the city itself there were evidences of progress, growth, industrialization, urbanization. The clean, beautiful subway was an old story, but not the ruthless leveling of ancient churches and whole blocks of houses to give Gorki Street and the other important boulevards added width. The shop windows were full of fine merchandise of every kind, though the prices were beyond the means of all but a fortunate few. Like it or not, I was forced to admit that Moscow in 1950 had the appearance of a city awakening from a thousand-year sleep.

In contrast to those we had seen on the way from the border, the people of Moscow were well dressed and looked well fed. The simple fact that they were all warmly dressed and were wearing shoes demonstrated the sweeping economic improvement in their lives since my last visit—though most of the shoes I noticed seemed to have been often repaired.

I found American touches everywhere I went—in the cars rolling by, in some of the architecture, but most of all in the mechanical equipment I saw. The orchestra playing at the Metropole asked me no questions this time about jazz. They played it a good deal of the time. And I had to smile because they billed themselves in lights as "The Moscow Boys."

The Muscovites I tried to talk with were as shy with strangers as in 1935. They were afraid even of hearing something critical of the Communist regime. Even that could get them into trouble. The magnitude of this universal fear of strangers and what they might say was perfectly demonstrated by a woman employee at our hotel whom Katerina liked. One day I suggested she come up to our room as my wife had some chocolate she wished to give her. The woman went white with fright, and seemed unable to answer. I noticed that for several days after that she scurried out of sight each time she saw us.

For some reason never explained to me, we were left to our own devices during our first days in Moscow. Perhaps the NKVD wished to make me feel free and also a V.I.P. Katerina did not take advantage of this extraordinary opportunity to see the city, but I did. Most of the Muscovites who dared to speak to me on the street asked the same question: "Did you ever see so many smiling faces as here, in our beautiful capital?"

I said no I hadn't. But I was not telling the truth, which was that I had never seen so many faces troubled by fear and worry in all my travels.

The peasants were still eating and drinking the same thing three times a day, I had found out: vodka, beer, black bread, and smoked fish. Yes, they all drank vodka and beer at breakfast, lunch, and dinner. The men drank vodka and beer half and half, as I'd seen the men on the train doing. The women drank either beer or vodka, but never mixed the two.

On January 20 Kovaliov telephoned and said that Korotkov wished to see me alone that afternoon. About three o'clock Kovaliov came to pick me up, and drove me to an apartment on Meshtchanskaya Street. The house was about two miles from my hotel. The apartment, on the third floor, was furnished in what would be considered lower-middle-class style in New York, but was rated as elegant here. It contained a radio, a phonograph, and a television set.

Kovaliov and I sat around, talking about music, until five o'clock, when Korotkov arrived. We drank several toasts and exchanged the usual amenities, and then the GPU official got down to business.

He began by joshing me about my reports on Dewey and Warren. "They could have been written for the New York *Times*," he said. "In fact, I suspect that is the newspaper you copied them from. It may be a surprise to you, Djon, but we also subscribe to the New York *Times*. I agree it is a most informative paper, though it never published precisely the sort of information about those two conservative politicians which we hoped to get from you."

Though he seemed in a good enough mood, what he was saying made me a little nervous. But he himself broke the tension by saying, "It is a good thing that Soble sent along your report on the secret meeting at the White House. We got that even before it was published in the newspapers."

I tried not to betray my surprise and I still don't know what Soble had sent in to fill out my dossier.

Then we started drinking toasts again. When my turn came, I held up my glass, and said, fervently, "I am sure that we all wish, from the bottom of our hearts, for peace between the United States and Russia."

That was the toast that only I drank. It was as though I had thrown the vodka into the faces of the two men. A moment later Korotkov, who detested the United States, began to tear into our government and the American way of life generally. He said if it were up to him he would not let one of his men stay in America for more than a year. He said the capitalist regime, with its easy living and emphasis on false values, was too corrupting.

"Isn't our food better than theirs?" Korotkov demanded. "Our cars? Our houses? Above all, our thinking? Did not we win the war without any help from our so-called Allies in the West—until the real fighting was over?"

Korotkov ended his denunciation of America's rottenness by proposing a toast to Soble. But he warned me against any social relationship with him. "You must have only a conspiratorial relationship with Abram," was the way he put the matter. (Abram, by the way, was Soble's real first name, and I never heard him called anything else by his superiors in the NKVD.) Korotkov also urged me to avoid contacts with any of Soble's friends or relatives, or other members of his ring. This was the policy all NKVD agents working abroad were expected to follow. It was shrewd, because if a single member of the spy ring either defected or was nabbed, he could turn in only his contact—in my case, Soble. The only member of the ring who could lead to more than one accomplice was Jack Soble himself.

Korotkov was so earnest about this that I realized why Soble begged me, each time I was to meet another contact, not to mention that he had introduced me to other spies in the ring or had divulged various secrets about the ring's operations.

When I asked Korotkov about the financing of my television company, he said, "Do not worry about money. We'll give you more than you'll be able to use. Meanwhile, I want you to meet everyone of importance in our Ministry of Cinematography and spend as much time there as you see fit. I put Kovaliov here at your service. I had planned to have your old friend Zubilin here to entertain you. I will bring him here if you would like to talk with him. But he is visiting his mother in Siberia."

"Seeing Zubilin is not necessary," I said, hoping he would not be swept away by this inspiration.

Three days later I got the going-over in that same

apartment for which the talk with Korotkov was merely a warm-up exercise. On the way there Kovaliov revealed that this day I was going to meet Leonid Dmitrievich Petrov, the deputy who ran espionage operations in the United States, under Korotkov's over-all supervision.

Kovaliov also warned me that I was not supposed to know Petrov's name. Now this is not the foolish hocus-pocus it sounds like: telling a man on trial—and that's what I was—some fact or some name and then immediately warning him not to reveal his knowledge of it; because if he slips up on that, how can he be trusted?

But that was routine. What was far more interesting to me was discovering the rivalries among the NKVD men. For example, I was not with Petrov for very long that day when I discovered he was Soble's most determined enemy within the framework of the NKVD.

He was a small, frail man, this Petrov, with a long, jagged scar that ran all the way from his right ear to the corner of his mouth. He talked English, but strictly the "dese, dem, and dose" variety. He began politely enough by saying that he wanted to make quite clear what was expected of me. Then he switched at once to the subject of Jack Soble. Though efficient in every way, he felt that Abram became entirely too thin-skinned when his relations with me were discussed.

Petrov next adopted the fatherly attitude of "This is going to hurt me, son, worse than it will hurt you." Saying he wanted me to understand that there was nothing at all personal in anything he was about to say, he poked fun at my Dewey-Warren report but blamed that all on Soble. "Abram trained you poorly. We need more meat in these reports," this Muscovite with the scarred face told me. "And this is a serious matter. Because we all need to get rough and tough at times. But he handled you with kid gloves." Meanwhile, Kovaliov was taking down every word Petrov was saying.

Petrov talked a good deal about the worthiness of self-criticism, making the point that one must regard oneself with complete detachment at all times, and be unceasingly critical in judging one's own actions. "I have no hope of making a Marxist out of you during your brief stay in Moscow," he explained, "but you can begin by practicing the self-criticism *we* all practice and believe. That is a cornerstone of Marxism."

Like Korotkov, he warned me against getting too fond of Soble. "Your relationship must remain conspiratorial, must never descend to the social level." Next he turned to the matter of my own finances. Did I really have millions of dollars? I nodded, but regretted the fib when he asked me to tell him in what countries I had my money salted away. I gave him fake figures which he wrote down.

Next he said, "Why do you not turn over all the money you have to Moscow?"

I told him I would think about it.

"What is there to think about?" he demanded. "Either you are a true Communist or not. If you belong with us your money should also."

"I think I can operate more efficiently for the Cause if my money is available at all times," I replied.

Petrov said he had never heard of such capitalistic rubbish. If I turned the money over to the Party, I could get whatever I needed any time I asked for it.

His next questions made it obvious that Soble had reported that I was a friend of Cardinal Spellman. The question was, "Could you place a member of

Soble's spy ring in the Cardinal's household? As the Cardinal's secretary, perhaps?"

Needless to say, I didn't encourage such proposals. But when we parted, I had the impression that Petrov was very pleased with the results of our interview.

At our next meeting it also became evident that Petrov had been assigned to make a special study of my background, connections, and character in order to determine what was the best way I could be used. This time Kovaliov was not alone when he picked me up. He was with Korotkov and Petrov when he came around for me. The table was set for dinner when we arrived. This session lasted for seven hours and was marked with much drinking of vodka.

Soon after we arrived Korotkov asked me a peculiar question. He called the housekeeper in and said, "Look her over." Then he sent the woman away. "Is she attractive, Djon?" he asked me. "Would you like to sleep with her?"

"She is not unattractive," I said, and smiled.

Korotkov explained that the NKVD had for some years been making a study of sexual preferences among men of all the nations of the world. They had assigned, he declared, hundreds of trained sexologists who were devoting their lives to this work. In Moslem countries they had enlisted the help of eunuchs.

"There are no better judges of feminine sex appeal anywhere, of course," he declared. "Today, as a result, we possess the greatest fund of information on sexual intercourse everywhere ever compiled."

Korotkov also described the schools for tyro prostitutes in which the students were instructed in all the arts of *amour,* refined and unrefined. Meanwhile, they were carefully indoctrinated. At the end of the course they were required to demonstrate their knowledge of the boudoir sciences.

"Americans go mad over these clever girls," he told me with a laugh, "particularly those in the Occupation forces. Americans are so inhibited that most of them have never even heard there is more than one way to enjoy sexual intercourse. Those who have heard that seem unable to believe it. The girls pass on to us everything these American service men tell them. Sex works far better for us than dope. At least, this is what we have found to be the case."

Finally I was given a list of notable Americans they wished me to cultivate. They wanted me to make friends with J. Edgar Hoover and keep a close check on what he was doing, and to make an attempt to recruit Helen Gahagan Douglas, then the Democratic congresswoman from California, to the Communist Cause. I once had mentioned to Soble that I knew Michael Farrel, the United States displaced persons chief in Vienna.

"Why don't you introduce Soble to Farrel?" they asked me.

At this point, Petrov tried to appeal to my vanity. "But isn't it absurd for us to try to tell an intelligent man like you how to go about this sort of work? I really think you should be telling us what you can do. For instance, there is Mrs. Douglas. You know her. Why don't you try to get her to help you?"

I can't say for sure even now what they were attempting. At that time her political opponents had been trying to smear Helen Douglas as a Red, though it was well known that she was a great liberal fighter against the extremists of both right and left.

Next they mentioned another outstanding Democrat, United States Senator William Benton of Connecticut. Couldn't I spot some friend in his office? And what about the State Department? Couldn't I place anyone there? To prove it could be done they told me that they already had a minor employee working in the United States embassy in Paris, who had been most useful to the Cause.

I kept saying the same thing over and over: I would see what I could do. They seemed satisfied with this, and finally said that they expected me to help Soble with his money transfers and currency movements.

Korotkov, at one point, shook his head over Soble. He wondered if Abram's success with the bristle factory had gone to his head? What did I think of that? I said I did not think that had happened or could possibly happen.

To me it remained astonishing how little the NKVD high command trusted its own operatives. Korotkov told me Jack would be my sole contact—with one exception. He, Korotkov, might require reports of me on his old friend at odd times. If so, he would send another man to check with me on whether Soble was deteriorating. The parol for this spy on other spies would be, "Did you know the general died at dawn?"

I assumed, of course, that Korotkov knew of Soble's plans for Albam, Myra, and possibly himself to work in the television company. So I had no hesitancy about mentioning it.

"No, no, no!" shouted the surprised General Korotkov. "They are to have nothing to do with it!"

The means for transferring the $350,000 was still the chief stumbling block. Korotkov had not yet won the approval of the NKVD higher-ups for any of the various plans so far suggested. Giving me $350,000 deposit on the purchase of fifty American films for $1,000,000 would not fool anyone, he said. The idea of giving me paintings worth hundreds of thousands of dollars in return for my films had also been abandoned for the same reason.

But I was beginning to pick up a fact here and there—that the payments to Soble were made quarterly, and that his bristle factory had cost Moscow $57,000.

At the next meeting, a week later, Kovaliov was very excited because this time their big boss would be at the conference. Though Beria was top boss, Fedotov was the man closest to him and also among the select few permitted to attend the Politburo meetings.

"Don't use anyone's last name while we're with Fedotov! Never interrupt him," Kovaliov said. "Make no criticism of Korotkov or Petrov, no matter what he asks you about them. And under no circumstances offer comparison between Russia and the United States."

After all that I expected to meet a smoldering volcano of a man. But Fedotov, who arrived with Korotkov and another NKVD man named Rodichenko, proved most pleasant. He introduced himself, asked about my health, wanted to know if I was enjoying my trip to Moscow and if there was anything he could do for me. He was particularly interested to hear the latest news about his old friend Jack Soble. After Fedotov told me that he and Soble had been good friends for more than thirty years, I decided to hell with these pussyfooters. I broke all the rules Kovaliov had just given me. I talked about everything I cared to. The others worried and quivered, but Fedotov was delighted. We discussed the arts, films, artists, entertainment for the masses, the opposing philosophies of Communism and capitalism, politics in various countries, and the countries' attitudes at the moment toward Soviet Russia. He said that the Soviets had tons of gold that they could dump on the market in order to devaluate the dollar and demoralize American economics.

Fedotov praised Charlie Chaplin highly, and said that if the comedian moved to Russia he could have anything he wanted, but that he was invaluable as a Communist weapon right where he was (in California at that time).

The others—Petrov, Kovaliov, and Korotkov—were amazed at his frankness and afterward took the cue from him in their behavior toward me. But they were really staggered when Fedotov, their big chief, sent word that his chauffeur could go home. He announced he himself would drive me home. That meant I was *in!*

In front of the hotel, Fedotov kissed me three times on each cheek and said, "If there is anyone you don't like, anyone who is annoying you and you don't want around any more, just let me know."

As I got into bed I congratulated myself that I was "in." The grilling in Switzerland had been merely a warm-up for the "long look-over" I had been subjected to in Moscow.

When we left Moscow on February 6, two or three days later, we were treated with the same courtesies as on our trip into Russia. We were seen off at the Moscow railway station by Trusov, Kovaliov, and Ivanov; the same sweet-faced Ukranian girl greeted us at Brest Litovsk; in Warsaw and in Prague we were met by the same courtly greeters.

We arrived in Vienna on February 12. By then I had had six days to think about my three weeks in Moscow. But what I thought about most were not my many sessions with the NKVD chiefs, but nineteen extraordinary theatrical productions we had seen while in the capital of the Soviet world. These included ballets, operas, musical comedies, plays by

Chekhov, and Shakespeare, and a satire on Truman. The productions were lavish on a scale no showman in capitalistic America could compete with. One Moscow show, for example, had an underwater ballet that alone cost a fortune. The decor of the theaters was first-rate, the seats were comfortable, the houses packed to the rafters every night. My one criticism was that the acting was a little old-fashioned. They were still using the Stanislavsky method of acting in its original form; no modernization had been permitted.

But to me the unforgettable show of the nineteen was one my guides appeared reluctant to let me see. This was a puppet show with life-size puppets. The opening scene was a bedroom, showing a male and female puppet in a double bed. The male was a reasonable facsimile of Joseph Schenck, the Hollywood movie tycoon. The woman was identified in the program as Miss Lay. The lover, who was soon introduced, was Mr. Pervertitis.

The next character was a puppet of Darryl Zanuck. He appeared with polo mallet in hand, dictated five scripts alternately to stenographers, and had twelve secretaries working at the typing. He fired a cannonade of orders about whom to fire and hire. The Zanuck puppet moved from one secretary to another, dictating a part of one story to the first girl and another part to the second, then jumping to another script. The audience roared at this sharp-edged satire of a Hollywood big shot in action. And it seemed to me amazing that these people even knew who Zanuck and Schenck were. The authors obviously were familiar with Hollywood. I went backstage but no one there—and there were all sorts of stagehands and other workers around—would tell me who wrote it, staged it, or produced it.

I told Kovaliov when he saw me off at the station

that he and the Ministry of Art should be hanging their heads in shame for presenting so shoddy an entertainment. I pointed out that it was the more regrettable because the bureau's other productions clearly showed the progress in theatrical production Moscow had made.

As I was getting on the train, I also said, "Everything else was fine, beautiful. I enjoyed my trip. But why did you have a man stationed at our door all the time we were there? He followed us everywhere we went. Was that friendly?"

He thought that over for a moment. "Very friendly," he said, without changing his expression. "We had him there for your protection."

The last thing Kovaliov said was that financing for my television project would be along shortly.

We both smiled as he said it. Who wouldn't? However, I felt secure, basking in Fedotov's favor—if only for the moment.

CHAPTER 9

The Mysterious Mining King

We had hardly checked into the Hotel Krantz-Ambassador in Vienna when the phone rang. A man, speaking English, requested me to go at once to the Café Mozart, a popular coffee house two blocks from the hotel. He said he had a very important letter for me. As I approached the Mozart I saw a man standing on the corner. He seemed to be watching me intently. But as I smiled and walked toward him, he turned and disappeared around the corner.

I walked into the café and sat down. Immediately I felt a tap on my shoulder, and heard someone whisper, "Quick! Follow me!" I wheeled around but already he was almost through the door.

It was Vitaly, Soble's new contact.

He kept me walking after him through the dark streets for four or five blocks before he allowed me to catch up with him. Each time I started to walk faster, he did also. At a deserted corner he popped into a taxi that was waiting by the curb. He left the door open for me. The moment I got in beside him the driver started off.

I started to ask him the reason for his extraordinary precautions, but he held his finger to his lips and nodded toward the driver. When the taxi stopped I saw I had been taken to the railway station in the Russian Zone of the city.

After watching the driver leave, Vitaly told me he had wished to warn me at once that the American embassy in Prague had taken a sudden interest in all my movements.

"You better watch your step," he said. "Your quick trip to Moscow and back has them puzzled, Djon. Wherever you go now they will be following you. Korotkov has given instructions that you are not to meet Soble again until we are sure you are clean. However, if we have additional information for you, Abram will contact you in Paris. When will you get there?"

"In a few days."

Vitaly thought for a moment. "If you are there by February twentieth, walk down the Avenue de l'Opéra at four in the afternoon. If not, do it the next day, or on the twenty-second."

"But I am not under surveillance," I assured Vitaly.

"You are wrong," he said. "The Americans were watching you all the time you were in Prague. That can only mean one thing: someone in the Foreign Department of the Czech government has been leaking information to them."

"How can you tell that?" I asked.

He looked at me in pity. "How else could they know so quickly that Ambassador Silin had kept pressing the Czechs to rush him approval of your visa?"

I was wrong. The United States had planted a girl in the Czech Foreign Office. On the other hand, the NKVD had their girl in our embassy in the same city. I was never told what happened to the NKVD's girl agent. She was either quietly dropped, or fed fake inside information that the American authorities wished her to pass on to the Soviet.

I did not arrive in Paris until February 21. Jack had been telephoning me, I was told, at the Raphael Hotel. I got him on the phone and he came to my room, ignoring the rendezvous Vitaly had arranged for us on the Avenue de l'Opéra.

When I asked him why he was so reckless, he insisted that what Vitaly had said was wrong about my being trailed by the Americans. He had been covering me himself to make sure I was not being followed. What had happened, of course, since my talk with Vitaly in the Russian Zone railway station was that word had been passed to our embassies to stop tailing me.

Soble questioned me about every phase of my trip to Moscow. After hearing the whole story, he dropped me some interesting information. The exposure in London of Klaus Fuchs as a Russian spy happened to be front-page news at the moment. When I asked Jack about that, he shrugged it off, saying, "We have two other Klaus Fuchses in London."

Jack also said that practically everyone in Artkino Films, the Soviets' government-controlled film-making unit, was "ours," meaning they did double duty as spies whenever required.

Jack revealed that, thanks to Korotkov's cooperation, he was having large quantities of the best Chinese pig bristles delivered to him in Switzerland for resale on the Paris black market. This was managed by smuggling the bristles across frontiers in Russian diplomats' luggage.

The arrangement of having Myra receive the payoff money in New York from the black marketeers was also working out very well, he said. Nevertheless, she was coming over with their boy Larry during the summer. But she would have to return in the fall so that the little fellow could continue his schooling over there, and also to continue banking the black-market money for him.

Whether or not this was true seemed unimportant. What counted was that Soble was confiding in me more and more. Once he asked me to urge Korotkov to send him an entire carload of Chinese bristles. Korotkov promised to arrange this when I mentioned the matter, but never did. Perhaps it slipped his mind. Perhaps he was informed that there was a good reason why his old friend should not obtain the bristles in bulk. In any event, the carload of bristles never reached Jack, who had felt that just one such shipment would solve all his financial problems.

Sometimes I could not help feeling sorry for Jack. I imagine anyone would who had to watch a man going down unawares to his doom. And disaster in his case seemed inescapable, for if the FBI did not get him, his own gang would. And I had contributed to his destruction by introducing him to luxury, to fine hotels and restaurants, to the world of big money. For Soble, of course, was dazzled by this glittering new world. For thirty years he had been living the Spartan existence of the dedicated espionage agent, in which he had to live on the run, never speaking what was on his mind, never trusting anybody but Myra.

Not that Soble had abruptly quit passing me a great deal of misinformation. There was one pure cock-and-bull story he told me about a "blond colonel" in the United States Army of Occupation in Germany who was supplying him with all sorts of secret information. But it was usually impossible to decide when he was telling the truth. Like most successful liars, he preferred putting enough facts in every story to give it an air of credibility.

It took the other Russians three full months to find out that I was not being followed by American spies. Meanwhile, Jack made another trip to Moscow. On getting back to Paris he congratulated me. He said I had made a great hit with the men there.

In Vienna I was given a new parol. Now the contact who approached me would say, "I am the representative of Almi Films."

To which I was to reply, "Fine. I want to see you." And then I would wait for him to conclude the parol with the words, "Mr. Vitus from Rome has a message for you." It was called to my attention that the parol was now using parts of the names of Vitaly Tcherniavsky and Korotkov. The first two letters of Vitaly were the first two letters of Vitus, and Korotkov's initials "A." and "M." were the first and third letters in the word "Almi."

This was probably told me to help my memory. When I tried to get written instructions by claiming that the parol was too complicated for me to remember, Vitaly refused to hand it over. The FBI, I knew, would have liked to see such written orders of the enemy—but I was never given one.

The secret agent preferred to spend as much as an hour making me repeat, word for word, the parol which he read off to me from a piece of flimsy paper about an inch and a half square. Sometimes I had to say it over twenty times to prove I knew it. Then he would twist the paper with the written instructions into a twirl, put a match to it, and watch it burn.

Sometimes each of several secret agents carried a part of an order or report. None of these made any sense until put with the others. They had all sorts of secret hiding places for such messages: a hidden pocket built into a belt, a tiny hidden chamber scraped out of a silver coin, or a place of conceal-ment in the case of a fine watch. They showed me that, when I had to write down anything, I could conceal the flimsies in the silver paper wrapping of a pack of cigarettes. The best trick was writing the message on the paper at the bottom of the pack. Some of the Communist spies could write in so mi-croscopic a hand that they could hide a long message under a postage or customs stamp.

I was then dickering for the Western rights to *The Fall of Berlin,* a Moscow film. But when this was finally screened for me, I bowed out. I said that it was so loaded with propaganda that the whole world would suspect me of being a Russian propagandist if I took it over. I later became interested in one of the best Russian-made films, *A Child of the Danube*. But negotiations collapsed on this deal also, this time because of too much involvement in red tape. I did manage to complete one deal with Moscow later on.

Nothing else of much interest happened until June 23, when I had a rendezvous with Vitaly in Vienna. As we talked I had the impression that he was await-ing a signal. Then suddenly he stopped talking and drove me over a devious route to an apartment house. He took me to a third-floor apartment.

Once there I tried to protest the delay in my television and movie deals with Soviet representatives. His face became very stern. He snapped, "Stop worrying about little things. There is going to be a civil war in the most sensitive area in the Far East within two days." Forty-eight hours later I picked up a paper and read that war had erupted in Korea. Vitaly also was able to predict—two years in advance—the trouble that would flame up in Indonesia.

That summer of 1950, I noticed that Jack was starting to do bewildering things. He had gone to the United States for a few weeks. When he returned to France in July, he risked his freedom by attempting to smuggle in a couple of cartons of American cigarettes. The French customs officers found the cigarettes. They took him to a small room, where they searched him. The only reason they failed to find the messages he was carrying to Moscow was that he had sewn these into the linings of his coat and trousers. "See how smart I am," he told me.

"You'd be a lot smarter if you did not take such desperate chances—just to smuggle in a few cigarettes."

As usual when he had not seen me for some weeks or months, he had large tales to tell me: now that "blond colonel" of his had alerted the Kremlin that the American High Command had made plans to invade and occupy all Russia; two hundred thousand North Koreans (still according to Soble) had been trained by the Red Army, which was preparing to train a half million more of them; the Communist forces had perfected a plan to seize General MacArthur, but MacArthur had foiled them by changing his schedule on that particular day.

He himself was waiting only for Myra to join him in a week or so with the rest of his report—before making another quick trip to Moscow. He said that the report was so important that Beria and the entire

Politburo would read it. He expected her within a week or so.

Jack also had a good deal to say about Jake Albam, his successor as chief of the spy ring in America. At first, Moscow had wanted Albam to work in a stationery store in Lower Manhattan. But Albam had refused this cover, and was now working in the herb business run by relatives of his.

He complained that Albam was doing very little for the Cause, but conceded that it was more difficult than ever to do any espionage work in the United States because the three-letter organization was becoming enormously efficient. The FBI had even driven one agent, "the Professor," usually dauntless and cunning, out of the States. "The Professor," who had never before had to take it on the lam, was now in Canada. But Jack was convinced that he himself was not being followed. "I'm okay," he assured me, and continued veering between reckless acts and extreme cautiousness. That summer, for example, he suggested we drive to a villa he had rented at Villerville, on the north coast of France, as a surprise for Myra and Larry, whom he expected within a few days.

But the shock when he brought me inside and I found the Zlatovskis there! The two couples had rented the place jointly for the summer! Considering the NKVD's stern rule against socializing among its secret agents, this was asking for important trouble!

But Jack said Moscow would never find out. Giving me a suspicious look, he added, "Unless you tell them about it."

Incidentally, this was the first time I met Jane Foster's husband, George Zlatovski. He told me he had got his honorable discharge as a lieutenant from the United States Army, Intelligence Division, in February 1948. At that point Jane called me into another room. She said that George needed a job desperately. Without one it would be impossible for them to stay in France. Could I help out, find anything at all for him? I promised to do what I could.

That was a promise that was to haunt me for a long time.

A remarkable thing happened during the last week in July while I was in Vienna. I had gone to a rendezvous with Tcherniavsky at the usual place, the viaduct near the entrance to the Prater. But his wife appeared instead. She was terribly excited.

"Vitaly could not come," she whispered in a trembling voice. "He is on important business, Djon. Could you meet him here the day after tomorrow at the same time?"

"Of course," I told her.

The next day the newspapers reported the mysterious disappearance of a Yugoslav citizen from a train while it was passing through a tunnel in the Russian section of Austria. He was the third Yugoslav who had vanished in that manner. On reading that, I of course suspected what important business had detained Vitaly. Actually it was one of a series of dress rehearsals for the abduction and murder of Tito, the Premier of Yugoslavia, who was playing footsie first with the Kremlin, then with the West.

A couple of days later I went to Badgastein, a health resort in Austria well known for its mineral baths. During the first week I interrupted my vacation to go to Vienna. I wanted to tell Vitaly I was fed up with waiting for Moscow to finance my television deal, and was also willing to forget all about a movie deal I had been talking over with certain Russian film representatives.

He urged me to be patient a little longer. "Go back to the baths," he said, "and stay there until you hear from me. I will check with Korotkov."

He said he would wire me if he had any word, signing the telegram "Czerny." If all had gone well, the message would read "Contract prepared." If he wished me to bring Soble along, he'd add the words, "Bring something with you."

"But how will you get in touch with Abram?"

This is when I made a stupid mistake. "That will be easy," I said, and showed him a wire I had just received. This announced that both the Sobles and the Zlatovskis would join me at Badgastein within two weeks. It was signed "Jack, Myra, Jane, George."

On seeing this, Vitaly went into a tantrum. He said each of them would have to be severely disciplined. "It is bad enough for them to travel together. But they must be mad to wire you they are coming. Not to mention signing their own names."

I went back to Badgastein. When the quartet did arrive, they were accompanied by the pretty young daughter of a Midwestern political expert. Jack boasted that Jane had started recruiting this girl, but that now he was taking over. He hinted broadly that the first step in her indoctrination would be the usual one: seduction.

He also told me that either Jane or George Zlatovski had been going on to Salzburg every day for him, mixing with the American officers stationed there, and bringing back important new information for him on each trip. I did not mention Vitaly's outburst against the four of them. I assumed they would hear from Moscow about that soon enough.

On September 2, just as I finished my cure, the telegram from Vitaly came. It read: CONTRACT PREPARED BRING SOMETHING WITH YOU.

Jack was usually eager to keep any rendezvous anywhere. But this time he begged off, saying he had made too many business appointments in Munich with bristle traders that he would have to cancel at the last moment.

"What in the world do you want me to tell Vitaly?" I asked him. "I know he has many questions he wishes to ask you."

"Take Myra to Vienna with you. She can answer all his questions. It is of the utmost importance that I meet Karl Gebhard in Munich. He is the man who is going to Canada as my representative. Tell Vitaly that I will be in Vienna in the next few days. Also advise him that I may not have my new report quite ready." Myra, he added, should be given only oral messages, as he did not care for her to run the risk of being caught with one on her person.

But instead of Myra, only my FBI man was on the train that took me from Badgastein to Vienna. When I went to the spot for our usual rendezvous in the Prater, I found Petrov there instead of Vitaly. I also noticed two groups of men, five in all, hovering near him like so many bodyguards. Three of them quickly disappeared, but the other two, I noticed, followed us.

Petrov grabbed my arm and walked me off—almost as though he considered me his prisoner. He said, "Where is Abram?" I told him that Soble had been detained in Germany on personal business. This did not satisfy Petrov, so I explained that he had offered to send his wife, but that Jane Foster had been taken ill at Badgastein and Myra had to stay behind to nurse her.

"Badgastein!" He exploded. "You mean you were all there together?"

I nodded, for I was certain that Vitaly had told him all about that and that he was just putting on a show to see how I would respond. He took me to the same apartment where Vitaly had interviewed me. As we walked there, he fumed and sputtered because I had come to our rendezvous wearing a bright yellow tie. "This is more than an indiscretion," Petrov said. "It is madness!"

Then he started fulminating some more about the group taking the baths together. "You are lying about this!" he thundered at one point. "*You* might be stupid enough to meet with the others, but Jack is too experienced to permit any such luncy!"

When I got bored listening to his abuse, I showed him the telegram signed with the four names. When he read that I thought he was going to burst with rage. The long scar on his face became as red as blood.

After a while Petrov permitted me to leave, but only when I agreed to meet him next day at noon at the same place. It happened that, as I left the apartment, I discovered that I was being followed by a man in a plastic raincoat. Wherever I went he followed me. I got annoyed, naturally, and started to play little tricks on him. If I was going out for a pack of cigarettes, I would step out into the street, bundle up my coat around my ears, pull my hat low over my eyes, look this way, then that, slink along, duck into doorways and up and down alleys, as though I were planning to blow up the city. I kept it up until the game wearied me. After that, when I saw him, I would shout, "Hello, faithful shadow!" But nothing would discourage him from tailing me.

When I reached the meeting place the next day I was met by Vitaly's wife. But as I turned, my other elbow was gripped by Petrov.

"Walk as though you're flirting with her," he whispered. I obeyed, paying her compliments as the three of us walked to an apartment at No. 10 Danhauserstrasse. This time Vitaly himself was there.

I was taken to a small room, where the two men left me. They told me to remain there until they came back. At intervals I could hear the footsteps of men walking past the door. There seemed to be four or five of them. When Vitaly and Petrov returned they took me to a larger room. Again they told me to wait until they returned. They said they were leaving the house. They warned me not to go near any of the windows, and advised me not to open the door under any circumstances.

As they went out I looked at my watch. It was 12:40. I just sat there, scared, unable to imagine what was going to happen next. That was just what they wanted, of course. Minutes crept by, then hours. Petrov returned first. It was then four o'clock. Vitaly walked in a few minutes later.

Petrov flew into a rage again over the yellow tie. As his anger mounted, he seized the quiet blue tie I was now wearing, jerked it violently, then pulled up the knot so that it was almost choking me. After a minute or two he released me. But before I could regain my breath he began criticizing the other clothes I had on. "They are too loud. They can be seen blocks away. But that yellow tie. That could be seen miles away!" He also became choleric once more about the Soble health group gathering at Badgastein.

Before I left he lectured me on using my own initiative for the Cause. "You have famous people for friends, yet you report nothing to us about them. You don't have to wait for big things to happen. We want to know about the little things too. You have never even told us such simple things as how an American citizen gets a routine visa from Paris to Vienna." Then he said, "Did it not occur to you that some of our men might find it useful to know

Ernest Heusermann? I want you to introduce me to him."

Heusermann, then the American film-control officer for the United States Army in Vienna, was later in charge of the Josefstadt Theatre there. Petrov's idea of involving him with the ring was ridiculous. Heusermann would have anyone thrown out of his office who tried to indoctrinate him. But not wishing to be garroted with my own necktie, I promised to approach Heusermann.

Petrov gave me two other assignments that day. The first was a peculiar one. I was to go to Belgrade, the capital of Yugoslavia, and get material for a report on the public opinion there of the merits of Soviet Russia and the United States. From what I learned later I have reason to suspect that this had some connection with the impending plot to assassinate Premier Tito.

They may have been trying to decide whether they enjoyed too much prestige among the Yugoslavs to risk losing if the facts about the murder plot against their leader became public. Or they might have wanted to find out whether there was enough resentment against the Americans there to try blaming the United States for the assassination. It is also quite possible that they were simply testing me to see if I would or could gather and deliver accurate information.

As my cover, I was to try to sell Yugoslav rights to *Carnegie Hall* and my other films. This, also, he thought would serve to put me in touch with people who had their ear to the public pulse: film distributors, theater owners and managers, and possibly some newspapermen.

My other assignment I could do immediately. This consisted of telephoning Myra at Badgastein. I was to say, "The people in the bristle business are very eager to see Abram in Vienna. If he will come at once, they will telephone him at the Hotel Alcorn within an hour of his arrival. But get him to hurry." I phoned Myra but she said Jack was still in Germany, though she would try to get my message to him.

I saw Petrov several times during his visit to Vienna. On each occasion he ended our talk with a lecture— once on the necessity of becoming a "more conscientious conspirator." Another time he rebuked me for thirty minutes because I had been ten minutes late. "Punctuality," he emphasized, "is essential." He also had me go over, endlessly, my parols—"Almi Films," "The general died at dawn." At our last meeting he told me to return to Paris. I would get my final instructions there. But this turned out to be merely a maneuver to get me out of Vienna before Soble arrived. With Jack's assistance, Petrov expected to score the biggest coup of his career as an espionage agent. This was information the Kremlin had been seeking for years: figures on atom-bomb production in the United States, along with precise information on the location of the bunkers where our A-bombs were stored.

This invaluable information was to be supplied by a man-and-wife spy team I had not met. If I could believe Soble—who told me about it shortly afterward —they had been working for some years close to Los Alamos and various other atomic-energy installations. The man, a nuclear physicist, Jack said, even had photographs of the bunkers. If the documents and photographs were as important as Petrov believed, getting them to Moscow would be hailed as one of the great strokes of Soviet espionage. He would be promoted. Colonel Soble would probably be decorated and become General Soble. Petrov wanted me and every other Russian spy moved far from Vienna for the time being, thus preventing a lot of jealous Comrades from claiming a share of the credit.

But on September 23, when I saw Soble in Paris, he taunted me for my disloyalty in not remaining in Vienna until he got there. When I told him that Petrov had ordered me to Paris, he called his NKVD colleague four-letter words in an assortment of languages. He said that Petrov should have listened to lectures about punctuality instead of giving them.

For Petrov failed to show up three times in succession for controlled Vienna rendezvous with Jack. Jack had brought to these meetings documents and records of the utmost importance which he wished to turn over to Petrov. These represented, he said, months of work by some of the shrewdest, most hardworking members of the Russian worldwide spy ring. Though he did not confide it to me at the time, these were the documents that gave the Russians the inside story, their first clear picture, of A-bomb production in the United States.

Consider Soble's spine-tingling dilemma as he stood that first evening in the rain, waiting for Petrov to show up and relieve him of his invaluable—and incriminating—documents. And it was raining in sheets. He was not supposed to telephone Petrov or anyone else. He did not dare return to his hotel room with the documents. If Petrov had been arrested there was every likelihood that police would be waiting there for him.

Usually, in such a situation, the espionage agent is supposed to destroy all the material he has brought to the rendezvous. But this was not a usual situation. The importance of the papers precluded burning or tearing them up.

In the end, after waiting, drenched by the rain, he telephoned Tcherniavsky, who came on the run, relieved him of his precious burden, and hastily arranged for Soble to meet the missing agent the following night. He did not show up on that second evening, and a third rendezvous was arranged. Again, Petrov did not appear.

Soble believed Petrov either was dead or had been captured by the enemy. But one day, almost a week late, Petrov rolled into Vienna looking a good deal the worse for wear and dissipation. It turned out that the stern disciplinarian had been on an extended bat. While waiting in Vienna to get in touch with Soble, he had run up to Prague to see a girl friend. He had been holed up in her room, drinking like a mad sailor and refusing to let the lady get dressed for four straight days and nights.

When at long last he showed up in Vienna, bleary-eyed and weak from sexual excess, Soble rushed him to the Russian sector, where he made the sodden Petrov telephone to Fedotov himself and confess his unpardonable debauchery. This was the NKVD theory of self-criticism in actual practice. But to me the supreme irony was that the stern agent, after managing to get me out of town while the atomic secrets were in transit, had managed also to get himself out of town when the big prize came in.

And now Soble had an additional reason for being resentful of Moscow. Whatever large reward he expected for the coup of getting the atomic secrets never came his way. Sometimes I looked at him in astonishment, remembering what an obscure-looking man in his ill-fitting clothes he had seemed at our first meeting only three years before, how modest his personal ambitions had been.

But now he was a big shot, at least in his own estimation. He had money flowing in from his factory like water, and was living like a king in Paris. His ego was inflated a little more each time he walked with me into a hotel or restaurant and was introduced to some famous Hollywood star, distinguished playwright, or showman of world renown. The idea that as my friend, and possibly my future business partner, he could rub shoulders with the great and glamorous people of show business even while serving the Great Cause of promoting world Communism all but made him dizzy.

All this, also, sharpened his desire to impress me with his importance. He had tried to do it by boasting of his success in the bristle business. That hadn't worked very well. He had also tried by dripping little bits of information to me about his activities as an espionage agent. That seemed to do the trick, for it served my purposes, of course, to pretend that this did impress me, and that I considered him a real insider in the strange, secret world of international spying.

The FBI urged me to lose no time in trying to worm out of Soble the identity of the husband and wife whom I long called in my reports to them "the atomic couple."

If I got started on the right trail, it was largely because Jack couldn't stop talking of the unspeakable rudeness of "that sinister clown of a Petrov." He kept saying that Leonid had been rude not only to me, to him, to Myra, and to little Larry, but to a very "important Communist sympathizer, possibly the richest in Central Europe."

Itching as I was to ask him questions about this, I resisted the impulse. Nothing could shut him up so fast as any sort of question. So I waited.

"This millionaire," he told me one day, "has absolutely refused to talk with Petrov. He telephoned

Moscow personally to complain of Petrov's rudeness. After that they sent Tcherniavsky to contact him."

And, little by little, Jack got into the habit of dropping me an occasional clue as to the identity of this millionaire fellow-traveler. Once he said that this man, though his family was among the wealthiest and most aristocratic in Austria, had always been a Communist sympathizer. Another time Soble described him as an old college pal of his. He said they had attended the University of Leipzig together. Due to the political upheavals of the past quarter century, his millionaire friend had lost millions of dollars invested in Czechoslovakian coal mines. But he had recouped these losses many times over, and had now emerged as one of the mightiest monopolists in the whole Balkan area. From Jack's various remarks I assumed that his mysterious mining millionaire had some intimate connection with the atomic couple.

So now the FBI told me they wanted all the information I could get about each of the three. It was the biggest assignment they had given me so far; it was also a puzzle that took us a long time to crack.

CHAPTER 10

I Hit the Espionage Jackpot

The mysterious mining king was by no means the only old college chum whom Jack Soble was trying to make use of in his espionage work. While briefing me on my Belgrade trip, he declared that most of the real "progressive liberals" in Yugoslavia had been classmates of his at Leipzig University in the early thirties. One day Jack told me their names and asked me to find out what had happened to these old friends since he lost touch with them. He said he would be particularly interested in any of them who might have emigrated to the United States and were working in the Yugoslav embassy, consulates, or commercial agencies there.

I left for Belgrade on the Simplon Express on October 11, 1950. Just before saying good-by to me, Jack said that Moscow's idea that I was a millionaire was costing me plenty of money. "This time," he said, "you must do something you should have started doing long ago. That is give Home an account of all your expenses on this trip. And while you are at it you might also put in a bill for the five-hundred-dollars-a-month rent you are still paying for that penthouse office in New York. If they do not pay you," he added, wryly, "I will—even though they owe me forty-eight hundred right now."

It takes two days to go from Paris to Belgrade by train. I arrived there at nine in the morning. Putnik, the Yugoslav Travelers' Bureau, had got me first-rate accommodations at the Hotel Moskva. I ate whenever I could at Belgrade's excellent Majestic Restaurant, there being no other good eating places in that city. Putnik also procured tickets to the opera, plays, and film theaters for me during my five days in the city. Disregarding my instructions from Soble, I spent most of my time with the film people there.

My report could not have cheered Home up very much. The Americans were in high favor with everyone I talked to in Belgrade. Everybody liked them, respected them. I could discover no similar affection for the Russians.

From Belgrade I took a Yugoslav plane to Zurich, where I changed to one for Vienna. While waiting in the transit room for this second plane, I suffered so severe a nosebleed that I had to send a porter for the handbag in which I was carrying my handkerchiefs. This inconsequential incident illustrates another odd

way in which the Communist-trained mind works; the
moment I mentioned this matter to Vitaly, he wanted
to know all about it.

"How in the world did you manage to do *that?*" he
asked. "You mean all you had to do was bribe the
porter and he got your handbag from the luggage
waiting to be put on the Vienna plane?"

"I did not bribe him, Vitaly. "I tipped him."

"Tip, bribe, what's the difference?"

Knowing by this time that it was impossible to convince any Communist that there is a difference between tipping and bribery, I dropped the subject. I
was beginning to realize that in the conspiratorial
world men like Vitaly live in, there can be no capitalistic tipping, only bribing. Basically, I suppose,
this is because, not trusting one another, how can they
trust foreigners, the enemy?

Whatever else I liked about Belgrade I cannot recommend the food—except at the Majestic Restaurant.
On getting back to Vienna I had indigestion for
several days and it was not until October 22 that I
was well enough to meet Vitaly at the Johann Strauss
Cinema at nine o'clock in the morning. He and his
wife were there when I arrived. They took me to the
apartment house at No. 10 Danhauserstrasse, where we
went into apartment 15. But when I started to tell
Vitaly my story he stopped me abruptly. He said, "You
must write that down. All Moscow is waiting to read
what you have found out for us about Belgrade."

He sat me down at a small table on which lay a pen,
two dozen freshly sharpened pencils, and a pile of
paper. He told me to include in the report these phases
of the trip:

1. The trip, with all customs details.

2. People I met and, if possible, addresses and the
nationality of each.

3. The attitude of each toward foreigners, and particularly the attitude of Yugoslavs toward Americans.

4. Sympathies of any of them with Moscow, and names of those individuals.

5. Did I feel safe during the five days I was in Belgrade? Did I think there was any suspicion of me? Was I watched? Was I followed? Would I repeat the trip, if asked to?

Vitaly left with his wife, after warning me not to open the door, turn on the radio, or make any other noise. At two p.m. they returned with sandwiches and hot coffee. Then they left again and came back a second time at seven. I had written seventy pages of notes. Vitaly told me to return next day as he might have questions to ask me when he finished reading the report. This time I was to come straight to the apartment. Next day Vitaly complimented me on my report but said he regretted that I had mingled with some White Russians in Belgrade. All White Russians, he said, were both untrustworthy and dangerous.

But nothing in my report interested him nearly so much as the incident in the Zurich airport. Once again he had me go over each detail. Had the porter actually left me alone while I opened the bag? I explained that I told him to wait there so he could take the bag back to the baggage room. Well, then, had the porter turned his back while I was opening the bag? I said that with my nose bleeding I had neglected to watch what he was doing. This made Vitaly cluck like a mother hen fretting over a mentally retarded chick.

The fact that I had seen an unusual number of priests on the trip also aroused the curiosity of this Russian spy. I had to explain that they were on their way to Rome to attend the proclamation of the dogma of the Assumption of the Virgin Mary. Then I made the mistake of mentioning that I happened to know one of the priests. He was Father Mix, a relative of the famous cowboy star, Tom Mix.

Vitaly questioned me for half an hour about Father Mix, though I protested I knew practically nothing about him. Then he asked whether I thought my friend Cardinal Spellman would attend the great ecclesiastical gathering in Rome. I said that His Eminence was not in the habit of asking my permission when he wished to go abroad. As I was leaving Vitaly asked me what my expenses amounted to on the trip. I told him $780. He asked me for an itemized account. The next day we met at the Lindenkeller Restaurant, where for some reason he insisted on carrying on our conversation in German, though we had spoken Russian during our last few meetings. He said he had wired Fedotov concerning the $350,000 promised for our television project, and expected a final answer during the next few days.

I then gave Vitaly the itemized expense account. He had the $780 with him, and promptly handed it to me. It was all in twenty-dollar bills, wrapped up in a sheet of brown paper. He had me sign a receipt. So now, having my signature for monies received, the NKVD could relax about me, feeling that they had me under their thumb. Their belief suited my purposes fine, as well as the FBI's.

Some time before, I had told Vitaly that I would be returning to the United States in the fall. He had two assignments for me on this trip: he wanted me to find between ten to twenty Americans who were loved and trusted throughout the United States, and to get them to come in a group to Moscow. These influential Americans could then see for themselves that the Russians truly wanted peace. Vitaly insisted that the Reds were willing to make concessions to such a delegation of Westerners. "We do not want to talk to your comedian progressives," he said, "but to men who can go home and convince the people of America that another world war is the last thing the Kremlin wants!" I was to hear this plea a hundred times from the lips of other Communist officials and spies.

And I, for one, am convinced that they did want peace, and still do, for at least the twenty or thirty years they will require to rebuild their agricultural and other resources which Hitler's Nazi armies so crippled and devastated. Then it may be a different story. For their leaders show no indication that they intend ever to abandon their dream of world conquest and domination. But, as many a true friend of peace has said, anything can happen in a world free of war for twenty or thirty years.

My second assignment was to get as cozy as possible with Cardinal Spellman and several other distinguished Americans, including an old friend of mine, Dr. Thomas Keith Glennan, whom President Truman had just appointed to the three-man Atomic Energy Commission. And as this was being written, Dr. Glennan was appointed Administrator of the National Aeronautics and Space Administration, or "Space Boss," as the newspapers called it.

Glennan had been studio manager at Paramount during the years when I was running the lot's music department. How they discovered that we had been good friends back in those days, I don't know. I wondered about that when Vitaly got out a clipping from the New York Times which told of Truman's appointment of Keith, and described his career. He instructed me to investigate the new AEC commissioner's political leanings and the state of his personal finances. I should also find out, of course, whether there were any shady incidents in his past. Was he a heavy drinker, for example? Did he have a mistress? Who was she?

What about his secretary? Was Keith honest? Could he be bribed? Vitaly assured me that getting the material to blackmail my old friend would make the higher-ups back home in Moscow very happy indeed. I said this was not difficult to understand.

I was also given some new parols and cautioned to reveal nothing about these to Jack Soble, as these arrangements were being made exclusively for me. Vitaly had been authorized to give me $50,000 in cash at this time if I needed some money for the television business. But, after talking this over, he and I agreed that it would be better to wait until the full amount was on hand.

This was another thing that greatly impressed Moscow. The NKVD was not accustomed to having offers of such amounts of cash refused by its secret agents. The idea that I was a big shot beyond financial temptation from either side was exactly the way the FBI wanted it.

After my return to Paris, Soble kept urging me to do something about getting a job for George Zlatovski. He said that George had recently been making trips almost every few days to Bordeaux and Fontainebleau to check on how much military equipment was arriving from the United States. It was important to the Cause for him to get the job that would entitle him to working papers.

I thought it over for a few days. Then I told Soble that if George would invest $5000 in a local film company, the head of that company might give him the job of assistant manager of the company's theater in Paris.

Though Zlatovski was able to raise only $3900, he got the job. Unfortunately, the manager of the theater was a man of the extreme right. Zlatovski, never a chap who could keep his mouth shut, resented the ultra-conservative views of his boss. They were forever getting into quarrels over politics. Within a few months Zlatovski talked himself out of the job he needed so desperately.

To complicate matters his wife, Jane, came to me shortly after he was thrown out of his job and announced that she was pregnant. It was George's baby, she said, but she did not wish to have it. Her parents in California had been violently against her marrying Zlatovski, she said, and she feared they would never forgive her if she became the mother of his child. Jane, who had been drinking heavily, also confided that Soble had promised to arrange for an abortion. Abruptly, she added that she was scared to death of him. She said that he beat her up often.

This was true. Jack himself had told me the same thing. He explained that he had to beat up Jane, and some of his other women from time to time, to keep them in line, to keep them loyal to him and to the Great Cause.

At the end of 1950 Katerina and I sailed for New York aboard the *Queen Mary*, and we continued on to Hollywood by train. But after little more than a month I was back in Europe again on business. I had done nothing about Vitaly's assignments. I decided to tell him I would work on them on another trip to the States that I would be making very soon.

This time I was traveling without Katerina. Frankly, I was not unhappy that she preferred to remain in California. It was bad enough trying to fool the Russians and my friends, without having Katerina questioning me as to why I was seeing various mysterious men and preferred going everywhere without her.

In Hollywood, by this time, I was being generally labeled a Communist. Even my intimate friends were disgusted with me. Those who did not suspect me of being a Russian agent thought me at least a fellow-traveler. Some thought I should share the fate of the "Hollywood Ten" who had recently been sent to prison for refusing to explain their connections with the Communist Party. It was dismaying to walk into a restaurant and find old associates looking the other way. It was shocking to encounter a man whom I had done professional favors for and have him ignore my outstretched hand. Some of them wrote letters to the FBI and the Senate Investigating Committee about my mysterious relations with Moscow. No, I did not mind leaving Hollywood behind me—at least until the real story could come out. But I kept wistfully wondering when that would happen. My counterspy job had already taken far longer than I ever dreamed it would.

When I next met Jack Soble in Vienna, I found him in a mental state approaching panic. He was so nervous that boils had broken out all over his body. He told me that everybody in his group seemed to be either quitting or about to quit. Among these, he said, was a Russian-born doctor who worked as a staff physician in a United States prison.

"And that man holds the Order of Lenin!" exclaimed Jack, mournfully.

He also lamented the defection of two brothers he knew, both naturalized Americans. One of them lived in New York and the other in Paris. Both had been part of his espionage gang at various times. Like the prison doctor, they had been wholehearted Communist workers all their lives, but now they were refusing to cooperate.

There remained the difficult problem of finding Zlatovski a job. George had tried to get a post of some sort with the American military forces in France, but had been turned down cold. Zlatovski thought this unfair because he was an honorably discharged ex-Army officer.

But Soble's real grievance was against the men at Home. After furnishing invaluable information to them—he now all but told me that this concerned America's atomic secrets—he had been ordered to stay away from the couple from whom he had got it, and also from me.

As though this weren't enough to make a man lose faith, the men of Moscow, despite their many promises to help him out in business, had sold 200,000 kilos of Chinese bristles to a merchant in Stockholm, a deal that could have netted him a profit of half a million dollars if they had only thrown the business his way.

Even when in so bitter a mood, Jack liked to reminisce, possibly to illustrate to me how much better things were in the good old years. This day he told me how he had emigrated to the United States with a group of other Lithuanians, all but one or two of whom, he said, were devoted to "the Communistic ideal." They had had a terrible time getting to the United States. Having come out through Vladivostok, they had been stuck in Japan for months. Finally they had managed to complete the journey, thanks to the kind help of a relative of his, a prominent Boston attorney who had agreed to vouch for them in their new country.

"He is a loyal American," Soble remarked jeeringly. "After taking all that trouble to get us into the country, he became suspicious. Speaking quite earnestly one day he told the lot of us that he loved his adopted country. The good old United States of America. In fact, he said he loved the land of liberty so much that he would strangle with his own hands any one of us who tried to hurt Uncle-Sam-land."

Jack was in stitches by this time. "What a fool!" he

kept saying, between guffaws.

Down through the years I had to listen to a lot of this infuriating sort of stuff, and hold my tongue. What I cannot deny is that I could sympathize with him because of the difficulties he was encountering in doing business with the Russians. For months and months I had been trying to buy certain foreign rights to certain Soviet films, and with no luck. When I seemed to have a deal set, the business representative I was working through would abruptly be replaced. When this happened, the new man never seemed to know what stage the negotiations had already reached. That meant we needed to start all over again. Or some other hitch appeared out of nowhere.

It was on February 21, 1951 that Soble at last began to leak to me the information we had so long been waiting for. Until then he had given me merely a few clues to the identity of his mining tycoon and "atomic couple." This was on an evening when he and I were dining in a Vienna resturant with a film man whom Jack was eager to impress. Attempting to be casual about it, Jack mentioned having recently been entertained at the home of a couple whom he described as the finest, richest people in Vienna. With a soft look in his eye Jack explained that this rich man had been the owner at one time of coal mines in Czechoslovakia. He had only lost control of these owing to the Communist coup there. And he had been negotiating recently to get them back, and seemed to have an excellent chance of succeeding.

Jack had been a fellow student of this tycoon at Leipzig back in the twenties. Some years later the wealthy man's brother had moved to Canada, where he had made a great success in the lumber business.

His eyes half closed as he sipped his brandy, Jack

went on revealing details that, put together with their own facts, I fervently hoped would help the FBI to identify the man. The rich man's wife and her sister were both university graduates, he said; both had doctor's degrees. He added that he had known both of these girls for many years, as had his brother Robert.

We were getting plenty of pieces of the puzzle. But when would he drop the *name* of the Communist millionaire who was involved in some way, I was sure by now, in the stealing and transfer of America's atomic secrets in the great deal that Petrov had come within an inch of wrecking?

Not long after this I managed, after endless tiresome dickering, to acquire the remake rights to *Marika*, a beautiful Russian color picture. But I had to fork over $100,000 in hard American dollars for them—too much to permit a profit, as it turned out. When I next saw Vitaly I complained bitterly about the tough bargain the Soviet cinema representative had driven, and also about the continued delay of the long-promised $350,000. I also followed Soble's suggestion and asked reimbursement for the $500-a-month rent I had been paying now for more than two years for the New York penthouse office.

Vitaly proved uninterested in the trimming I had got on the *Marika* deal or in what he called the trifle in rent I had laid out for the unused New York office. But he could make me a definite promise concerning the $350,000. All I had to do, he declared, was get Keith Glennan on my television company's board of directors. If I could manage that, he guaranteed I would be rewarded at once with the full amount.

Like Soble, Vitaly was very worried about the spreading troubles within the NKVD itself. "Too many of the Comrades are running away," was the way he put it. There was plenty of trouble, not only among Soble's people, but in Hungary and Poland as well, and even in Vienna, while we were sitting there talking together like true Comrades.

When I asked him to set up new contacts for me in the United States before my trip there, Vitaly promised he would try. But, he said, the FBI was making things tougher all the time. The three-letter organization now had a band of investigators well trained in politics to harass Moscow's espionage men.

Did I know any FBI men? When I said "No" with a straight face, he wondered if I could "get something" on the Bureau's chief, J. Edgar Hoover. I said this would prove a waste of time, as Mr. Hoover had many underworld enemies who would have got something on him years ago, if possible. He then asked several questions: Were all FBI agents university graduates? Did they come from wealthy families? Were they highly paid?

I told him I did not know but I could find out the answers for him very easily. Vitaly then said that if I got this information for him, and Keith Glennan agreed to become a director of my company, the $350,-000 would be handed to me when I came back.

On my way to the States I stopped in Paris to see Jack Soble. The time I spent there with him gave me a good example of how and why at least one Communist agent's loyalty to the Cause was being rapidly undermined. He had been awarded a medal for his work on the atomic secret but felt this was inadequate and inconsequential.

I spent the next six weeks or so in the United States. Just before returning to Europe I flew to Washington, where I visited with Keith Glennan in his office and had lunch with him. Having first obtained the FBI's permission to do so, I broached the suggestion that he become a director of the television company. He looked up the regulations governing outside activities of commissioners of the AEC and told me that there would be no conflict of interest if he became a director of my company.

I had explained that I had not as yet obtained the necessary backing. I wished I could tell him the real story, but it was, after all, just talk. No matter what happened, Keith would never actually get involved.

From Glennan's office I went to the Department of Justice Building, where I joined a party making a tour of the offices of the FBI. This was the public tour regularly made each day by visitors from all over the country. At the suggestion of the Bureau men I was working with, I took back to Europe with me both the literature available to all comers and also application forms which the men who wished to join the Bureau were required to fill out.

Five days later, when I handed this literature to Vitaly in Vienna, he could hardly believe his eyes. The application form was almost too much. It was another example of the naïve astonishment that greeted my story about retrieving my own handbag at the Zurich airport.

"If you got all these documents so easily," Vitaly said, "it must have been a trap. You must have been followed everywhere you went in Washington."

I shook my head. It was all becoming quite monotonous. To change the subject I showed him a gold police badge I had been carrying around with me for twenty years or so. This is one of those "Honorary Los Angeles County Deputy Sheriff" badges that thousands of Southern Californians have been given down through the years. They are supposed to help you when you get traffic tickets or have other small troubles with the authorities in Los Angeles.

He asked me so many questions about this that I

ended up wishing I had kept the badge in my pocket. A hundred times Vitaly asked how I had managed to worm my way into this important police organization. When I said they were easy to get, he just scoffed, saying I was too modest for my own good.

And when he had finished marveling about the badge and complimenting me on my achievement in acquiring it, he returned once more to his idea that I had been tailed in Washington. Nothing I said could dissuade him about that.

Next he asked me if I had seen Cardinal Spellman or any other representative leader while I was in the United States. What was the reaction there to President Truman's abrupt dismissal of General MacArthur from his Far East command? Did I know anyone who had been investigated by the McCarthy committee?

Next came a flood of questions about my visit to Keith Glennan. He made me put down the exact location of Glennan's office in the Atomic Energy Commission's building. What was Keith's manner when he greeted me? When I put down the truth—"Cordial"— Vitaly demanded, "How cordial?" He wanted Keith's precise words. Had he slapped me on the back? Expressed regret that we old friends saw one another so seldom? He was eager to learn the name of Keith's secretary. Was she young, old, married, single, pretty, plain? When I told Vitaly that I hadn't even learned the girl's name he shook his head as though saying, "I'll never make a spy out of you, Boris."

He kept coming back to Cardinal Spellman, as the other high-ranking NKVD officials had. That had puzzled me, but no longer. They seemed to be convinced, all of them, that His Eminence was a member of the FBI. As ludicrous as this sounds to an American, it seemed perfectly logical to anyone in the Russian spy network.

At this meeting, as at most of those with NKVD officials, there was talk of international developments. I learned that there had been military maneuvers along Siberia's arctic seacoast. Vitaly felt that Tito must be eliminated and revealed that at the moment Moscow was dealing in its own way with seventeen Yugoslav nationals.

On May 9, with Soble and Zlatovski, I flew to Zurich, I on my business, they to meet a Swiss contact. We were joined at the hotel by their wives.

I had never seen Soble so ill and nervous before. He said he had received a letter from his brother, the doctor, telling him that the other doctor who treated Gubichev, the spy in the Judith Coplon case, had been interrogated by the FBI. But they had not questioned Soble's brother. "Coming on top of what happened to me," he said, "why shouldn't I be ill? I'm spitting blood, that's all. That is the matter with me."

In the parlance of the Russian spy ring, "spitting blood" means that the police are after you. Soble said that the French police had visited his bristle factory and spent hours asking about all his travels. What alarmed him most was that the gendarmes had refused an *apéritif*.

"You know what that means, don't you?" he said.

I nodded, sympathetically. When the French police refuse a drink it means they have such grave suspicions of you that they prefer not to make the slightest friendly gesture toward you. What they have reason to think of you is no laughing matter—or drinking matter, either.

"Only after the major came to my defense did they leave the factory."

The badly shaken Soble wanted six months' vacation from all spying work. He wanted me to tell Vitaly that the French police had grilled him for hours at the suggestion of the FBI. Also that his brother, the doctor, *had* been questioned by the FBI.

Now in my opinion, five years before, Soble would have taken all this in his stride. But he was beginning to deviate. I could see that, as he went on with the reasons why he needed a half-year vacation. He was sick, he said. So was Myra. The wife of one of his brothers had cancer. None of this is supposed to matter when the Cause is involved.

But something even more important than my awareness of Soble's weakening allegiance to Moscow happened on that visit of ours to Zurich. While we were waiting in the railroad station, I saw Soble meet a handsomely dressed man. He was about five feet eleven, rather fat, weighing I would say about 250 pounds. He had thick lips and wore a gray hat. They embraced, and I walked away. When Jack rejoined me, he said, "That was the rich Austrian manufacturer. He will be in Paris in June and in New York in August."

And on June 10, 1951, one month later, the talkativeness of Jack Soble enabled me to score my second real coup as counterspy. In Paris, when I told him that I had been forbidden to contact him, he seemed terribly shocked. So, while I still had him in a bewildered mood, I accused him to his face of lying to me. I told him that I had better obey the orders of our superiors in the NKVD and have nothing to do with him. This frightened him, because if I did obey he would be cut off from all contact with Moscow.

"What do you want me to do?" he asked. "How can I prove my friendship?"

"Trust me," I told him. "Prove you trust me."

He waited, unable to figure out what I was driving at. "All this beating about the bush about your mine-owning millionaire!" I said. "Why are you afraid to tell me his name, if you are so good and faithful a friend of mine?"

This was taking the risk of alienating him. But it worked. I had chosen the right moment to ask.

"Low Beer," he said.

"Low Beer? That sounds like a phony name to me."

"But it isn't. That's the millionaire's name—Paul Low Beer. His wife is Alice Low Beer. They have two or three children. He is transferring lots of money right now to Swiss banks. He runs businesses in Sweden, New York, London, and other cities. But he feels that Swiss bankers are the safest in the world."

After leaving Jack I was so elated that, forgetting I was fifty-six years old, I ran down the boulevards of Paris to a café on the Champs Élysées where my FBI friend and his partner were waiting.

CHAPTER 11

When Spies Fall Out

During the summer of 1951, trying to make peace between the Zlatovskis and the Sobles became almost my main job. It was obvious that if our superiors at Home heard that the members of our espionage ring were quarreling bitterly among ourselves they might drop the entire group. As this would have ended my usefulness to the FBI with my work uncompleted, I kept trying to patch things up.

The inter-family scrapping did not start over any resentment of the adulterous relationship between Jack and Jane. It was provoked by that familiar symbol of capitalistic enterprise, an icebox. I mean the old-fashioned wooden kind in which you put a big cake of ice in the top half and a pan underneath to catch the water as it melts. In Paris, during 1951, these were still difficult to come by. Jane Foster Zlatovski insisted that the precious wooden icebox was hers. She had loaned it to the two young American girls who had turned over the apartment to the Sobles. On being told of this, Myra insisted that this was news to her. She had understood when she took over the apartment that the icebox was part of the deal.

Unable to get back the wooden refrigerator, Jane painted a caricature in oils of the three Sobles and sent it to them, labeling it "The Holy Trinity."

As usual with such quarrels, the icebox came merely as the last straw. Jane had long been at her wit's end because George could not find work. They both blamed Jack Soble for luring them to Paris with the promise that he could get Zlatovski a good job. They also said he should have compensated by letting them meet some of the higher-ups in the NKVD. They insisted his real reason for refusing was that he wished to hog all the credit for whatever work they did for the Great Cause.

In June, George made a special trip from Paris to Vienna, hoping to induce me to arrange a meeting with some NKVD contact there. I told him I was too busy. He then said that he and Jane had written a letter he would like me to pass on for them.

"This gives your reasons for asking for such a meeting?"

"Yes, it does," he told me.

Getting in possession of such a letter, needless to say, would give FBI written proof that the Zlatovskis had been working as members of the Russian espionage system. I told him to bring the letter to my room after midnight. But it turned out to be typewritten, and the FBI had told me that one written by hand would be much better for their purposes.

Because the letter was written in English and ten pages long, I had an excuse to make him produce a hand-written letter. I pointed out that no one in Moscow was likely to read a letter of that length, particularly one written in English. I suggested that he write a short synopsis of the contents in Russian and to return with both the original letter and the synopsis next day. These I agreed to pass on for him.

George agreed, but before he left he told me more about his money woes. He was getting $150 a month in disability pay from the United States Army, he said, and until they quarreled with the Sobles he had been getting $150 a month more through Jack for his espionage work. I noticed that he said nothing about Jane's also getting $150 a month from Moscow. Now that his pay as a secret agent had been cut off by Jack, he did not know how they were going to live.

While he was in a talkative mood, I asked him what he knew about the undercover work done for Jack by his factory assistant manager, Jacques Ajer; by Michel, Jack's nephew; and also by the so far unidentified "blond American Army colonel" stationed in Germany. George shrugged, and I really don't think he knew. But he said that Jack exaggerated the importance of everything he did, and minimized everything George and Jane did.

The next morning, bright and early, Zlatovski was back with the original letter and a two-page synopsis in Russian. The synopsis was handwritten and he had signed it with his code name, "Rector." The ten-page letter was signed "Rector" and "Slang," the latter being Jane's code name. The letter outlined their grievances against Abram, and asked for a personal interview which would give them a chance to answer all questions concerning their grievances.

I turned over both letters to the FBI. The Bureau

kept them, for nothing could have been achieved for our side by passing them on to the enemy.

But when I saw Vitaly about a month later, I discovered that the letter could have done little damage to Jack's standing. That had already been done. Vitaly told me to inform Abram and his group that they must quit operations for the next two years. Abram, he said, had hurt the Cause by talking too much. But the worst thing Abram had done, he said, was to introduce the agents of his group to one another.

I had to think fast, think of something to say that would impress him enough to reconsider this drastic decision. I knew that when I told Jack Soble he would be both relieved and indignant. But to me it simply meant the end of the job I had been trying to do with the FBI—with the work not even half finished. So I said the only thing that occurred to me that I thought might work.

"Do you wish me also to stop working for the Cause for at least two years?" I asked him.

The frontal approach caught him off guard, I think. He said he would take up that matter with Moscow. I was well aware that the NKVD considered me a special case. Jack had boasted in Moscow that I was his prize recruit, a man who knew celebrities of a dozen different countries. That is why he had introduced me to his superiors while refusing the same privilege to the Zlatovskis and the others in his group. To him, George and Jane were just two more conspirators working under his orders.

Until I heard from him again, Vitaly said, I was to stop all activities. Lately Moscow had been reliably informed that my movements were again being followed, this time by the FBI. Until I was "clean" again I should stay away from everyone in the Movement. But before we parted he gave me a strong hint that I would not be dropped permanently, no matter what happened to Soble and the others.

"I had another assignment for you, an important one," he said. "But now I've had to give it to another agent. Incidentally, we would pay almost anything to get something on either President Eisenhower or J. Edgar Hoover." Several weeks later, on August 1, Moscow notified me through Vitaly that I was "clean."

My frontal approach had worked perfectly!

The FBI was eager for me to get contacts in the United States. At my urging, Vitaly set up arrangements for controlled meetings with new contacts both in Los Angeles and in New York. In Los Angeles the meeting place was to be on South Hope Street, between Sixth and Seventh Streets; in New York on Fifty-ninth Street, between Fifth and Seventh Avenues. I was instructed to arrive with a piece of music in my hand. The parol would remain the same—Almi Films.

The rest of this meeting—I had no hint that it would be my last rendezvous with Vitaly—I spent listening to his comments on the international situation. He declared that Malenkov was trying hard to win over Stalin to a program of immediate war. However, he pointed out that the Kremlin's other leaders were at the moment much more interested in Asia than in Western Europe. He also spoke with enthusiasm about a fantastic new weapon the Soviet was about to test for the first time. This proved to be a new bomb which Washington did not even know the Russians were experimenting with. Vitaly also spoke of the speedy progress the Soviet's nuclear scientists were now making in the development of earth satellites. This six years before Sputnik!

After two months of traveling I got back to Vienna in late October, and I telephoned Vitaly's number. A

stranger answered when I identified myself as "Riabov," the code name Vitaly had told me to use when
phoning him.

The stranger told me to be at the Tabor Cinema at
six o'clock. I put in an appearance there with the
usual roll of sheet music. When approached I went
through the Almi Films parol with the new contact.
Holding my arm he walked me to a car parked a short
distance away. Behind the wheel there was a chauffeur,
who had kept the motor running. The moment we got
into the rear seat the car started off. My new contact
introduced himself as Aphanassy Ivanovich, but neglected to give his last name. It was Yefimov, he told
me a good deal later on. He took me to an apartment
for our talk, as Vitaly had always done.

At this first meeting Aphanassy explained that he
was the Russian member of the Four-Power Allied
Economic Commission in Vienna. This meant that he
served every fourth week as chairman of that Commission, alternating with the American, French, and
British commissioners.

I noticed he was not wearing his uniform, and asked
him why. He smiled, explaining he wore it only during the day while officiating as Russian member of the
Commission. "At night," he said, "while performing
my extra duties I find civilian dress more incon-
picuous."

These extra duties comprised a heavy work load. My
new Vienna contact was in complete charge of all
espionage work in Austria, Hungary, and Yugoslavia.
Of course, I found that out only later.

This first meeting was very brief. Aphanassy explained that he could talk to me far more intelligently
if he had an opportunity to read and digest all the
reports on me and also my dossier.

We made another appointment for January 23,

1952, same place, and time, 5 p.m. Once we were in the apartment again Aphanassy said he could not understand why the United States did not recognize Red China and North Korea without further delay. The war there was too big a drain on both great powers. Furthermore, what could either side get out of it? Moscow was gradually finding out that there were too many disloyal elements in the so-called "people's democracies" to keep such satellite countries in line for very long. Suddenly, he asked me, "Why was Attorney General J. Howard McGrath fired by President Truman?"

"I do not know," I told him.

"I regret that," he said. "Djon, why don't you take more interest in politics?"

I just shrugged. It is difficult to know just what NKVD men such as Aphanassy are after when they ask you something like that. It is possible that the workings of American politics do mystify them. On the other hand, I repeat, one thing is sure: they are always testing you, trying to find out if your sympathies have shifted, listening for the chance remark that will betray a weakness or character flaw. There are few accidents in one's encounters with Russian espionage agents. If you run into one of them unexpectedly at a restaurant or a theater, it was planned that way. If you find a beautiful woman sitting next to the seat you have reserved on a plane, the Soviets may have planted her there. Even when their conversation appears casual, there is some purpose behind it. They have no small talk. They like to think they are working for the Cause all the time. They would prefer, if they could manage it, to have no loyalty to anything or anybody but Home.

So this day, when Aphanassy said, "Too bad about the big thing," I shook my head gloomily. I had no idea of what he was talking about, but I was all ears.

"Three of our best men were killed," he said then. "An American, an Italian, and an Englishman." I since have decided that he was referring to a recent atomic bomb test. But at the time I had no idea of what he was talking about. Whenever I was in the dark like this I tried my best to seem entranced by whoever was speaking, not so much by what he was saying as by his personality. Hero worship, even of so shallow and transparent a kind, few men or women can resist. I had had good luck so far in and out of the spy world, using that look of adoration.

Just before we said good-by that day Aphanassy asked me, "What about Keith Glennan *now?*" He had heard that Gordon Dean, head of the Atomic Energy Commission, had resigned. If Keith became chairman, would he still be able to serve on my television company's board of directors? He seemed pleased when I assured him it would make no difference.

At our subsequent meeting that week I was asked dozens of questions about Glennan, and whether it would be possible to plant one of "our men" as a secretary in Cardinal Spellman's office. "No," I said, "it is not possible." He repeatedly demanded that I tell him what I knew about Bill Montgomery. I insisted that I knew no one by that name, but this just drew a pitying smile. I still know no Bill Montgomery. I suppose Aphanassy had been given the wrong name.

The most important thing these conversations revealed to me was that Moscow's uneasiness over the once-dedicated Sobles was still growing. They had instructed Abram to lie low; the best thing he could do now, Aphanassy said, was to come home and straighten out his financial affairs. None of his superiors had heard from him for six or seven months. Would I please persuade him to lose no more time in getting in touch with Korotkov?

At each meeting he repeated all this. Finally, I reminded Aphanassy of Tcherniavsky's warning to me to stay away from Soble. After conferring with Home, Aphanassy authorized me to confer with Soble when I next went to Paris.

By this time I thought I knew Jack Soble as well as one can hope to know a secret agent. And I could imagine but one reason why he had not communicated with Moscow for so long a period: he wanted to defect but had not been able to figure out a safe way to do it, and was stalling for time.

What puzzled me utterly—and promised to be important for me to find out—was what in the world Moscow wanted of him. It wasn't a question of liquidating him. To do that it would be unnecessary to bring him in from Paris. For very little money they could have professional thugs kill him right there in the French capital.

The one logical explanation seemed to be that Jack Soble knew something that the NKVD considered of first importance, something they wanted to make sure they had complete information on. If this was so it must be information that would be equally valuable to the FBI. And later, when I discussed this idea with the Bureau men, they seemed to agree.

So it was that both sides assigned me to the ticklish and sometimes blood-chilling task of staying with the defecting espionage ace until he was ready to give up his mysterious secret.

On March 18, 1952, I met Jack near the Paramount Theatre in Paris. We walked together to the Avenue de l'Opéra. I wasted no time on the amenities, but told him straight out what Aphanassy had said.

"Can it be true," I said, "that you have not sent a report to Moscow in all these months?"

"No, it's a damned lie," he replied. He insisted that Myra had traveled to Germany to deliver two letters to a contact there. In addition, there were two letters he had mailed himself to the Soviet embassy in Paris. "But what are they worrying about? Each of these four letters explained the same thing, that I am spitting blood. This is not suspicion on my part," Jack added. "It is a fact."

He said that Professor Ravetzky, his family doctor, was also an intimate friend of the Paris prefect of police and that the prefect had permitted Ravetzky to look over his dossier. It contained the dates of all the trips Jack had made in recent years in and out of France. When Professor Ravetzky asked the police official about this, he had confided that they were particularly curious about Soble's dozens of trips to Vienna. He had added, "This is because your patient claims to be traveling on factory business. And there is no bristle business of any account there."

Two detectives had recently visited the factory again. Jack was not there, but they had questioned Jacques Ajer, his assistant and fellow Communist, for hours. The wheels within wheels were whirring faster and faster, it seemed to me. As I well recalled, M. Ajer was the gentleman whom Moscow had chosen to check upon Jack.

"Myra hasn't been able to sleep nights," Soble declared. "She insists that Jane and George must be responsible for all this trouble, and also that they may be working for the FBI. They are just the type, she thinks."

Jack definitely knew that the Zlatovskis had been trying for months to get in touch with the NKVD behind his back. They would not hesitate, he was sure, to undermine him and Myra with Home.

"Exactly what the Sterns tried to do to me," he

said, bitterly. "Not only are they trying to get to the people at Home behind my back, but Jane has written a malicious letter to Myra, accusing her of being a provocateur!"

"How did they get into your group in the first place?" I asked him, wondering whether he would tell me the same story he had once before. He did. It was that Martha had known Jane Foster in Washington years before, and had introduced Jane to him. She had also introduced Jane and George, whom Jane quickly recruited. George was then, of course, in the Army Intelligence Division.

Jack denounced the outrageous behavior of the Zlatovskis until he ran out of words. As always, it seemed ironic to be listening to an espionage agent expressing horror at some bit of human treachery. They themselves stopped at neither abomination nor deceit.

As I've said, I often felt sorry for Jack. I don't suppose you can associate with any human being that long without discovering a few endearing characteristics. I liked both Myra and Jack. They could have been good friends of mine under different circumstances. And despite my determination to destroy them before they could destroy me and everything I lived for, it was a wrench for me that day when Jack told me it was Myra's birthday. They were celebrating with a dinner at Dominique's, and he invited me to join them there. I said I would drop in after dinner.

After I left Jack, I called up Dominique's and ordered a bouquet of long-stemmed roses sent to the Sobles' table right after they arrived. I got there about nine-thirty or so, and offered a champagne toast to Myra's health and long life.

That afternoon I had urged Jack to come to Vienna with me and face the music. This he flatly refused to do. Korotkov was his one hope, he felt. He promised to write him a letter. In a short while we adjourned to the men's washroom, where Jack again refused to obey Aphanassy's order to return to Vienna. I then suggested that he at least give me a signed statement that he was refusing.

With an annoyed shrug, Jack got a piece of paper and wrote in Russian, "Our friend will explain the nature of my sickness. Ludmilla has also been ill." He signed it "Peter."

That was all I could get him to write. He said it was enough because Korotkov would recognize his handwriting. Giving me a sly look, he said, "That is, of course, if he ever sees this."

"Who is Ludmilla?" I asked.

"Myra."

"And your code name is Peter?"

"You ask too many questions, my friend," he said.

After the FBI photographed this two-sentence note, they told me to pass it on to Aphanassy. They congratulated me on getting it, for this, like Zlatovski's handwritten letter, was convincing visual proof of a connection with Moscow.

A few days later I reached Vienna with Jack's brief note. I urged Aphanassy to recommend to Home that Abram be allowed to return to the United States. "They may cancel his passport if he stays in France. And he is spitting blood there." As usual, Yefimov was writing down every word I uttered. When I gave him Jack's note, he examined it and promised to wire Moscow at once for a decision. He intended also, he said, to airmail Home the note itself together with his report on my recommendation.

He gave me Moscow's answer at our next meeting. This was that the men at Home understood Abram's situation perfectly, and had no objection to his going to the United States. Their one condition was that he meet Korotkov for instructions. This would take only a single day. The French could make no objection to Abram's going to Switzerland, and it was absolutely essential for him to meet there with his dear friend Korotkov. The instructions he would get from Korotkov, Aphanassy emphasized, concerned the handling of Soble's present group in America and the chances of organizing there another cadre of agents.

Fifteen days before the date Abram desired for the rendezvous, he was to write, naming it.

"To whom?" I asked, possibly a little too eagerly.

"Abram knows very well whom to write to," he told me, giving me a sharp look as he added, "and also how any such letter should be worded. He knows, too, the city in Switzerland where we will be expecting him."

Aphanassy explained that from Switzerland a waiting plane would take Abram either to Moscow or to Czechoslovakia, where he would get his instructions. Jack could then immediately start on his long journey to the United States. Aphanassy said that my job would be to assist Jack in the United States and that Abram would tell me all the details the first time he saw me in New York.

"Abram cannot possibly find anything wrong with this assignment," said Aphanassy. He then forced me to say this entire rigmarole over and over until he was sure I could repeat it to Soble word for word. He even corrected my inflection. I told Aphanassy that, if he really wanted Jack to come to the rendezvous with no further delay, a personal letter would impress him more than anything else possibly could. He nodded.

Late in March 1952, Aphanassy Yefimov handed me Korotkov's letter to Jack. Hand-written in German, this reply, a brief letter, began, "My dear old friend" and expressed regret that the recipient had been ill, along with the hope that his physician, the professor, would cure him quickly. He trusted that they could see each other again very soon. It was signed with Korotkov's initials, "A. M."

As I tucked this in my pocket, I congratulated myself on obtaining additional proof of Soble's spying activities. I also could not help wondering how Soble, after reading this, could avoid making the trip. Meanwhile, the mystery of why the Russians were taking so much trouble and being so patient in their efforts to get him to Prague or Moscow was becoming more intriguing every day.

When I got back to Paris, Soble was not there. After hours of telephoning, one of my calls was returned by Myra. She said that Jack was traveling in Germany, but would be back next day. He did come back and, to my surprise, seemed quite pleased with both the verbal instructions I gave him along with Korotkov's letter. Needless to say, I gave this letter, like all the other messages, to the FBI first to copy. He said that even if his old friend Sasha had not signed it he would have recognized his German writing. With a fond look in his eye he studied the ink the general had used, and even held the paper up to the light so he could examine the water mark.

In contrast to the last few times we had been together, Jack was in very high spirits. It turned out that he was about to close a bristle deal for a New York firm that would net him a personal profit of $5000 or more. The deal involved 12,000 kilos of bristles, he said. But an even greater cause for his jubilation was a cable he showed me. This was from the president of the New York firm, and said: COME OVER HERE EVERYTHING CAN BE ARRANGED. The word "everything," Jack explained, meant that his passport problems were solved.

The next day I called on the Zlatovskis and got a pleasant surprise. George, that one-man international unemployment problem, had got himself a job revising a technical dictionary for the Library of Public Instruction of the French government. Part of his salary was being paid by Unesco.

Though the Zlatovskis were willing to make almost any sacrifice for the dubious privilege of working again for the NKVD, they stopped at the idea of a reconciliation with the Sobles. Jane was a headstrong and tempestuous woman. Once, in a drunken fight with her husband, she had thrown George's only pants out the window of their flat. Though he begged her to go down in the street to retrieve them, she refused, and the luckless George had to run down in his shorts to get them back.

The day he told me about his job he said he would give me a copy of the technical dictionary as soon as it was published. "I want you to pass it on to Home so they can see what sort of work I am capable of doing." They preferred to work for the Cause in either France or Switzerland.

I had been told that our government would very much like to have both of them back in its jurisdiction as quickly as possible. "I am going to California soon, George," I told him. "Wouldn't you and Jane like to live there for a while?"

His eyes brightened. "I'd like to get into some sort of construction work there," he told me.

I agreed to look around for him and to write if I found anything suitable for him out there. But when I got to the Coast shortly afterward, he wrote me saying that he and Jane had changed their minds about returning to the United States. He did not say why. They may have feared that Soble would betray them. It is also possible that Jane, as her friend Martha

Dodd had done years before, had come to suspect the truth about me.

May 6, 1952, promised to be another important day for me. It was the first Tuesday in the month and I was in New York. This meant that I could go to the rendezvous—58 West Fifty-eighth Street—and meet the new contact Aphanassy had given me—with the FBI photographing the whole affair. The time was three o'clock in the afternoon, though Aphanassy had argued that any time during the evening would be much safer. At the FBI's suggestion I had held out for an afternoon meeting, claiming that while I was in New York my theatrical business kept me busy evenings. The FBI wanted a daylight meeting so that they could get a better likeness of the contact.

When nobody came, I started to wonder if I had got some detail of my parol confused. My instructions were to carry under my left arm an album of phonograph records from a current Broadway musical-comedy hit. I was also sure of the address and the time, and also that I'd been instructed to walk up and down in front of the apartment house there.

But where was the contact who was to come up and say, "Did you hear those records?" and know me by my reply, "I have just bought them at Liberty Music Shop on Madison Avenue"?

I began to feel ridiculous about the whole business, particularly knowing that an FBI man was concealed nearby with a camera ready. To add to my annoyance, the doorman of the building was eying me belligerently.

When it became fairly obvious that the doorman was about to demand why I was marching up and down in front of the place, I walked away in disgust, chucking the album into the first cellar I passed.

On June 3, the first Tuesday of the following

month, I once more waited for the contact. To my irritation, he did not show up then or on the first Tuesday of two subsequent months.

But meanwhile something far more important had happened. During the first week in June I had phoned the bristles dealer who had cabled Jack "Everything has been arranged." He informed me that Jack was even then on the high seas, and would arrive on the tenth. This New York businessman thought a good deal of Jack's business ability. He was impressed by Soble's extensive connections in the trade in Germany and said Jack had done a large amount of business abroad for his firm.

Meanwhile I had run into one of Jack's brothers, the doctor, on the street. I had met him several times at the Soble apartment on Washington Heights. I was sure that Jack had told him that I was involved in espionage work, so I had no hesitation about telling him that, as far as I knew, Jack had quit working for the Soviets more than a year ago.

"I wish I could believe that," he replied fervently. "How I wish it! I never shared Jack's dialectical ideas, even though I tried to help save him, as any decent brother would. But now he is in one hell of a spot. I don't know what I can do to help him. I don't know what anyone can do."

He now had a flourishing practice, and disapproved of Jack's work for the NKVD—so much so that he had begged Jack a year before to quit and come back to the States.

"He shouldn't have waited until the very moment when his passport is expiring. He knows damn well that, having only lived here for five years, it would arouse the government's suspicion if he stayed abroad as long as he has. I am going to stay away from him, believe me," the doctor told me. "These FBI men are not only brilliant, but they have counterspies working for them all over the world."

I recalled Jack's telling me that his brother had been interrogated by the FBI, and said, "I suppose you were bitter at being questioned by the FBI. It must have been quite embarrassing."

"I was never questioned," he said. "And I don't know why. After all, Valentin Gubichev, Judith Coplon's friend, and Mrs. Gubichev were both patients of mine. And the FBI questioned another doctor, a surgeon who performed an operation on Gubichev. Why do you suppose they didn't come near me?"

I didn't know, and said so.

What seemed more important to me was trying to figure out Jack's motive in lying about this. Why had he told me that his brother had been questioned by the FBI? Was his only reason the fact that I would pass on the story to my Soviet contact in Vienna? Or was there something else behind it? Could it have any connection with the information that his superiors in Moscow suspected he had withheld from them? Or was he beginning to suspect that I was a counterspy?

When Jack arrived aboard the S.S. *Liberté* the bristles dealer and I met him at the pier. The next day Jack came to my room at the Hotel Meurice. He said he had gone to Bern but the new man who met him there did nothing but shout at him about the plane that was waiting to take him to see Korotkov. Jack said he insisted on telephoning Korotkov instead, and finally convinced his new contact that it would be suicidal for him to go anywhere but the United States, because the French police were watching him so closely now. "I told him," he said, "that my whole group was all right, with the sole exception of the Zlatovskis." But he got the fellow to promise that he should not have to do any more espionage work until his American passport was extended.

Jack told me even that much reluctantly. At the moment he was too worried about his passport troubles to talk for long about anything else. Myra, he said, had gone to see the girl in the United States embassy at Paris, where they had always been renewed almost automatically. But this time the girl took up the passport, saying it would have to be sent to Washington. Jack intended to hire a lawyer to get him an extension.

"But whether I get the extension or not," he said, "it certainly looks as though they have a file on me in the State Department."

Jack was broke. He wanted to borrow $1000 from me, but I told him I was short myself because of the interminable delays in getting the $350,000 I had been promised.

"You will never get that money, Boris," Soble told me, "because they are convinced you are such a wealthy man. You have played that part too long and too well."

It did look as if all my efforts had been wasted. But that seemed unimportant compared to the discovery that I made on my next trip to Vienna.

CHAPTER 12

When It's Liquidation Time in Moscow

New York is one city that lives up to her reputation of being a perfect summer resort. She smiles upon us all then as she displays her thousand beauties. You can see her special glory, whole brigades of smartly dressed, long-legged women, emerging from their winter cocoons of ermine and mink into diaphanous frocks and gowns in which they appear as pristine and elegant and charming as so many jungle butterflies.

It also seems to me that there are more footloose lovers and out-of-town honeymooners in New York during the summer. You find them wherever you go, whichever way you turn. You see them laughing and drinking in the cafés and dancing on the rooftops of hotels. You run into them at the Broadway shows, come upon them on Fifth Avenue, wandering hand-in-hand in and out of the shops. They stuff themselves aboard the crowded Hudson River excursion steamers and into the glass-covered sightseeing buses that zigzag through the Manhattan streets. They venture to the top of the Empire State Building, climb all over the Cloisters, gravely inspect the Hall of Fame, and dive into the tumbling waves at Jones Beach. I sometimes think that it is they who give New York each summer the look of a city that will remain forever young and vital and exciting.

But for the hard-pressed, frenzied, fearful Jack Soble, New York through the summer of 1952 was nightmarish—because of the terror growing inside his skull. Meanwhile Myra, on whom he greatly depended for companionship and moral support, was in Paris, trying to sell the bristle factory. He also missed his son Larry.

I think Soble feared that my attitude toward him would change completely when I learned that he had run away from the Communist underground and had not asked for permission to come to New York. My friendship, I think, meant a great deal to him. The idea that I could raise large sums of money inspired him with the hope that I would not let him down if his financial situation became intolerable.

Everything harassed and frightened him—everything that was happening, and much that was not. He was in the position of a man trying to jump—in middle age—from the center of one hostile world into another.

His loyalty was still to Communism but the good life he had come to savor so much could be found only in our capitalistic world. He was trapped between these two worlds, suspended in space between them, as it were, and kicking wildly to gain a foothold in one before relinquishing his position in the other.

Enemy or not, it was a grim and heart-rending experience to watch this once tough, shrewd, resourceful gamecock of a man gradually being eaten up by self-pity. And I *had* to watch. Watching and waiting and encouraging him to betray himself was the job I had promised the FBI I would do. But I did not like it. The truth is that only a monster could have enjoyed the pitiful spectacle Soble made.

A hundred times I found myself impelled to hold out my hand to him, and say, "Jack, will you *never* stop torturing yourself? You're in an impossible situation. Give yourself up. The FBI is not the NKVD. It will give you every possible consideration."

But Jack Soble was not ready to abandon Communism as an ideal. He and Myra had believed in it too long and sincerely. They still saw it as the salvation of mankind, as the last hope of humanity for world peace. They had given the best years of their lives to it, risked everything they had again and again. To them, as to so many others, it was both a political creed and a religion.

One day that summer, though, I did think he was ready. He had just denounced the callousness of his superiors in the Soviet espionage department. "They are barbarians," he told me. "They have no manners. How little, for example, do they appreciate a fine woman like Myra? They always wanted to send her on dangerous missions. It means nothing to them that her life may be in danger. And look at the man they made our boss here! Zubilin—a brute, a drunken bully!

They are barbarians, I tell you, brutes, beasts!"

I heaved a sigh of relief, thinking the long agonizing struggle was over at last. "Let's drop them," I said, quietly. "If you believe that, Jack, we could—"

But he did not let me finish. As though to atone for what he had just been saying, he interrupted me. "There is still Korotkov," he told me. "We can always turn to him in a pinch. *He* can be trusted with anything. So what have we got to lose? Let's at least give them one more chance."

Yet in his next breath he started taunting me for believing, simpleton that I was, that I would ever get the long-promised $350,000 from them. "It is always the same thing, never action, never the money. They will just talk on and on about it, I tell you, I know!"

Jack got some perverse satisfaction, of course, out of the idea that he was not the only victim of the endless snafus of his fellow-Communists. Once he told me that not long before another secret agent and he had written down a list of a hundred and fifty espionage men and women they had either known or worked with, and found they now knew the whereabouts of only three of them.

"Some of the others may, of course, have defected— and got away," he said. "If so, they were the only lucky ones."

Jack was also upset just then by the sensational exposure of Russian espionage activities in London. On June 24, William Marshall, twenty-four, a radio operator in the British Foreign Office, was arrested. He was charged with passing secret information to Pavel Kusnetsov, second secretary in the Russian embassy there. Marshall was sentenced later to five years in prison for violation of the British Official Secrets Act. Being a foreign diplomat, Kusnetsov was merely expelled from the country and sent home; nevertheless,

Soble's sympathies were all with the Russian, whom he pictured as another victim of Moscow's inefficiency. Kusnetsov had been for a time Jack's contact when Kusnetsov was an attaché to the Moscow embassy in Paris. That seemed to bring the case home to him.

"They should have protected Kusnetsov," he kept telling me. The fate of young Marshall, the catspaw who was disgraced for life and sent to prison, did not interest him in the slightest.

I made two trips to Europe that summer. The first concerned only my business interests abroad; I stopped briefly in Zurich, Vienna, and Paris, but had time to see only film people, and was back in three weeks.

In New York I found Jack more pessimistic than ever about his chances of getting his passport renewed. He had written Myra that he wanted Larry and her to join him in New York by the end of August, whether or not she had sold the business by then. There was Larry's education to be considered, he said.

My second trip to Europe got me there in time to see Myra off on the ship to America. Jacques Ajer, the factory manager, had been trying to buy the bristle factory, she said, but had not been able to get together enough money. I helped her pack, and I got her steamer accommodations for her.

The big surprise of the trip came in Vienna when Aphanassy told me that Jack never had made the trip to Bern which he had described to me so vividly. When I mentioned it, Yefimov said, "Abram never went to Switzerland at all. He skipped out of France without consulting anyone. Not even Korotkov knew he was leaving and is as puzzled by his behavior as the rest of us. When next you see Abram, remind him that we still hold him strictly responsible for the fifty-seven thousand dollars he owes us. We want him to give us a personal accounting of that money."

Yefimov gave me another surprise when I complained that my new contact in New York had not met me at 58 West Fifty-eighth Street. "I went there four different times," I said, "on the first Tuesday of each month." He smiled, and drew from his pocket a beautiful color picture. It showed me throwing my album of records down the cellar steps.

"The contact was there, but did not approach you," Aphanassy explained, "because on none of those four afternoons were conditions right for a rendezvous."

Yefimov did not show up himself at our next rendezvous, at Vienna's skating rink. Instead a girl— Granitscha, a pretty youngster who had served us vodka and food at our other meetings—came and took me to the apartment. This time an Armenian, an amiable man named Christopher Georgevich Petrosian, was waiting for me. He said he was Aphanassy's boss and had sent him on an out-of-town assignment.

By this time I had become convinced that Soble's prediction that I would never get the $350,000 would prove correct. In fact I had canceled the lease on my penthouse office in New York some months before. But Petrosian seemed so friendly I thought I would make one last try with him. When I got the same old excuses, I shouted, "All right! The hell with you fellows! You've been promising me this money for several years, and nothing has happened. I do get more and bigger *promises* all of the time. Of promises, I admit, you never run short."

Petrosian said he was amazed at my attitude.

"Fine," I told him. "Perhaps I'll get some action then."

They were more eager than I to get the television project started, he said, but a man of my experience should realize that government bureaus everywhere were the same—slow, never in a hurry, forever blocking and delaying everything with their red tape.

As this was my last attempt to get the money, I felt entitled to the last word. "So Home encouraged me to rent a penthouse office in New York for five hundred dollars a month and let me keep it for three years! I made no use of it. I was only in the place twice. Eighteen thousand dollars of my money was wasted, and you—"

Petrosian said, "Patience!" So maybe *he* had the last word.

Petrosian had new instructions for me to transmit to Abram Soble. Moscow agreed that, since Abram was in New York, he could stay there permanently. However, there were two conditions. He must return the borrowed $57,000 at once, and as soon as it was feasible he must return to Vienna and confer with Korotkov. Meanwhile, any message he had to send Home I could transmit for him. Petrosian was particularly emphatic about one other thing: when I got the money from Soble I must not bring it to Europe with me. I was to put it in a safe place in America until I received orders about how to distribute it to the underground workers there for salaries and expenses.

Petrosian talked to me freely about the battalions of propagandists the Kremlin had planted in France and England to create dissension between the two countries. Like all the other NKVD officials, Petrosian lavished on me many suggestions of how the United States, if it had any sense, would insure world peace. Ike's campaign promise to fly to Korea if elected, annoyed him. He thought if Eisenhower sincerely wanted world peace he would fly straight to Moscow instead of Korea.

Petrosian predicted that if the United States did not cooperate a bombshell would be exploded in the Middle East. Petrosian knew what he was talking about. Even then he was preparing to go to the Near East to line up political leaders in Egypt and other countries in the Mediterranean powder keg on Russia's side. The shrewd Petrosian was particularly well suited for the job. He had mastered Arabic and other Oriental languages, and was well connected with most of the men in the Near East who counted, including Nasser. Aphanassy later described to me the fantastic new assignment he had been given to help along the Soviet Cause in that supersensitive part of the world. This was the recruiting of Christian and Moslem priests who would work for the Communists in Morocco. The difficulty, he complained, was finding enough French priests who both spoke Arabic and did not mind doing such jobs.

My business that time detained me in Europe until December. When I finally saw Jack again in New York he denied with great heat that he either had defected or had left France without Moscow's permission. "It is their old technique," he said. "They will never admit the truth if a lie serves their purpose."

He listened carefully as I told him of what our new NKVD boss in Vienna had said. But he was not going back, he declared, to make the financial accounting they demanded. Instead once again he would write a letter to Korotkov.

"The same old stuff?" I asked him.

"Of course not," he said. "I have something exciting to tell them. I have a wonderful new man working for us now. He is feeding me information that will make the men at Home lick their fingers with delight each time they read his reports. My new man's name is Slava." This was the way he hoped to distract Home from their demand that he return the $57,000.

Then he sat down and wrote the same old alibis about how his passport difficulties made it impossible for him to go to Europe. As soon as he had the trouble straightened out he would go there. Meanwhile he suggested that Korotkov send a man to take over the bristle factory. But Soble admonished the general to make sure that this Comrade both knew the business and was loyal beyond question to the Party. Soble did not seem to realize how funny this was, considering his own position as a man who had defected and also was being asked to account for $57,000 of the Party's funds.

He wrote entire pages boasting of the sensational work that Slava, his mysterious new man—he referred to him as "S" in the letter—was doing. This particular *billet doux* was sixteen pages long, all written in code. To this code Jack gave me the key. An X after a word indicated that this word (or the phrase it was part of) meant something else. The X he put after "California" meant that it was the code word for "South America." "Main hospital" was for "main duties," and so on.

A new New-York-controlled rendezvous had been arranged for me in Vienna. It was at the Simón Bolívar statue at the Sixth Avenue entrance to Central Park. But once again I appeared there on four different days without being approached by anyone. On the fifth day—it was March 3, 1953—a stranger came up to me. He identified himself as "Ivan," and we went through the prearranged rigmarole.

"Did you play those records?" he asked.

"No," I replied, "I just bought them at the Liberty Music Shop on Madison Avenue."

"Fine," he said, completing the parol. "Let's hear them together, then."

(Incidentally, an FBI man photographed this meeting. Through his pictures "Ivan" was identified as Vassily Molev, an attaché with the Russian consulate in New York.)

"Ivan" and I walked across Central Park South and down Sixth Avenue to Howie's Restaurant. We selected an isolated table and ordered coffee. After the waiter served us and went away I slipped him the letter. But when I tried to give him the code he stopped me. "Ivan" said he saw no point in knowing the code. He had heard I was returning to Europe soon, and suggested I pass it on to the proper person.

When I got to Vienna shortly afterward Aphanassy had already received the letter. He wrote down the code as I gave it to him. He seemed terribly upset about something, and I asked him what was wrong. He had been sent out of town on a week-long assignment recently, he said. On coming home he found his wife and baby gone. Frantic with worry, he phoned General Korotkov in Moscow.

"Of course your wife and baby are safe," Korotkov told him. "We thought it best to get them here in Moscow until the danger is over."

Though I had learned not to ask questions I couldn't help exclaiming, *"Danger!"*

Aphanassy acted like a man who had a secret he very much wished to confide. He started walking restlessly up and down the room.

I waited patiently and in the end he told me that the dangerous assignment, the most important of his career as an espionage agent was nothing less than the assassination of Tito, Dictator of Yugoslavia.

He had been away to check on the details, and to give last-minute instructions to the four aides assigned to help him. One was a pilot, another a naval expert, the other two civilians. But each was able, cool-headed, and ruthless. The whole party was going to the job disguised as Catholic priests.

"If I seem nervous," Aphanassy said, "it is with reason. The date set is March twenty-eighth, just eleven days from now. But if anything goes wrong that night, we plan to eliminate Tito sometime in June."

He sighed and shook his head. "It is, as you can imagine, a very complicated proposition to arrange a political crime of this importance. I never had to learn so many different parols and signals. I have to keep them all in my mind at the same time."

I was with him a good deal during the next few days. His tension mounted steadily, hour by hour, as the time for Tito's assassination came ever closer.

On March 28, 1953, I kept listening to the news announcements on the radio. I bought every newspaper I saw. Next morning I sent for more before I was even out of bed. But as far as I could find out not one word had been published or broadcast about the assassination attempt.

At a meeting with Petrosian that May he explained —without realizing he was doing it—that the assassination had been canceled, literally in the nick of time. He said this without mentioning Tito's name. He said that he had sent Aphanassy on a mission of the utmost importance, and then had to call off the assignment at the last moment.

"I saved Aphanassy's life," Petrosian declared. "If I had failed to reach him, he would surely have been liquidated. Even so, he is in the hospital with a nervous breakdown. But he would have been in his grave by now if not for my efficiency."

"Was the job *that* important?"

"Important! It was the liquidation of so important a person that the newspapers would have called it the political crime of the decade."

Moscow, it seemed, had changed its mind about Tito just as the five killers, all disguised as priests, prepared to murder him. Home had decided belatedly that Tito was not a hated and dangerous enemy, but one of Russia's best friends. My guess is that it was equally lucky for Petrosian that he got word to Yefimov in time.

Petrosian gave me Korotkov's reply to Jack's latest letter. This was kindly in tone, typewritten in German, and signed only "A.M." It expressed amazement that the relationship between the Sobles and the Zlatovskis had deteriorated to the degree it had. Korotkov said he wished to see Soble in Vienna, but that the meeting could be in Switzerland if Abram preferred. As far as the financial matter was concerned, Abram must not assume that he necessarily shared the views about this "of some of our representatives." In fact, he would not be surprised if Abram (whom he referred to throughout as "the recipient") proved to be completely in the right.

Of course, that year, 1953, was crowded with events that were to shape the future of Russia, and of our world as well. Stalin died on March 5, and the terrific tug-of-war among the handful of men who wanted to replace him began almost immediately. Lavrenti Beria, head of the Soviet secret police, was dismissed on July 10 as an enemy of the people, and executed toward the end of the year. The repercussions rocked the Russian espionage system to its foundations—and were to keep rocking it and ripping it into embittered and opposing segments for years afterward. With Beria's downfall, all his favorites came automatically under suspicion. Agents such as Soble, who had named a son after Beria, were lucky if they were not liquidated as "saboteurs." And everyone who had admired Beria tried frantically to disassociate himself.

By June, Aphanassy was out of the hospital. We had arranged a rendezvous for the fourteenth, but only his chauffeur, Alexei, showed up. The chauffeur explained that neither his boss nor any other NKVD official could meet me; they were all too concerned with the disorders in East Berlin for any conferences.

But I saw Aphanassy just four days after that. He seemed tense. He confirmed the idea that his nervous breakdown was a result of the last-minute change to cancel the assassination of Tito. But he had been given a medal, by Beria personally, and a promotion in rank.

He said that Beria had told him of a new apparatus the Soviet's scientists were developing. This, he said, will forewarn Moscow of coming atomic attacks up to 633 miles away. Beria also said the NKVD had an exact check on the atomic weapons stored in France, and that Molotov had been able to place a woman on Churchill's office staff and a man in Anthony Eden's office. (A month later, of course, Aphanassy was hoping fervently that everyone in Moscow would forget he had ever mentioned Beria's name.)

In July, when I returned to New York, I found Soble loaded down with new problems. Both Myra and his brother were now urging him not to have anything further to do with Moscow—in other words, to defect openly. Jack was also in a tizzy because Leonard Lyons, the newspaper columnist, had recently published an item saying that "a daughter of the former ambassador to Germany during Roosevelt's regime" was being summoned to testify before the Senate subcommittee investigating subversive activities. This, of course, was the so-called McCarthy committee.

"That means Martha, of course," he whispered. "She won't talk."

"Well, what are you worried about, then?" I asked.

"I'm thinking of Stern. If they ever start asking him

questions, we'll all end up in Leavenworth."

(But Martha avoided appearing before the subcommittee by pleading she was suffering from amnesia. Her husband was never summoned. Not long afterward the Sterns moved to Mexico City.)

My conversation with Jack took place in a bar. We went there because Jack refused to accept Korotkov's letter in my hotel room. He took the letter into the washroom of the bar and did not return for fifteen or twenty minutes. But when he came back to our table he was smiling.

"I am not afraid to go anywhere to meet Korotkov," he said. "I just want to be sure of one thing: that I can count on him meeting me personally."

However, Myra, his brother, and Jake Albam remained apprehensive because of what had happened to Beria. They kept saying that now no one in the NKVD, including his friend and protector, was safe. They said things would continue that way in Moscow for quite a while. Overnight they convinced Jack that it would be madness to go to Europe, to say nothing of Russia, with the situation so unsettled. They also insisted that he quit communicating with Home through me.

He was not ready to take this drastic step. But he did say that Korotkov should give him specific instructions. "What could be more specific than the instructions in his last letter?" I asked. In the end all I could get from him was another letter, the same sort he had been having me take to Vienna all along.

When I got to that city I realized at once that Myra, Jack's brother, and Albam were right in warning Jack that the whole Russian espionage system was still whirling in turmoil. At first, Aphanassy was reluctant even to meet me. When I finally managed to arrange a rendezvous he came, looking like a man awaiting certain doom.

"For four days in a row now," he said, "I have not been able to get a single phone call through to either Korotkov or Fedotov in Moscow. Each time I call, somebody else answers, somebody I do not know. I fear the worst for our old friends, Djon. It is true that I managed once to speak to a supervisor I know. But after that one call I could not even get him on the wire! And when I asked the supervisor to have Vitaly Tcherniavsky call me, he said, 'Impossible, Comrade. He and his wife are being interrogated day and night, and in separate rooms! The interrogation of hundreds of other Comrades also goes on, night and day. Ever since Beria was arrested, Moscow has been in turmoil.' "

"But what about Abram's letter?" I asked. "What do you want me to do with it?"

"Disappear!" he said. "Meetings now are wrong. I only met you today, Djon, because I have so much respect for you." He wrung my hand. "This may be farewell, Comrade!" he said.

However, eleven days later, when I saw Aphanassy again, he seemed to have regained his old assurance. He accepted Abram's letter without hesitation. Despite eliminations of personnel on all levels, he thought the NKVD's worldwide organization was rapidly returning to normal.

Now that he felt safe himself, Aphanassy shrugged off the wholesale murders of Beria's favorites. "After all," he said, philosophizing, "to preserve the system requires continuous examination and re-examination of each of us."

(But he found out he was mistaken about the ending of the liquidating process in December, when Beria and six of his officials were executed. How many others were killed or imprisoned we will never know.

I have reason to believe that almost all the people in Vienna to whom I had been delivering messages were liquidated, either then or a little later on.)

In October 1953, when I was back in New York, Soble's spirits were at their lowest point since I had known him. His passport extension had not been granted. That made him fear the worst. "My file by this time must be in the hands of the three-letter organization," he said.

What truly infuriated him was learning that his dossier in Paris had just been taken out of the French Police's hands. His physician friend, Ravetzky, had written him of this. "They had somehow got me mixed up with a French Communist, the son of a baker!" he said. "Yet there is not the slightest similarity between our names. So I am in the clear over *there* now, when it is too late! When I can't get back!"

On November 3, 1953, I told Jack I was leaving for Europe next day. He came over that afternoon with a copy of the State Department's latest letter about his passport, which he wanted passed on to Korotkov. Though Myra was continuing to insist he give me no more letters to deliver to Korotkov, he wrote another now at my urging.

This was on three sheets of hotel stationery and was written in German in pencil. It was another demonstration of Jack's impressive talent for saying the same things in different words. This one said a mutual friend, Dr. Slanzer, had received a position in one of our best clinics. He was now the leading doctor in one of its departments. To achieve this, he had passed the state examinations after seven and a half months of preparations and trials. Family members were getting along nicely, and some of them might visit Europe in the spring and look up the recipient.

After reading this aloud to me, Jack translated it.

"Dr. Slanzer" was Slava, "clinic" the War Department; "seven and a half months of trials and preparations" meant that the State Department had, after much deliberation, finally cleared Slava for work in Europe; "family members" meant Slava and other members of Jack's group.

"My health has been miserable," Jack also wrote. "I had to have a blood analysis taken and hope I have not got tuberculosis. I hope to come to the South of France during the winter." Jack explained that this meant his passport troubles were not over, that he was still under investigation and could only hope he was not in a dangerous position, and that the matter did not have any political implications. He told me to advise Korotkov that he would continue his political activity whether or not he got the financial aid he needed.

I had so many business matters to attend to in Italy and London that I did not get the opportunity to deliver Jack's messages until Christmas Eve. Aphanassy's chauffeur, Alexei, picked me up. There was another man in the car, a blond, youthful Latvian, whom he introduced as Igor Vassilievich Sokolov.

Alexei drove us deep into the Prater forest to an isolated house, a neat-looking, freshly painted dwelling with one curious feature: one could enter it only by a flight of stone steps leading from the garage in the basement. These stairs led to a small room off a larger, well-furnished living room. On the way, Sokolov explained that he was replacing Aphanassy for about a week.

We sat down in the living room, and Sokolov read the letters aloud to me in impeccable German.

The following week, Alexei drove me to the same house in the woods to meet Aphanassy. When I praised Sokolov's manners and appearance, Yefimov explained that Sokolov was one of sixty or so young men who had been recruited for the system from among students at German universities. "We take them to Russia and train them in our own universities for recruiting work in East Germany," he said. Sokolov, for example, now had seventeen men working there for him, all of them with technical educations. "But even after these young fellows are given important positions," he added wryly, "we never quite trust them. We think it wise to watch and check up on them constantly." Korotkov was coming to Vienna soon to see me, he said. "We can have only a short conference today, Djon," he added, "I have some instructions to give a French labor priest."

"A what?" I asked.

"During World War II," he said, "thousands of workers in the war plants of France became discontented with their low wages and long hours. The French government, hoping to quiet the workers, arranged with the local Catholic dioceses to send young priests to work in these plants. The priests, working without pay and purely out of patriotism, were expected to prove an inspiration to the malcontents. Instead, these young, idealistic padres were outraged by the laboring people's plight. And the young priests became leaders of the men, advocating reforms for the workers. Some of them proved easy to recruit to our Cause, and have been working for us ever since."

When we drove into the garage under the house I noticed a big black sedan standing there. In the anteroom were two priests—or men dressed as priests. While Aphanassy and I were talking in the larger room I heard a shot, not in the anteroom but not far away from it.

Aphanassy was neither surprised nor disturbed. He looked at his wristwatch, nodded, and said, "Well, that's over with. And it was done on schedule."

As I left, there was but one priest in the anteroom. And he was on his knees, praying. Downstairs the black car was still there. I had not a doubt that one of the priests I saw had just been executed only a few feet from where Aphanassy and I sat talking.

I was stunned, but tried to conceal it. The Communists pride themselves on their indifference to human suffering, and to death itself. I was supposed to behave just as callously.

But I knew that day, if I had ever doubted it before, that helping to smash these killers, these ruthless destroyers of human life, was the most important thing I had ever had to do in my life. God willing, I would continue doing that just so long as the FBI felt they could use me.

CHAPTER 13

The Man in the Black Suit

Ironically enough, Jack Soble seemed to have found his way out of his labyrinth of woe just at the moment the Inostranni was undergoing the biggest shakeup in a generation—particularly his branch, of which Yefimov said, "The entire conspiratorial setup in the United States is being sharply scrutinized by our biggest men."

What promised escape from all his troubles was a good job with a Canadian brush company. He was in Montreal when I returned to the States early in 1954, but I saw him in New York a few days later. He looked healthier and happier than he had in many years. Jack gave all the credit for that to Canada. He confided that he had already figured out an angle which he and his new boss were counting on to make their fortune. This involved a scheme which would enable them to cash in heavily on the fact that Canada, unlike the United States, had no embargo on bristles imported from China and Russia. Jack said they planned to import huge quantities of such foreign bristles for use in paint brushes. They were going to mix the imported bristles with cheaper domestic ones, bleaching them to disguise their origin. These superior paint brushes would cost four dollars a dozen to manufacture in Canada, but would bring twenty-four dollars a dozen here.

There were other important advantages, Jack believed. "Even a man in my situation," he said, "can move there on just a landing card. Not only that; I can become a Canadian citizen within five years! There is a brother of Low Beer living up there," he said. "He made no bones whatever about having been a Communist as a young man in Vienna. And that did not make a damn bit of difference to the Canadian officials. He has built a good business there for himself! There is a tolerance for all political beliefs in Canada that you cannot find in the United States. The best thing of all is that Canadian passports remain valid for ten years! I would never have been in the trouble I'm in now if I had had one of those instead of an American passport!"

Finally I interrupted him, and got tough with him for the first time. For Aphanassy had told me to insist that Soble subordinate his business and personal problems, when talking to me, to those matters of interest to Home.

"You've been talking for forty-five minutes," I said, "and you have not said one word as yet about your assignments. Now we'd better take *that* up."

I waited, but he was too startled by my new attitude to reply. "You did not even ask me if I had any message for you from our Comrades abroad," I went on. "And I have instructions for you. *Instructions* this time, not requests."

Jack looked at me thunderstruck as I repeated the instructions exactly as Aphanassy had dictated them to me. "One, you are to introduce me to Slava. Two, you are to get him to turn over his reports directly to me. Three, you are to supply me with a written list of the names and addresses of all your Soviet collaborators. Four, in the future you are to communicate to me only verbally your personal needs, requests, and desires. These I will repeat to the right people verbatim." After letting all this soak in for a moment, I added, "I will not accept a 'no' from you on any of these instructions."

Then it was my turn to be astonished, because Jack burst into tears. He sobbed that the Soviets had not been cooperating with him and now I too had turned against him. But I forced him to repeat the new instructions again and again until I was convinced he knew them by heart.

Before we parted we arranged for another rendezvous for the following Thursday evening at five p.m.

I met him in the lobby of my hotel. As I had expected, he refused to go upstairs to my room with me. "You want to put me in chains!" he kept saying in Russian. I was to hear that from him many times.

We walked down Sixth Avenue to Tom's Place, a bar that did not look too crowded. There we sat at a table and ordered a drink. One thing quickly became obvious. Jack intended to keep on stalling, no matter what the consequences. He had alibis galore for not complying with the instructions. In spite of myself, I had to admire how logical and sensible he made these sound.

He was unable to introduce me to Slava because

Slava's wife refused to permit such a thing. I must remember that Slava was an important man now. The
poor man had been in trouble with the Federal authorities back in 1946 when it was discovered that he
had accepted $500 from Chaliapin, our ring's agent in
San Francisco—not only accepted the money, but
signed a receipt for it! But recently, after a great deal
of hard work, Slava had obtained clearance to move
to a post in Europe. Mrs. Slava did not wish him to
do anything to cause the clearance to be withdrawn.
In just two months, if the transfer came through, he
would be moving on to a post either in Paris or in
Bonn, Germany. He would sail for Europe, if the
transfer came through in time, between June 15 and
June 30. That would enable Slava to meet me, or any
other secret agent designated, in either Paris or Berlin
early in July.

Before I had a chance to object to the "ifs" condi-
tioning all this, Jack began to sing the praises of the
mysterious Slava. "Slava is tall, handsome, blond, a
native-born American, and only thirty-six years old! A
linguist too! I'll let you know the moment his transfer
comes through," said Jack. "Meanwhile, we'll arrange
the details of the rendezvous and parol. If Berlin is
the meeting place, Slava will be there in front of the
Amfro Hotel at eight p.m. on the date selected. If it
is Paris, the perfect place would be in front of the
Hotel L'Aiglon, on the Boulevard Raspail!"

With that settled, Jack announced that he was in a
position to do me a great favor. All I needed to do to
get rich quick was give him $10,000 to invest in the
Montreal brush company. However, I proved slow and
stupid about seizing this offer. He suggested an alternative. I was to get his friend, General Korotkov, to
deposit the $10,000 in his, Soble's name in the Crédit
Suisse.

"This will do me a great deal of good," said Jack. "And meanwhile I will be traveling all over Canada and the United States, establishing better connections with my many contacts." He pointed out that Korotkov could do him the favor with no inconvenience, as Sasha always had at his disposal a fortune to spend on his espionage workers in Germany without accounting for it. From all this talk, I guessed, of course, that Jack was skating on perilously thin ice at the brush factory in Montreal.

I next saw Soble eight days later at my room at the Hotel Essex. He had again lost his jaunty air. Now he said that he must have not $10,000 but $25,000, and at once. If he did not get the money he could not become a partner in the brush company in Montreal. He was so distraught about this that for once he seemed to have forgotten his rule of never talking in an unchecked hotel room. He sat down at the writing desk with some hotel stationery before him, and said, "This is the most important letter I have ever written in my life. You must help me, Boris, you must be on my side."

He wrote the letter, then wrote two more. He read all of them aloud to me when he finished. As I listened, I could not see how he expected the three letters to help him. He was still stalling, still using the same old tricky evasions that had fooled no one in Moscow when he tried them before.

In addition to the three letters, Soble gave me a small piece of paper on which he had written the names of his Canadian contacts as well as others. The names were: "Roman," "Belov," "Sasha," "Oscar," "Mendish," and "John L."

I protested that these all sounded like more aliases, while he had been instructed to give me the real names and addresses. But Soble protested that the men in

Moscow would know who the agents were because all except "Mendish" had originally come with him from Lithuania. When I guessed that "Belov" meant Jacob Albam (whom he usually called "Belova") and "Roman" a brother of his, Soble admitted I was correct. I told him he was mad not to give me at least the real name of Slava to take back to Vienna, along with his unsatisfactory letters. Soble waited until we were riding down in the hotel elevator together. Then he said, "I will give you his first name—it is Elliott."

I went with him to the street, and watched him walking away until he turned the corner. His broad shoulders were braced as though he expected to fight his way home through a hurricane.

When I turned the letters over to Aphanassy in Vienna he had them copied, and then sent the originals on to Moscow. Before our next meeting, on May 4, he had heard from Home. It seemed that our superiors in Moscow were almost as displeased with me as with Abram. "Each time you come back from the United States," Aphanassy said, "you bring only a new excuse or an alibi. This time you were instructed to refuse to take a 'no' from Abram, yet his excuses and alibis are again all you brought us. You did not even force him to introduce you to the various individuals in his group."

I did not know what to reply to this. It seemed a bad time to show him cablegrams I had been getting almost daily from Soble, imploring me to get him some money. The tone of these was so desperate that I took a chance.

Aphanassy Yefimov read them, then gave me an appraising look. "Don't you think there is only one way to settle this?" he asked.

I shrugged, waiting to see what he would say. "If you are so interested in getting money for your friend, why not go personally and talk to the men in Moscow who are holding it up?"

I reminded him that my last trip had aroused the curiosity of the American diplomats in several embassies. "We will take care of that," he said. "We will send you to Moscow on a plane on which there will be no other civilians."

I said I would think this over, and I did. I also talked the proposition over with the FBI. I pointed out that there was no reason to think that the NKVD entertained serious suspicions of me as yet. But I also said that, with the Soviet espionage system still in turmoil, no one could do more than guess about that.

A few days later Aphanassy treated me to an expensive meal at a restaurant. While we ate he asked me if I had made up my mind.

I decided that my position—with him, at least—was strong enough to gamble on an ultimatum. If nothing else, it might show where I stood with Home.

"Unless Korotkov comes here," I said, "I am going to leave Europe. I have made tremendous sacrifices for the Cause. I cannot wait around forever for firm instructions about what in the hell to do about Soble or anything else. Anyway, what promise made to me have you ever kept?"

"Don't leave Europe, Djon," said Aphanassy. "When you are next in Vienna Korotkov will be here to talk everything over with you."

I thought I had established that day that I would not be treated again as a misbehaving child—for a while, anyway. But at our very next interview—this was at a fish restaurant in the Russian Zone that overlooked the Danube River—Aphanassy gave me a real grilling. All his questions concerned Soble and Soble's group. The questions were asked in a stern, business-like tone, and he took down my answers in a small notebook. Did I know Slava? How many times did Jack mention Slava to me, and in what connection? What did I know about Abram's relations with Slava? One of the cables from Soble had come from Mexico, and I was asked about that. How did Abram get to Mexico? Had I helped him get there? What were Abram's plans for the future? What did I know about the brush company in Montreal?

Aphanassy said he believed that Korotkov might soon visit Vienna. I waited for him as long as I could, then left on urgent film business in London and also in Zurich. It was July before I returned to Vienna. I got there just in time to attend a small farewell dinner given for Aphanassy. He had just been promoted to the post in the Near East which he had once told me about. But Yefimov did not like to leave Vienna now that the time for that had come. He and his wife had been happy there, and he thought it a good place to bring up his infant son.

The following week Korotkov made his long-promised visit to Vienna. I must say I was flattered, on arriving for our first rendezvous—this was behind the New Berg Theatre on the morning of July 16, 1954—to find the general himself waiting for me. After exchanging the usual inquiries about each other's health and family, he took my arm and walked me deeper into the Russian Zone. He lost no time in getting to Soble's case. "Can you explain what has happened to our Comrade?" he demanded. "Abram has been a true Communist, a great worker and a selfless Comrade for so many years!"

On hearing that I was equally bewildered, Korotkov exclaimed, "It must be his surroundings that overwhelmed my old Comrade. Easy living! Radio, television, the press, all appeal to everything corrupt in our men!"

Korotkov felt that if such a steady, loyal Communist as Soble could be swept off his feet by the luxuries of living in the United States, none of his secret agents would be safe there. He had sworn never to expose another of them to "Western malaria" for more than one year at a time.

"Soviet Russia is growing in strength each day," he boasted. "When the time is ripe we will strike, Comrade. In one day we will wipe out all the American air bases from Spain to Alaska." He drew in his breath sharply and added, "And on that very same day the one hundred most important Americans will die. Some of them will be poisoned, some crushed under falling rocks, some in unavoidable automobile accidents. The sooner these capitalistic exploiters, these bloodsuckers of the poor are liquidated, the better! Have they ever done one thing that entitles them to escape such a fate? Today there are no real workers whatever in America, and no peasants. All Americans, rich and poor, young and old, have by now become corrupted, and are enslaved by the dollar and the fear of losing their own security."

By then we had arrived at our destination, a house that was dilapidated on the outside, but was furnished quite elegantly. The floors were covered with thick Oriental rugs. There were many *objets d'art* and rare books in fine bindings.

General Korotkov started to point out some of his favorite volumes, but broke off with "I want you to stop at *nothing* in getting Abram to Europe. Don't hesitate to use threats." He looked straight at me. "You can tell him that I instructed you to carry out these threats if he ignores my summons this time."

When I left General Korotkov that day, my head was spinning. The talk about threatening Soble's life impressed me far less than his eagerness to get Jack back to Vienna. Why? It would be simple to let Soble drop out of the espionage picture, equally simple to kill him. There could be but one explanation of why Home had been patient for so long with Soble. The men there must be convinced that he had held back some vitally important information—possibly as life insurance for himself. Why, otherwise, should they continue playing year after year this international cat-and-mouse game with him?

And when I continued to be urged by one Russian agent after another to visit Moscow, I could not help asking myself, "Does Moscow believe I know whatever important secret Soble is withholding in hopes of saving his life? Is that why they are so eager to get me behind the Iron Curtain?" Meanwhile Slava did not come to Europe, and that summer I began to wonder whether Soble had invented him.

But it became apparent that Korotkov believed in Slava's existence. He kept telling me, in other conferences we had that summer, that I must get Slava's report—and in Slava's own handwriting!

"My heart aches for Abram," he said, "but I must leave his fate now completely in your hands, Djon."

During one of our last meetings he confided that Malenkov, other high-ranking officials, and he had completed their blueprint for a thorough reorganization of the American division of Inostranni.

General Korotkov considered the espionage set-up in the United States his worst failure. In a rueful tone he told me, "My appointments have turned out most fortunately everywhere else in the world, Djon. And I do mean everywhere—Germany, France, Belgium, England, Japan, and the rest of the Orient. But in America my men have failed me, utterly failed me. Even Zubilin, I see now, was not the right man."

Korotkov, as usual, made no secret of his hatred of

the United States. But he said that thanks to the incomprehensible behavior of Abram, Malenkov was insisting that he go there and straighten out the mess Zubilin and his old friend had made of their jobs.

This he saw as additional reason for Abram to come to Europe without further delay. Who could brief him better than Abram on the situation, coach him on matters of personal behavior? Before taking any action he wanted to discuss the qualifications and character of each man in the espionage group there. Most important of all, he wished to consider where and how new recruits could be found. These must be strong men, he said, devoted heart and soul to the job of advancing worldwide Communism. Though he had never been in America, he was sure that the comforts and luxuries his secret agents had found there had demoralized them. This is why he must have men of iron will to carry on the work.

"Idealists, you see, have something soft in them—always," he declared. "And that soft side, exposed to sufficient temptation, will corrupt them."

During a previous talk, Korotkov had asked whether Soble, Aphanassy, or Tcherniavsky had ever spoken to me in a complimentary way about Beria. He also wanted to know whether Tcherniavsky had ever gossiped about Beria. My answer to all such questions had been "No."

Suddenly, he thrust a long folded piece of paper at me. "Sign it!" he said.

I did, signing "Boris Morros" without reading what was written above.

"This paper merely says," he explained, "that neither you nor Soble was ever close to Beria."

"Is it important?" I asked.

"It certainly is," he told me, giving me a glassy smile that made my skin crawl. "You may be shot for signing this paper. But it is not your business to ask questions, is it?"

At the FBI's suggestion I stopped off in Paris on my way home. I was asked to find out if the Zlatovskis had changed their minds about returning to the United States.

"We haven't changed our minds," Jane told me, "and never will."

She was sure now that State Department investigators were on her trail. A woman who had worked with her in the OSS at Vienna years before had sent her that warning. This was based on the fact that Jane's friend had been exhaustively questioned by State Department men. The woman had been asked to write down for the investigators everything she could recall about Jane.

But my visit produced rewarding results, nevertheless. Jane, who had been suspicious of me for years, had suddenly experienced a change of heart. Or perhaps she saw me as her and George's last hope to renew contact with Moscow. In any event, she wrote a short note which she asked me to pass on to General Korotkov when I next saw him. This requested a personal interview, and was signed "Slang." Being in her handwriting, it was important potential evidence of her membership in the Soble espionage ring.

My next meeting with Jack in New York was as unsatisfactory as the others. He had repeatedly cabled me to rush him $5000 and was angry because I had not done so.

"Stop talking about money," I snapped. "Tell me about Slava. That is what I'm here to find out."

"They know all about Slava in Moscow," was all I could get him to say. "They ought to remember when Slava gave Chaliapin a whole satchel full of papers back in nineteen forty-five, when the United Nations was formed. And how can they forget his services to them in Alaska and at Cologne?"

He wrote another letter—a ten-page affair—reiterating everything that he had written previously, about his need for money, his passport troubles, and the splendid work his Canadian contacts were doing for him. About the only progress I made was learning that Slava was his nephew, the son of a sister who had recently died. In the letter Jack stated that this nephew's name was Ilya (not Elliott!) Wolston. He also said Wolston had not come to Europe because he had been driven to the verge of insanity by his mother's death. But he was now recovering from his grief, and would leave for Europe very soon.

That defecting might prove the luckiest thing Soble ever did was a thought that occurred to me when I reached Vienna again in October 1954. The first two times I called the usual number—U-47306—there was no answer. The third time a man answered whose voice I did not recognize. He arranged a rendezvous for the following day when I identified myself as "Riabov." But when we met he was so aggressive I suspected that the NKVD had been taken over lock, stock, and barrel by the military.

"You are alone?" he asked, without bothering to identify himself. "I thought you would be with Soble. Or at least with the other one, 'S' " (meaning Slava).

When I tried to explain, he said, "You'd better go on to Moscow. They want to see you there." I pleaded, as usual, that I had too much pressing business to attend to, but that I would be happy to meet Korotkov in Vienna, when he could manage a trip to Austria.

On November 5 this same man brought me to a second-floor apartment on Foulmangasse. Korotkov was waiting. He actually appeared crushed by Soble's refusal to obey his orders. He said he was also disappointed in me, but Abram was the one he could not understand at all. "What has come over my old friend?" he asked. "Down through all our years of comradeship I could depend on his word. But now, what has happened to him? How could he have changed so much?"

For obvious reasons, the FBI wanted the relationship between Soble and Moscow to be maintained, no matter how precariously, for as long as possible. All I could do now, though, was show Korotkov the cables I had just received from Soble begging for money, and describing his desperate financial state.

Korotkov's affection for his old friend was truly sincere. I am convinced of that. After listening to me, he agreed—despite Soble's stalling—to reconsider the entire matter. But then he asked, "What in the world can I do if he continues to cause me so much trouble?"

"Oh, he will come out of it in time," I said.

"And if he does not? I suppose then there will be nothing for me to do but order him liquidated."

I got away from him that day as fast as I safely could. It was something, even in that mad, menacing world I was living in as spy and counterspy, to hear a thoughtful, sentimental man like General Korotkov talk with so little emotion of ordering the murder of one of his oldest and closest friends.

I suppose that is what made me hesitate at another meeting three days later when Korotkov wrote something in a tiny notebook and asked me to sign it. He covered what he had written with his hand.

"Let me read it, Sasha," I said. "Until now I have signed every scrap of paper you handed me, without reading it," I said. "This time I would like to know what I am signing."

General Korotkov kept the notebook in his hand

for a moment. Finally, with a shrug, he handed me the notation. It said:

"When I asked Djon why he questioned Aphanassy about Beria, his answer was 'Curiosity!' When I asked Djon if Soble asked him to inquire about Beria, he said, 'No!' "

When I protested that I had never discussed Beria with either Aphanassy or Soble, the general tore out what he had written in the tiny notebook and threw the scrap of paper away. I could not be sure what his motive had been, but thought it likely that, finding himself under fire as a Beria disciple and supporter, he was trying to prove that his men at least had had a detached attitude toward their chief.

During our next rendezvous, Korotkov said arrangements for his trip to the United States were about completed. I would be notified of his arrival and we would meet in New York. But I was to say nothing to Abram about his visit. However, he authorized me to assure Soble that the money he needed would become available on January 5. "I want you to bring your passport to our next meeting," he told me.

But as he said this, the chauffeur, Vladimir, without knocking first, rushed into the room. He was about to blurt out something, I'm sure, but Korotkov put his finger to his lips. The next thing I knew Korotkov had impatiently pushed me out of the room and locked the door. For a moment I stood in the corridor, not quite knowing what to do. From the locked room there was not a sound.

But in a few minutes Vladimir, looking shaken, and gray as a corpse, joined me.

"Come on," he said roughly.

"Just a moment," I told him. "I want to say good evening to the general."

"Don't bother," the chauffeur muttered. Seizing my

arm, he hustled me toward the door and outside.

I had not dared ask Vladimir any questions that evening as he drove me home. My next appointment with Korotkov was at six p.m. on November 16. Vladimir met me and led me through the streets to where his car was waiting. There was a man in the back seat whom I had never seen before. He was wearing a black coat and a black hat. There was something about his bearing and his straight-as-a-ramrod posture which gave me the impression that he was a military man wearing civilian clothes for the first time in years. As Vladimir opened the door and I got into the car next to this stranger, I noticed, in spite of his Vandyke beard, that he also bore a strong physical resemblance to Charles Bickford, the Hollywood movie actor.

Without greeting me, he leaned forward and whispered an address to Vladimir, who promptly headed the car into the Operngasse underpass, which leads into the Russian Zone.

When the car stopped, neither of us had uttered a word. My companion got out of the car first and I followed him. We walked down the street, stopped before an apartment house, went in, and walked up several flights of stairs. We entered an apartment and took off our coats. There seemed to be no one else there. I had decided not to show how nervous I was, no matter what happened. I had decided not to speak —as though it were some child's game we were playing —until he did.

But I could stand it no longer, and asked, "How long do you think we will have to wait for Korotkov?"

"We do not have to wait for Korotkov," he said quietly.

"Why not?" I said. "He asked me to bring my American passport."

His next words I will never forget. They were, "Alexander Mikhailovich Korotkov is no more!" He said this utterly without emotion, like a man telling you the time, or the score of a baseball game.

"What happened to him?"

"He is gone," this Russian Charlie Bickford said. "We do not have to worry about it. We will forget him."

"But he wanted to see my passport," I said, fatuously.

"You can give the passport to me," he said.

I reached into my inside coat pocket, got it, handed it over. He opened the passport, glanced at it, slapped it closed, slipped it out of sight. "I have one question to ask you," he said. "Do you wish to continue working for the Cause?"

"Of course."

"Perhaps you will be given the chance," he said. "That all depends on what happens tonight."

My skin began to crawl. There was no mistaking the menace in his tone. Like everyone else in show business I have never underestimated my ability to charm people. But if I ever knew anything in my life, it was that there was no chance of charming this Russian robot out of anything. As soon try to tame a lion with a smile. I was sick with fright. I am sure my eyes showed that as I watched him go to his overcoat and reach into the pocket. He took out a sheaf of letter-size paper and some pencils. He put these on the table.

"Sit down!" he said, pointing to a chair. When I complied he said, "You are to write down everything concerning yourself, your background, your family, and the state of your personal finances, also all the Soviet contacts you have ever had. You are to describe your relationship with Abram, from start to finish, also your relationship with the other members of his group, most particularly the assignments given you by our late Comrade, Alexander Mikhailovich Korotkov."

At that moment Vladimir, the chauffeur, came in and whispered something. "I have to go away for a little while," said the man in the black coat. "I hope when I return you will have written the report I want. Leave out nothing."

I seated myself at a table. Empty sheets of white paper never seemed more intimidating. I was too scared to write anything. I was too scared to think. I have not the slightest idea of how long the man in the black coat was gone. When he came back he found me still sitting at the table, staring into space. I had touched neither the paper nor the pencils.

"There are many kinds of persuasion, Comrade," he roared. He was about six feet two inches tall, and had muscles like a truck driver's. I was convinced that he would crush and mangle me if he got in a bad enough mood. I guess I was as near hysteria that day as I have ever been. Still, I won out over the impulse to giggle. I don't like to think what would have happened if I had not.

For a moment he seemed puzzled about what to do next. Then, with a grunt, he slipped into a chair near me and pulled the paper and one of the pencils from under my nose. Slowly and laboriously, he started to write. When he finished he shoved the sheet of paper at me. He had written down in Russian a list of twenty questions.

I got up my courage then, and attempted a little pleasantry. I told him that a long time before there had been an American magazine called *Liberty* and that for years its best feature was a list of the same number of questions. "The answers were on another page," I said. "They printed them upside down, I think, so you couldn't cheat it too easily."

For a moment he was confounded; then suddenly he shouted in my ear, "Stop babbling."

I stopped. He declared that I had better understand that he had come all the way from Moscow for the one purpose of meeting and examining me. "I am not going to leave this room until you have answered all the questions—to my satisfaction. Neither are you."

He waited for a moment, then added, "Either you are going to answer to me, Mikhail Petrovich, or you will sever relations with us as of this moment. Evasion won't help. Answering the questions halfway won't help. And, Djon, if you do not care to cooperate, you should leave the room—or try to."

Towering over me, he put his hands on his hips. I reached a trembling hand toward one of the pencils on the table. I knew that if I did not cooperate, I would never walk out of that room, that he would kill me with no more compunction than he would have in killing a cockroach.

Once I grasped that it was a question of survival, I saw that I, the little roly-poly man from Hollywood, would have to defeat him with my mind alone. I couldn't outwrestle this man, outfight him, outjump, or outrun him. I had to outthink him. Only some mental jujitsu that would catch him off guard could save me. Meanwhile, I must do anything, say anything, to gain time.

It was by then eight o'clock in the evening. But Mikhail Petrovich was in no hurry. He told me that the best way he could help stimulate my memory was by discussing each question with me at length before I wrote down the answer. He meant, of course, that I was to write down only what he wanted me to.

His first questions were:

1. What assignments have been given you?
2. When did you first meet Korotkov?

3. Who introduced Korotkov to you? Describe the circumstances, also the parols given you at that time.

4. How long have you known Soble, and how did you meet him?

5. What do you know about Rector and Slang?

These required only simple answers, but not necessarily short ones. For example, in my answer to the question about Soble, Mikhail told me to include the number of times I had seen Abram in Europe, the number I had been at his factory, also a good deal of information about each relative of his whom I had met, along with that person's legal name and present address. In addition, had I met Jacques Ajer?

6. What is your recommendation regarding Soble?

I recommended that Moscow send him $12,000. That brought only a frost-bitten jeer from my inquisitor. Mikhail said that every cent invested in the bristle factory came from Moscow, regardless of what Soble had told me about it. I then mentioned that Korotkov had also promised to get Jack a settlement, and immediately I regretted it. It was Moscow's opinion, Mikhail said, that Korotkov had handled both Soble and myself very badly. Korotkov had trusted Soble too much and, as a result, Soble was dangerous because of what he knew.

I pricked up my ears. The mystery again? What did Jack Soble know that made him so important? Maybe this ham-handed bully would spill it.

And he was talking on. Soble had been very wrong to evade a face-to-face explanation at the Center. At first I didn't comprehend what he meant. The Center? Then it dawned on me that to the new crowd NKVD headquarters was not Home but the Center. If Abram had been less cowardly, he was grumbling, if he had made an honest attempt to cooperate, every sort of money, and any other assistance he required, would have been given him.

I tried to explain Soble's passport troubles, but Mikhail had not the slightest interest in these, and said so. He next made my hair stand on end by spilling the secret. It was that Soble had detailed information about Trotsky's followers not only in the United States and Europe but throughout Russia itself.

When I heard that, I knew that I had at last solved the riddle of Moscow's continued interest in Soble. And it was the big prize I'd been waiting for all along. But the next instant I was wondering if I'd be given the freedom to pass it on to the FBI.

I tried hard not to give myself away. Mikhail was saying sternly that I must impress on Soble, the next time I saw him, that Moscow was interested in the most important assignment he had ever had. Looking at me strangely, he added, "When you tell him that, do not mention the Trotskyites."

"How can I tell him without mentioning the Trotskyites?"

"Just say it is the most important assignment he has had—in the past ten years. He will know what you mean. The reason he is out of favor at the Center is because he has delivered nothing at all lately on this assignment. He has failed us and he knows it!"

During the discussion about whether money should be given to Soble I mentioned that Abram had long been begging me for a personal loan. I said, "That shows how hard up he is!"

That only provoked another lecture. One of Soble's main faults, Mikhail said, was constantly demanding money. When this windy, rather one-sided phase of the conversation was over, the scowling Mikhail asked if I agreed with his analysis of Soble.

Not daring to say anything else, I said I did. He then told me to recommend that not a nickel be given to Soble, but without mentioning that he had advised it.

After that, we went on to the next question:

7. Why did Abram drop Rector and Slang?

My answer was, "Their emotional instability convinced him they are unreliable."

8. Do you agree?

9. Why do you agree?

I cited Rector's irrational behavior after I got him the job in the movie theater.

"But they are well connected with the American Army's Intelligence Service," Mikhail said. "A member of that service is visiting them this evening. And Slang used to write us excellent reports, though we have not heard from her in a long time. Is this because she quarreled with Soble's wife? Is that the reason you disliked and distrusted this true revolutionary, and refused to carry her reports to Vienna?"

Without even giving me a chance to reply, he accused me of being a sentimentalist, meaning I was not a true revolutionary.

In my own defense, I pointed out that Rector and Slang did not trust the Sobles. "They will not give me a report to pass along to you," I explained, "because I have been unable to convince them that I come from you, and not Abram, whom they now consider their worst enemy."

10. What do you think should be done about Rector and Slang?

I said that, if Home believed them useful, I should be given convincing proof to show them that the assignments I brought came through me from Moscow, not their enemy, Abram.

That made Mikhail laugh raucously. "What kind of proof do they require?" he demanded.

I suggested a letter, or they could give me Rector's

parol, if one still existed. "I'll handle it," he said, "so she will know you come from us."

11. Have you met "S" (meaning Slava)? Do you agree with Soble's high opinion of his character and ability, and what do you recommend for his future?

Mikhail seemed delighted when I explained that I had not met "S." He said I should recommend that this agent be turned over to me. But he also made me write down all I had heard about "S" and that my information about him come solely from Abram.

12. What do you know about "B"?

As "B" was for Belov or Belova (alternate code names for Jake Albam), I was forced to discuss again the matter of money.

This time the subject caused Mikhail to fly into a rage. He told me that the Soviets had given "B" not only money but also a small fortune in diamonds. In fact, they once transferred the lump sum of $25,000 to him through Soble.

Mikhail instructed me to add to my answer to question 12 the suggestion that Albam be turned over to me. My first assignment involving him would be to obtain a complete report of his activities over the past two years, and his plans for the future.

13. What are your impressions and opinions of Vitaly Tcherniavsky, Aphanassy Yefimov, Igor Sokolov?

I got by this question simply by saying I had found them courteous and cooperative. What Mikhail was chiefly interested in, as it turned out, was whether they had discussed Beria with me at any time. I swore that none of them had.

By this time I was becoming a little more relaxed, because, I think, of his frequent references to assignments for me. I reasoned that even a Communist could not expect a man to be a spy and a courier for

Moscow after he was in his grave.

The next half dozen questions I answered as skimpily as I dared. These included:

What is the history of the members of your family in the United States?

What is the background of your relatives in Russia?

What is your financial situation?

At that last I complained that the Center seemed to take for granted that I was a millionaire, which simply was not true. I attributed the error first to Zubilin, then to Soble. Both of them, I asserted, had been deceived because like everyone in pictures I lived in the finest hotels, spent money lavishly, and jumped for the check. "Practically everyone in the film business does that," I explained. "It is expensive window dressing, but it pays off, usually."

I told him I recently had invested in land in the Austrian Alps which I believed would prove to contain beryllium deposits. Mikhail had me write a description of my holdings, and suggested that I bring a sample piece of crystal beryllium from the property to our next meeting, along with any chemical analysis I had obtained. He warned me never to let the mineral-greedy American authorities know about my potential beryllium deposits.

By that time Mikhail seemed to have calmed down enough for me to tell him about the note I had signed for Korotkov. I did that as a calculated risk. I was sure that he already knew about that paper, but he might be pleased at my show of sincerity.

I had once more misjudged my man. "You do not *know* what you signed?" he said, starting to work himself up into a rage. He leaped up and hammered his fist on the table. "What in hell are you saying? How could you sign something like that without reading it first?"

I couldn't explain. I did not know why I had done it, except that I had trusted Korotkov to some small degree—something I never intended to do with this fellow.

"And now we do not know where this note is," he screamed, "or what is in it!" He kept hammering the table with both fists. "And now there is no Korotkov to tell us. There never will be a Korotkov we can ask."

I waited for his fury to subside. It took several minutes. Then he stabbed his finger into my chest.

"But don't you be the one to tell Abram that his protector, the great General Korotkov, is gone!"

"I wouldn't think of it," I said.

At last he came to the final question. "Why are you working for the Russian Communist Cause?"

I told him the truth: that it was to protect my folks in Russia. When he looked skeptical, I added, "Not that it did me any good. Two brothers of mine were killed by you Soviets."

He replied, "It must have been for a good reason."

That did it. Abandoning all caution, I started to yell at him. Now it was I who was slamming my fist on the table. I knew that yelling at him might cost my life, but I could not worry about that now. Hearing him sneer at my dead brothers, who had been murdered by his kind of thug, was too much to bear.

The amazing thing was that it worked. He calmed down. In a moment he was telling me the sad story of his own life. He was born in the most wretched circumstances; his father and mother had both died before he was three months old. And so, though he was merely a poor orphan and brought up in an asylum run by the charitable Moscow government, he knew what he was fighting for. The masses! He was ready to give his life for them, the masses, the millions of oppressed slaves in the United States and other capitalistic countries.

As for my brothers, unless they died serving the Cause of the Revolution, their fate did not interest him, he said.

That did it again. I pressed my luck by yelling at him again. I told him, "Every time that I work for the Soviets I risk my life. For the Revolution! Every time I enter the Soviet Zone I risk my life for the Cause." But what was *he* risking, a big young man like him bullying a little old fellow like me? What could I do to him here, with his own people all around him, outside the door, everywhere? I was alone, unprotected!

Again I got away with it. He sat there for a long time, staring at me in utter disbelief. And when he spoke again he conceded me a great deal, considering his mood of contempt of a few minutes before. "As long," he said, "as your main purpose is a revolutionary purpose, then you can help us. But I tell you with the utmost seriousness that you better keep your promises. From now on you must prove yourself by your deeds."

It was four o'clock in the morning when I walked out of that house. A little to my astonishment, I was still alive, still in one piece.

It was my worst ordeal—so far.

CHAPTER 14

Spies on the Run

Before my next rendezvous with the monstrous Mikhail Petrovich, I conferred with the FBI men who were assigned to guard me.

"This is getting dangerous, Boris," they said after I told them of my all-night ordeal. "If you want to quit right now, we won't blame you. It will be all right with us."

I thanked them. But I did not quit, though I was scared of this new gang as I had not been with the others. But there was something else that made it impossible for me to quit, an emotion new to me. I was devoured by a desire for revenge. This new bunch had gone too far, these underground workers, secret agents, conspirators, spies, saboteurs. Having been with them so much I had come to detest them. I was sick to the point of revulsion of their tricks, their despicable lies and traps and acts of cruelty. I was disgusted with their rigid, Simple Simon philosophizing, their whole "You're for us or against us" attitude, their conception of good and evil. Most of all I was disgusted with their maniacal pride, the pleasure they took in their acts of terrorism.

What the man in the black suit did at our next rendezvous was typical. I was taken again to the Operngasse apartment house, but this time to a different apartment on the same floor. Unlike the other, where my inquisition had been held, this one was tastefully furnished, and awaiting me on the dining-room table was a feast fit for a king. Now that I had been taught my lesson I was being shown—as though I were a twelve-year-old schoolboy—how well I would be treated if I stopped being so naughty and careless!

After we had dined and drunk the number of vodka toasts usual on such an occasion, Mikhail Petrovich got down to business. And this big brute, to give him his due, was a most efficient organizer of underground activity, the best I had had a chance to observe in action.

A good example of his cleverness is the mail drop he devised in Vienna before he returned to Moscow. For the drop Mikhail used a prominent optical firm from whom I had regularly bought lenses and other motion-picture-camera equipment for years. It is unlikely that the firm or any of its employees ever suspected that their respected establishment was being used by the Russian espionage bureau. My opinion is that none of my letters ever reached their shop. This was because a postal worker was ordered to deliver them to Vladimir, the chauffeur, instead of to the optical company's mailbox. His tipoff was "Paul Scott," which Mikhail told me to write on the envelope flap of the letters I sent. As he started to explain all this to me, Mikhail produced two of the firm's catalogues, marking in each the names of those items I was to use as code words. These included:

Minilux for Abram (Jack Soble).

Kleinstbild for perlon, a material possibly used on the exterior surface of airplanes.

Minigrand for information concerning this exterior surface.

Projector for Orlon, and if used for this exterior surface.

Optische for Rector (George Zlatovski).

Spannungspruefer for Slang (Jane Foster Zlatovski).

Universal for beryllium.

Katalogue for message.

Prisms for meetings, with cities to be written out, and dates in consecutive figures. (For example, April being the fourth month in the year, April 3 would be written 43.)

Toleranz for passport.

Gewicht for references to Cardinal Spellman, Glennan, and Louis Lurie.

Anstalt for Vienna.

Skala for a trip or voyage.

Compensator for Boris Morros.

Patent for money transfer.

I was told to write the letters in any language but Russian, and to use business phraseology so that each of the messages would read like an order. For a quick, practical check, Mikhail had me mail sample letters from Zurich and Paris. He wanted to find out if the postal employee was on the job. He was.

Mikhail seemed to think I was a bearcat for undercover work in quantity, and kept piling assignments on me as fast as he could think them up. He thought I would take this as a flattering tribute and proof positive of his faith in me. He even made me boss of the Soble spy ring, replacing Abram. The fact that Soble had not done one thing for Moscow in at least two years did not in his opinion diminish the honor he was paying me.

Though I was going to be in Paris for only a short while, he insisted I visit the Zlatovskis' apartment on the Rue de Mazarin at least three or four times. I was also to write a report offering my opinion of whether he was too stupid and she too drunk to be permitted to work as secret agents of the NKVD again. Later in Paris I did phone their apartment several times, without getting any response.

But the heavy assignments were in the United States. There Mikhail really expected me to put my small button of a nose to his grindstone. First of all, I was to tackle Soble, and find out whether Jack had gone to Mexico recently on his private business or in the interests of the Cause. When I asked, "What about Abram's Canadian contacts?" I was told not to waste my time on them. But I was to convince both Soble and Albam that I was now their boss. I was also to replace Soble as Slava's only contact in America. On seeing Slava, I was to get all his reports dating from years before, even though these might since have lost their value. Mikhail, like the others, emphasized how pleased he and all Moscow would be if I could force Soble to come to Europe.

My principal assignment for the trip was a beaut. I was merely to find out the chemical formula the Americans were using on the bodies of their supersonic planes to reduce skin friction. While I was at it, I could also learn the production technology of this plastic, which Moscow believed to be a mixture of Orlon and perlon.

In whatever spare time I had I was to cultivate my relationships with Cardinal Spellman, Keith Glennan, and Louis Lurie, a prominent California Republican.

This briefing meeting with Mikhail lasted seven hours. Before we parted, he gave me the usual pep talk on the Soviet Union's mighty future. He also tried to make sure that the feast did not turn my silly little head. The chauffeur, Vladimir, would be my Vienna contact. Mikhail said that Vladimir, unlike Vitaly and Aphanassy, was not going to be soft-hearted with me when I did not toe the line. Vladimir, he said, was a fine, upstanding representative of the new school of military intelligence. Furthermore, the men now in charge in Moscow—Malenkov, Khrushchev, Bulganin, and Molotov—were all iron men.

(I suppose this should have alerted me to the possibility of personal danger, but I had been hearing for so long about how tough all the Russian Communists were that I paid little attention.)

In later meetings I was given a new parol. Now I would appear at the Tabor Theatre with a newspaper folded under my left arm, my gloves in my hand. The man who approached me would say, "Have you seen Paul Scott lately?"

"Yes," I was to answer, "I saw him three or four days ago in Rome." To this his reply would be, "Fine, Djon."

At the end of 1954 I contracted pneumonia in Vienna and was rushed to a hospital, where an inexperienced nurse made my condition worse by giving me the wrong sort of penicillin. As soon as I got on my feet I headed for California and Palm Springs, to convalesce. But I did not neglect, meanwhile, to keep in touch with Vladimir through coded letters.

When I returned to Hollywood in the middle of February 1955, the FBI tipped me off that Jane Foster was now on the West Coast. She had rushed there from Paris to see her mother, who was critically ill. When I was unable to locate Jane I telephoned her father, whom I had once met at the Zlatovskis' apartment in Paris. On that occasion he had told me—with Jane listening, a grimace of disgust on her face—that he wished for only one thing before he died. This was that Jane would discover and admit to him how wrong her political beliefs were.

Fortunately Dr. Foster remembered me. He promised to have Jane get in touch with me. She phoned me later that day and I told her I could meet her at the Ambassador Hotel. To my surprise she seemed desperately eager to see me. She was at La Jolla, she said, but would get up to see me that evening, if possible. La Jolla is only a little more than a hundred miles south of Los Angeles, and Jane arrived at the Ambassador shortly after ten. After buying her a few drinks at the bar, I took her to a room I had hired especially for the talk with her. I told the barman to send up a fifth of bourbon, cracked ice, and several bottles of 7-Up for me.

I was a little apprehensive of what she would say when she saw the room. It was one of those very large sample rooms designed for the use of traveling salesmen who need a good deal of space to display their sample line. Jane had never seen such a room before and asked what it was. She accepted my explanation, and gave the room only a cursory check, principally to make certain that the doors were locked. They were, but there were two FBI men in the next room.

Jane, who had never trusted me in Paris, said plenty that night. She drank steadily, and the more she drank the more she talked.

Like Soble, Jane was now in a frenzy. At one point she said that I was the only person in the United States she could trust or talk to with freedom and candor, and I believe she meant it. In November she had got a cable from her father saying that her mother, whom she loved more than anyone else in the world, was dying. Though she knew coming to the United States might mean disgrace, or even a term in Federal prison, she had rushed home on the next plane. She spent the next four days at her bedside. "I could not bear the idea of mother dying without having a chance to say good-by to her. I now have the satisfaction of thinking that spending all that time at her bedside helped her recover temporarily. I hope so, anyway."

Jane had been in California only a few days when a member of the Security Division of the State Department called on her. He questioned her for three hours, then picked up her passport. She was bitter about the intensive grilling he had subjected her to. "He asked me about an article I wrote for *The People's World* years ago," she said. "Also about some pictures of mine that were published in *The Daily Worker*. I told the fool that I had not the slightest idea how the *Worker's* editors got hold of them. At one point I got so mad that I slapped the investigator across the face with my passport!"

As was so true with Jack, what the government was *not* doing distressed her even more than what it was.

The psychological theory that nothing upsets a guilty person so much as uncertainty was certainly working out in their cases.

What was rattling her most, Jane explained, was that the State Department man had spent most of his time questioning her about the people she had known before 1940. Jane kept saying, between healthy swigs of bourbon, "You would think they would ask me about the Sterns and the Sobles. Those four are all under suspicion right now. The government must know—or at least suspect—*something* about my relations with them. Why aren't the State Department people asking about what I've been doing in the past fifteen years instead of trying to dig back into ancient history? Why should what I did during the thirties seem important to them *now?*"

But no matter how drunk Jane became she never abandoned all precautions. For example, when I asked her outright that evening, "Were you ever a Communist?" she used an old Communist trick. While nodding her head "yes," she said defiantly, "No, I never had a Party card." This just in case the room was "bugged."

Later on, in the course of that long evening, it did seem that the bourbon she was gulping down might cause her to talk. Once she exclaimed, "I signed a Communist card in 1947, but I was drunk when I did it. They don't seem to know about that. They'd really have me, wouldn't they, if they knew about that card? The State Department hates me," she said. She had become convinced of that when she went to Washington to plead for the return of her passport. "State knows how violently anti-Dutch I was when I lived in the East. They know about my Indonesian activities. I suspect that in picking up my passport they are holding me as a hostage. They may think that George will be tempted to come back here just to be with me. But if George did return they would try to deport him to Russia.

"But I have written him that he must not come back under any circumstances. You know, the State Department in Paris once asked George for his passport but he refused to give it up."

If I had not been on serious business for the FBI that night I would have asked her the question that I had often wanted to ask other Russian workers: If they considered living under Communist rule desirable for the whole world, why were they invariably reluctant to be deported to that land of benevolence?

Like most alcoholics, Jane did not stick long to the same point of view. A moment later she said that George was not bright and talked too much. In fact, she said, she was thinking of obtaining a Mexican divorce. "Do you know of a good Mexican divorce lawyer you can recommend?" she asked plaintively. But in the next moment she was defending George, and blaming the Sobles for all their troubles. I explained that I would soon be able to give her a code word to prove that I was working directly for our superiors in Vienna, and not through Soble.

"Jane," I asked, "what do you want me to tell the Soviets about your troubles here? They'll ask me."

"Nothing," she replied.

Next, she went back to the mystifying interest of the State Department in her early career. In one of a series of interviews Ruth Shipley, head of the Passport Division, had questioned her for an hour. "Miss Shipley liked me. I put on a good-convent-girl act with her," she said. "It was so good that Shipley told one of her assistants that she thought she ought to look into this case personally. But it will do me no good. Her hands are tied."

During all this official interrogating Jane had admitted only what she thought the Department already knew about her: that she had been a member of a left-wing Washington book store, and had been in a group that picketed the White House in the early thirties demanding recognition for Russia. Mild stuff like that. Nothing they could send you to prison for. She had even recklessly signed an affidavit declaring that she had never been a Communist, but merely a left-winger, though aware that this could get her indicted for perjury.

On telling me all this, she hastily swallowed the rest of her drink. As I mixed another for her, she started to scream imprecations against the Sobles. But she declared she would never tell anyone in the American government that he was a Russian agent. "The very worst I'd ever say about him, Boris, is that he had once been a black-marketeer."

Suddenly wheeling on me, she demanded, her face contorted with rage, "Could you be working for the FBI, Boris?"

I pretended that this crazy idea amused me. Apparently that lightning flash of intuitive suspicion flitted out of her mind as quickly as it had come, because she did not refer to it again.

"I loathe this country," she declared. "I'd die if I had to live here. Do you think Home can get people out of the country?"

I told her that Home had done it for others and I would ask them to do the same for her.

"You are a good friend, Boris," she said.

At this point I asked her for the second time if she had ever been a Communist. She repeated the tactic of nodding her head while denying it verbally. But when I suggested she write Home a letter, explaining why she wanted to be spirited out of the United States, she proved how much smarter she was, drunk or sober, than any of the men conspirators. "A letter," she asked with biting scorn. "Do you think I'm crazy?"

She left shortly after that. It was fifteen minutes to one. The session had lasted for almost three hours, during which Jane had drunk up almost the whole fifth of bourbon.

Eleven days later I was freezing my ears off in Toronto, where I had gone to see Jack Soble. An FBI man accompanied me on the train as far as Buffalo, briefing me for hours as we traveled north. The last thing he said was, "Bring him across the border, if you can. I'll be waiting here for you."

As the train continued on its way through the ice-covered fields of Canada, I wondered if this could be the beginning of the end for Soble and his whole spy ring. It had been the most fascinating and important experience of my life, but, now that the chips were down, it could not be over too quickly to suit me. This part, bringing them in, was no fun. The sessions I had had with the terror-wracked Jack had also taken a lot out of me. And that long evening of listening to the raving and ranting of Jane Foster Zlatovski had taken more. The quicker I could wrap the whole thing up the better I would like it.

I had been unable to get accommodations in advance, and found Toronto jumping with visitors. I got in at eight-thirty and almost froze my ears off as I traveled from one hotel to another. Finally I got a room at the Edgewater. I phoned Jack at the Park Plaza at once and said I would be right over there. Looking more thin and harried and woe-begone than ever, he was waiting for me in the lobby. He suggested we walk around the corner to the Murray Restaurant.

"I can't stay in that room upstairs another minute," he said. "Myra is in Montreal. Being away from Myra makes every night seem a thousand nights long."

"You certainly look terrible," I agreed, after we were seated in the restaurant. We ordered coffee and dessert.

He did not reply until the waiter went to the kitchen. "I sure *feel* terrible. But you ought to see Myra. I'm afraid she's going to have a nervous breakdown. As you know, she's haunted by a fear complex. Both of us think you are acting like an idiot," he added. "What *are* you, a noble fool? Unless you're getting a lot of money out of it, why in the world do you continue making these visits to Vienna?"

"Why not?" I said. "Are you challenging my loyalty to the Cause?"

"I never knew whether you were loyal or not, Boris," he said wearily. "Sometimes I thought you must be doing all of it just for thrills. Yet only a jaded man would do such a thing and, God knows, nobody ever accused you of being jaded. So I'm mystified about your motives. And I have been for a long time." With a sigh, he went on, "But how in the world can you be so careless? In all my life I have never seen anything approaching your recklessness. Do you imagine for one moment that the American authorities are not following you? But even if this weren't true, Boris, there is another thing I should warn you about: either the Soviets will double-cross you, or they'll use you to double-cross me. But let's get out of here. I can't bear sitting here any longer."

"Okay, we'll go to your room, and talk there."

To my annoyance, when we got outside he insisted that we walk the streets as we talked. "For God's sake, Jack," I kept saying, "it's below zero tonight—let's get inside."

"No, I'm too restless, I tell you." Then he started to complain about his troubles, but I told him, "Look, friend, I'm freezing here because you insisted I come up. I interrupted an important business trip to Chicago to talk with you, to spend an hour or two with you. But I did not come all this way to hear you crying."

He looked at me as though I had kicked him in the face. But I went on relentlessly. "Let's forget the sentimental mush for once. I have a message for you, a very important message."

He looked at me with terror in his eyes.

For Jack, of course, my big news was going to be the liquidation of Korotkov, the one man in Moscow he trusted and looked upon as his best friend and staunch defender. Among other things, the FBI had stressed how vitally important it was that I tell him that story as dramatically as I could, and at the moment when it would have the cruelest and most devastating emotional impact on him. In his bewilderment and horror it was quite possible that he might go voluntarily with me to the Bureau and tell the FBI everything it wanted to know.

I began by describing my series of meetings with Korotkov, as though he were still alive.

"The first two of these conferences," I said, "were devoted exclusively to you, your activities, your problems. But let us go straight to the essential matter. Your old friend, whose paternal forbearance and patience with you has often amazed me, now suspects that your Mr. S., your smart, shrewd loyal Slava, does not even exist."

He winced as though I had pinched him. When he talked it was like listening to a frightened child.

"I never—expected—Sasha to turn on me *this* way."

"He thinks *you* have turned your back on him.

What else can he think? You deliver nothing. Your fabulous protégé is neither seen nor heard from, nor does he write a single three-line report. Your habit of forever demanding money has Sasha more disturbed than ever. Now he thinks *he* may be penalized for not getting a financial accounting from you. He kept asking me how he could explain to Home something he did not understand himself."

Jack had been walking so fast that I almost had to run to keep up with him. But these last words stopped him in his tracks. We were on a corner, under a street light, and we stayed there. He seemed to be unaware of the cold, but I wasn't. I had the mad feeling that I was freezing, not starting with my extremities, but from my insides out. Every pound of my fat little body seemed to be congealing. It made me even colder to watch what Jack was doing. In his abstraction, he pulled off a glove, scratched his face, put the glove on again, took it off, scratched his nose, put it on again.

Still following the FBI's script, I described how Vladimir, a burly man I had never seen before, had met me and taken me to the conferences with Korotkov. "Each time Vladimir was a little less respectful," I said. "I felt he was laughing at Korotkov behind his back, and soon expected to be laughing in his face. And"—I paused dramatically—"that is exactly what happened, Comrade Soble."

"Tell me," he whimpered. "Tell me, please! *Please!*"

I waited a moment, then went on. "The next time I went to a rendezvous, Korotkov was not there. Instead, a brutish military fellow was waiting in the car. He was wearing a black coat. He did not say anything at all to me on the way to the apartment house in Operngasse. Then when we were inside I looked around, I did not see Sasha—"

Jack's face was contorted now in an agony of suspense. "What happened? Hurry up, for God's sake," he pleaded. "Stop torturing me. What did they do to Sasha when he came there?"

"He did not come, Jack," I said. "I asked for him, but he did not come."

"What, what, what—" And now Soble was gibbering. "Tell me, Boris, for God's sake. *Don't torture me like this.*"

"Well, this big man in the black coat," I said, with deliberate slowness, "looked at his watch!"

"Go on! Get on! What about Sasha! Boris, tell me—"

"How can I tell you anything if you won't keep still?"

He tried, Jack Soble. How he tried—with his gloved hands pasted over his mouth. But he was unable to hold back the groans that kept creeping through the gloves like animal sounds.

"This man in the black coat," I said, "looked at his watch. 'Stop worrying,' he said. 'Korotkov is no more.' "

I expected Jack Soble, with his last human resources punched from under him, to screech. Instead, standing there on that snow-and-ice-covered street corner, in the middle of the night, he started to cry very softly for his old friend who was dead.

"Liquidated!" he said after a while, like a man in a dream. "But why am I surprised? I knew—Boris, I knew—when Beria—" He broke off. "But this is the end," he said out of the twisted corner of his mouth. "Men like Sasha were the best thing they had, the only good thing, I tell you. So it is the end—at least of the regime that we have always known and respected. You can tell them all for me that they can go to hell. They are butchers! They are sadists, tyrants. And I'm not a fool. If they ever got me to go to Europe I'd never come back alive."

Jack hardly listened as I gave him the rest of Mikhail's message. "You cannot get out of going to Europe any longer," I kept telling him. "This new gang will not accept your passport troubles as an excuse. They will give you a fake passport any time you want."

"I am not going back," he insisted, adding that I should not take such a chance either. I think he still liked me, sincerely, and was afraid Home would order me killed if I put myself in their clutches again. Brusquely I ordered him to hear me out, and told him that Home had officially made me boss of the group in his place. But at this time they wished me to direct the activities only of Slava and Belova. They were not interested in his Canadian agents. What they wanted was the information he had been withholding on the counter-revolutionists all over the world who called themselves Trotskyites.

"Come on, let's start walking again," he said. As he walked, he talked. He would turn nobody over to me. He had no information on the Trotskyites, had never been assigned by Home to get it. "I have only one message for Moscow. Tell them for me to go to hell. Tell them I am no longer in sympathy with the Soviet Union. Tell them I said it is no longer safe for us to meet."

When he started bemoaning Home's ingratitude for all his courageous achievements in Spain, Germany, and the Balkans, I decided the moment might be at hand to try my Sunday punch. But now he asked me two favors. He wanted a loan of $1000 to take Myra to New York, where she could be examined by better doctors than were available in Montreal. The other favor was that I should refuse to see the man in Vienna ever again.

I never got a chance to use that Sunday punch because of what he said next: "No matter what the Communists do, I'll always be true to them, ideologically."

I knew then I was licked, and would have to go back with an empty bag—no Soble, no information on the Trotskyites in America—to the FBI man waiting for me in Buffalo.

The last thing Soble said to me when we parted that cold winter night was pitiful. "Give me the money I need, Boris," he said. "I have lost everything that I invested in the brush company. I am no longer one of the owners, just a salesman. All I want to do now is make an honest living."

I promised to see what I could do, and let him know. But the FBI did not want me to lend him any money. Obviously, he would have to move back to New York if he remained broke.

When I got back to New York the FBI gave me Jacob Albam's phone number, and a list of questions to ask him; they had me memorize these and the information I needed to contradict him in case he started lying.

Albam was living on Riverside Drive. When I phoned him he proved affable and readily agreed to my suggestion that he visit me in my room at the Barbizon-Plaza. He said he could come on February 28, between six-fifteen and six-thirty in the evening.

If he came and talked, it would mean that I had got important interviews with three of the principal members of Soble's spy ring in three cities thousands of miles apart, within seventeen days. He showed up, and on time.

My first words to him were, "Belova, now you belong to me." That was the phrase which he had been told Soble's successor, as chief of the spy ring, would use to identify himself.

He smiled when I said that and I went on, blithely. "What are you doing now, Comrade?" I picked up a pencil, prepared to write down his answers, as I knew Albam would expect me to do.

"I am working as a foreman—of sorts," he said, "in my brother's herb business." He said he was happy at that work even though he was paid only $60 a week, plus a modest annual bonus. His wife had become a social worker and earned slightly more than he did. She, too, liked her job.

Albam was worried about one thing that evening. Dropping his voice to a whisper, he said, "She knows nothing. *Nothing!* And how am I going to explain to her my meeting you like this?"

"She knows Jack Soble, doesn't she?"

He nodded.

"Tell her I asked you to help me find him." That suggested excuse seemed to relieve him of all his apprehension. A man being questioned by someone working with the FBI, and worrying that his wife should suspect him of meeting a blond on the sly would have been comical—under other circumstances.

I next said, "By the way, Jack once told me that you asked him for money to pay a lawyer who helped you get your passport."

"That makes no sense at all," said Albam, but quite calmly. He quickly explained that he had applied for a passport a few years before. Hearing nothing from the State Department, he had written a letter to Washington and had been informed that the matter was still being investigated.

"It is true that I did consult a lawyer," he said, "and he advised me that my application was probably in the hands of the FBI, but that this was the usual procedure."

Unlike the other espionage agents, Albam was a placid soul. "I am not going to travel abroad, so I need no passport. When I do, the government will probably give me one." Then he added, and again without rancor, "I cannot understand what has happened to Jack. Why should I make up a story like that about asking for money to pay my lawyer?"

"When I saw Soble in Toronto a few days ago," I said, "he talked a good deal about Ilusha Wolston, his nephew, being dangerously ill with grief over his mother's death."

Albam shook his head. "Jack should turn novelist," he said, "if he is going to tell stories like that. Wolston has been insane for several years, certainly long before his mother's death. Unless I am mistaken, he is too ill mentally to realize his mother is dead. He is a physical wreck, a psychotic who more than occasionally goes berserk. He is also a recluse and lives on a farm most of the time. As though that were not enough, recently I was told by a doctor that he had cancer."

When I questioned Albam about this doctor, he explained that he was Soble's brother, hence Wolston's uncle.

I told Albam that his first assignment from me would be to get Slava's telephone number and address, as well as an up-to-date report on his mental and physical condition.

He did not have this information in time for our next meeting but said that he would continue working on it. On this occasion I discussed some of the stories Soble had told me about his handling of the undercover workers' money.

"Is it true that he once gave you between twenty-five thousand and thirty thousand dollars to invest in business and that you lost it because you are such a poor businessman?"

"Not a word!" declared Albam. He seemed to be sincerely puzzled at the story. "Jack gave me no money for that business. I borrowed only three thousand, and that from my brother. I did lose this three thousand, but not because I'm such a poor businessman. What I should have had was a lot more money to invest, but rather than ask my brother to risk a small fortune I withdrew from the partnership."

When he saw me looking at him quizzically, he said, "That is easy to check upon. I gave the Sobles receipts for every penny either of them turned over to me. I had to; they insisted on that." When I asked him whether Jack's story of once paying Albam $100 a week over a period of quite some time was true, Albam again said that Soble had been lying.

If Jake was telling the truth, my friend Jack had been chiseling thousands of dollars for years, robbing the organization to which he had dedicated his life.

Albam explained that since coming to the United States he had been paid in all $10,000 by secret agents. But Soble had not given him anything whatever to do for two or three years. Seven of the ten thousand had been given him by another contact soon after he came to the United States. In 1949 Myra, carrying out Jack's order, had given him approximately $2000. Since then Jack had given him small amounts from time to time, usually passing the money to him in a Manhattan newsreel theater. But these sums did not amount altogether to $1000, he believed.

"You can confirm this through the Sobles," he declared. "They have receipts for every dollar of this, as I told you."

I asked Albam to write a report for me on this and his activities since coming to America. He did, signed it "Belova," and gave it to me. I turned over this report to the FBI, and it was the chief evidence fac-

ing him not too long afterward when he was indicted by a Federal Grand Jury for espionage.

A few days later I ran into Jane Zlatovski as she
walked into the Barbizon-Plaza. I took a step toward
her, but she put her finger to her lips and whispered,
"Not now, please."

She either was being followed that day, or thought
she was. That chance encounter was the last time I
ever saw the unhappy California woman painter, who
had betrayed her country and so fiercely hated it.

CHAPTER 15

On a Spot Called Danger

A few days after the talk with Jacob Albam I headed
once more for Vienna. I wondered if this would be
my last rendezvous with the Russian secret agents
there. I also wondered if I would ever get back.

I appraised this new gang from Home, or the Center, as tough men of very unstable temper, to put it
mildly. As a precaution, I had sent to the optical-
company mail drop some of the information about
the perlon and Orlon composition that Mikhail had
requested.

This information had been supplied to me by the
FBI and, of course, would prove inadequate to help
them solve their technical problems. Furthermore, I
would have to inform Vladimir and Mikhail that the
material was used not to eliminate skin friction on
jet-plane bodies, but in the tires of such planes. The
FBI had figured out that the Russians had been having both sorts of trouble with their jets, and someone
along the line had got them confused.

Experience had taught me one thing. Bosses nowhere appreciate being told that they have made a ludicrous mistake. This was truest of the tough sort of bosses that that pair of Russian hoodlums were.

This was bad enough. But I had failed to bring Abram back with me, or even a report on Slava. About all I could tell them was that Albam was ready and willing to go to work. And he was probably too old to be of much use.

I met Vladimir on the night of March 26, 1955. He picked me up at the Tabor Theatre, then drove me for hours around Vienna, in and out of the Prater, while we talked. Needless to say, it was not a happy ride for me. Each time Vladimir heard something he did not like he either stepped on the gas or jammed on the brakes, stopped the car, and turned to me menacingly.

I did not try to soften my account of Soble's reaction to my announcement that he must come to Vienna with me without any more foolishness. "That man would not even go as far as New York with me," I said. "He is bitterly disappointed at not getting the money he needs."

"Did you lend him money?" demanded Vladimir, stamping on the gas so hard the car all but jumped into the air.

"Not a penny," I said, virtuously.

"Do you think he would have been more cooperative if we had sent him the money?"

"I have no doubt of it, even though Belova says Abram told him he quit a year and a half ago in Switzerland, gave a contact there fifteen thousand dollars, and also announced he was through working for Home."

"Working for *what?*" roared Vladimir, angered that I hadn't said "Center." This time he jammed on the brakes so abruptly that I was almost pitched head first through the glass.

Now all this was being done deliberately to rattle me, of course, and I must admit that Vladimir succeeded quite well in this aim.

"Working for what?" he repeated.

"Pardon me," I replied, meekly. "Working for the Center."

Starting the car again, Vladimir accused me of getting mixed up on the perlon-and-Orlon assignment. He said that what I had brought concerned the landing gear of jet aircraft, though I had been asked to find out what the United States Air Force was using to preserve the plexiglass surface of the canopies of their jets. I denied this, insisting I had brought back precisely the information I had been assigned to get.

Fortunately for me, the FBI had furnished me with some information about the manufacturing of the canopy materials. These were made, I now said, at the plant of the Kellogg Company in New Jersey.

"And they are also tested there?"

"No," I declared. "They are tested at Wright Field, in Dayton, Ohio."

"How do you know *that*?"

"My informant was General Burke of the United States Air Force. He is an old friend of mine. He told me all this at dinner in New York. I was taking him to a show that night, called *Silk Stockings,* a musical comedy." (I gave Vladimir the real name of the general, which, incidentally, is not Burke.)

At this point Vladimir stopped the car and gave me a pencil and a piece of paper. "Write down," he said, "exactly what he told you."

Obediently I wrote, "After the show, General Burke and I conversed. I found out from him that the Air Force uses Orlon and perlon in supersonic planes, not to combat air friction, but to prevent blowouts in tires when aircraft land at high speeds. The Orlon and perlon are woven into the fabric of the tires. As far as the friction in the air is concerned, other so-called 'hard plastics' are used in the transparent glass canopy that is over the pilot's head. Without these hard plastics the heat causes the material in the canopy to bubble. This, of course, obscures the pilot's visibility."

On reading this, Vladimir asked, "Does General Burke have stock in the Kellogg Company?"

"Could be," I answered.

I next handed him a one-page letter I had received from Keith Glennan, confirming an appointment with me. He thought this document was important enough to pass on to Moscow. But he was less impressed by my report on my evening with Jane Foster. "Slang blames much of her troubles on her husband's loud mouth," I told him. "Not having the code word she wanted from me, she refused to believe I came directly from you, and not Abram. Slang has always been suspicious of me because I have not this proof I'm working for the Center."

If this interested Vladimir, he gave no hint of it. He continued to praise and denounce me, alternately, until he dropped me off near my hotel.

I was greatly relieved at our next meeting, in the Prater. He said he had communicated all my messages to Mikhail in Moscow and now had the comments on my work. Mikhail was, of course, bitterly disappointed over my failure to deliver Soble. But my information on the tires was a good start. They now wanted the composition and the technology of the tire cords, and more information on the hard plastics for the canopy. Moscow also wished me to approach one of our greatest atomic scientists who had just been unceremoniously relieved of his post with the government. I was to point out to this famous man that in Russia scientists had much more freedom and, if defectors, were treated in a much more lenient fashion than in "the Fascistic United States"!

As had happened so many times, I also had to listen to a lecture on "Current Events and Their Significance," together with the usual platitudes about Marxism's showing up the pitfalls and corruption of capitalism for the disgraceful things they were.

Like the other secret agents I had talked to, Vladimir disliked being sent to the Far East, an assignment he was expecting. He explained that the Chinese were forever demanding more arms and the Soviet representatives had endless difficulties trying to please them. Even the old smoothie, Malenkov, he said, found it almost beyond his abilities to get along with Chou En-lai. Molotov and Mikoyan also had failed, he said, in their relations with the Chinese, but he thought well of the chances that Khrushchev, Zhukov, and Kaganovich would succeed with Moscow's "Oriental partners."

Mikhail Petrovich was in Vienna early in the following month and I had the tiresome job of going over all the same ground with him that I had covered with Vladimir. Mikhail proved much more forgiving than Vladimir over the Orlon-perlon mixup, and also thanked me warmly for bringing the true picture of Soble's attitude, no matter how bitterly disappointing it was.

"How, by the way, did he react to the news that Korotkov has been eliminated?" he asked.

"It completely demoralized him."

"Ah!" he sneered, "a Korotkov lover. Our Abram is a cooked goose."

Because the FBI had asked me to keep the door

open for Soble if I possibly could manage it, I said, "I do not think that even now Abram is lost to us."

Mikhail was not even mildly interested. "The Center can be relied on to make the right decision about him," he told me with finality. He told me to stay away from Soble, and also from Albam. He then asked, "What about Slava's report?"

I had no recourse but to tell him that Slava apparently was insane much of the time and that his report existed only in Abram's imagination.

"Then stay away from Slava also, of course," Mikhail said. "Meanwhile the Center will be pondering what to do with the old and new groups in the United States."

He added that he had an assignment for me that would keep me busy on my next trip there. It was highly commendable that I had learned what I had so far from such a great military leader as General Burke. But this time he wished to make certain that I understood precisely what the Center wished me to find out. He insisted that I memorize everything he said, instead of putting it down on paper.

Mikhail deeply regretted our misunderstanding. He said that he thought the world of me. He then asked abruptly, "Have you brought along your checkbook?"

This frightened me, because I didn't know the purpose of his question. When I produced it he examined it as though he had never seen one before. He kept pumping questions at me. He wished to know all about the stubs, the drawing of checks, the cashing of them, when and where you could cash them, who would accept them, and other elementary facts Americans learn in grammar school. After absorbing my answers he said brightly, "I see your bank is the Crédit Suisse in Zurich." He handed the checkbook back to me. "Now, if you please, sign four checks and give them to me."

"To what amount?" I asked.

"Oh, I will fill out the amounts later on."

I could see my reputation as a millionaire vanishing right there. "You'd better be careful of the amounts. There isn't much money in that account."

"Oh, I won't make out any check for more than a small sum, say two thousand dollars. And we will reimburse you for whatever money we borrow from you in this way."

I swallowed a lump. "If altogether the four checks amount to more than a thousand," I said, "they won't be honored. That is about all I have in that bank now."

"Why not put some of your other money there, Djon?" he asked to my great embarrassment.

I had to confess that I could not do that at the present time because all my cash was tied up in my various film, mining, and optical companies.

"It is dangerous for me, Comrade," I argued, "to have money transferred in this way to a fellow conspirator. And I'd better have the name of the person to whom you are going to give these checks in case the bank calls me for confirmation."

He laughed that off, and I could think of no way to avoid signing and handing over the checks. But I did ask him not to draw more than $300 on any of them. I numbered the checks consecutively. As soon as I got the chance I hurried to Zurich, where I gave Siegfried Mahler, director of the bank, the numbers of these checks and asked him to see that none were cashed if drawn for more than $300. I am sure the poor man was bewildered, not understanding how checks signed by me could be drawn in larger amounts than I wished. And it was hardly a matter I could explain.

I could not tell whether my reluctance to give Moscow carte blanche with my money was going to endanger my life. But I was aware that the Center might decide at any moment to wash its hands of me along with Soble. The vital question then was whether they would label me "To be liquidated" or "To be forgotten."

I learned that the Center was through with me when I returned to Vienna in May after a quick trip home. On the tenth I had an appointment with Vladimir but he failed to show up. On the next day a stranger approached me. When we completed the "Paul Scott" parol he asked, "Have you completed your most important assignment?"

I shook my head. "I was not in the United States long enough for that, but I will be sure to do that on my next trip."

"Unless you complete that assignment," he told me, "and within the next few months, you will have no reason to get in touch with the Soviets again."

"I would like to speak to Vladimir about that," I said, "or better still, Mikhail Petrovich."

"I am sure you would," he said, and walked off. I never saw him again.

As soon as I could safely do so I jotted down this description of him: thirty-two or thirty-three years old, 155-160 pounds, five feet eight, blond with very curly hair parted on the left side, gray-blue eyes, clean-shaven, homely, having large ears and a mouth full of gold teeth. He had no hat and was wearing brown shoes and a khaki trench coat.

The next day Siegfried Mahler telephoned me, saying that a man had attempted to cash one of my checks at the bank's branch in Lucerne. The check was made out for $2000. The man appeared to be an Englishman and gave the name Leland John Gladwin. He was told to return in a few days, after the bank had communicated with me, but never did.

Though it looked as though the jig might be up, I wrote again on July 1 to the optical company from New York. In this letter I claimed to be making progress toward discovering the secret formula for weaving perlon and Orlon in the landing tires of the Air Force jet planes. Before I left for Europe I had some of this information and enough on the manufacture of the hard plastics to cover myself, though naturally not enough to help the Communists.

On this trip I telephoned my contact's number—U-47306—several times. Vladimir came to the phone only once. All he said was that until I had some progress to report concerning my "important assignment," it would be a waste of time to try to contact Mikhail Petrovich.

Though I announced that this might be my last trip to Vienna, I was unable to contact Vladimir. I continued to call U-47306 repeatedly through most of that summer. I finally saw him accidentally when my car bumped into an Opel he was driving. I held up my forefinger to indicate to him I would like to see him that night. He shook his head, holding up two fingers. I interpreted this to mean he would meet me the following evening instead, which he did. He was at the Tabor at the usual time, six p.m. He walked away on seeing me and permitted me to catch up with him when he was sure we were not being followed. When I complained bitterly of having to wait so many weeks before seeing him he said that I was not to worry, and that after this when I called I would have no difficulty in reaching him. I said, as though heartbroken at the idea, "Possibly you don't need me any more. Is that the reason I've been having trouble reaching you?"

Vladimir shrugged and said, "There will be thousands of more chances." He dropped me a grave warning. I had recently been shadowed by orders of the Center. "You did not report to us your visit to Herr Waldbrunner." Waldbrunner was a Socialist who was then minister of reconstruction in Vienna.

"What chance did I have to report anything? You fellows didn't even answer the phone when I called."

"Herr Waldbrunner is a very interesting man," said Vladimir thoughtfully. "He speaks Russian well, was once Austrian ambassador to Moscow. Even more significant, he has recently been in the United States." In a sharp tone of reproof he demanded, "Now, Djon, what was the purpose of your visit?"

"If you are so efficient that you shadow me," I said in a surly tone, "you should not have to ask that. You should be efficient enough to know why I went to see him."

Vladimir pretended to take my annoyance as a great joke. "Ah, Comrade," he said. "You know too many people but do too little for the Cause. Now what progress have you made in your assignment?"

I pointed out that in this trip also I had been able to spend only a few days in the United States. I did manage to see my friend General Burke, but I had been able to get little information during our brief interview. The general had told me that the military only draws up specifications and awards contracts. This was why he was not fully acquainted with all the manufacturing details of the jets' landing gear. And I had not wished to arouse the general's suspicions by persisting when he was obviously reluctant to tell me this military secret.

Vladimir told me to keep working on the Orlon-and-perlon formula. "But you can forget the plastics," he added. "We have already obtained all the information we require on those—from other sources."

Vienna was being returned to the Viennese that summer. With the four powers pulling out, Vladimir said, his group would move elsewhere, though he himself would be stationed at the Russian embassy. I could reach him by calling the old number. If I called before ten a.m., he would know I wanted to meet him at the Tabor at six p.m. that day. If I called after ten, that would mean I would be there the following evening at six.

But when I was in Vienna during October the phone was answered by a stranger who denied Vladimir was in town. Instead he suggested that I go to Moscow for the Christmas holidays. "You will be welcomed there," he told me. "You will be welcomed by all your friends there."

"I'll see if I can change my plans and go," I said. Three days later I called to say that due to pressure of business affairs I was unable to make the trip.

This stranger knew that I had moved from my hotel to a *pension* and asked for my new address. I replied that I had never heard of addresses being given in this fashion over the telephone. All he wanted, he said, was confirmation of the telephone number. The stranger then asked me to be in Vienna at the beginning of the new year. He also instructed me to write no more letters to the optical company. "If you are no longer able to maintain contact with our representatives, we will be able to find you."

"Find me where?" I asked.

"Either here in Vienna, or at your home in the United States."

During the next three weeks I was unable to arouse anyone at that number. Was I out? Was I through? On Christmas Day I was in Vienna and tried again. After many phone calls I finally got an answer. "This is Riabov," I said. "I would like to speak to Vladimir."

"When can you go to Moscow?"

"I cannot say right now."

"You *must* say."

I started to tell him the reasons, but before I could say anything further he hung up. My repeated calls to the number after that failed to get any response at all.

But one morning at eight I was awakened at my room in the *pension* to which I had moved. It was the maid summoning me to the telephone.

"This is Riabov," said still another voice that was strange to me.

Whoever it was had got his signals mixed. But when I explained that I was Riabov, he seemed to get more confused than ever. He had started speaking in German, but now he switched to Russian.

"When are you going to the Center?" he said.

"I will not be able to go."

"Then you will have to wait for your next assignment," he said.

"What other messages have you for me?" I said.

"None. I have only orders to make the arrangements for you to go to Moscow—when you decide to go."

"I will call the number in a few days."

"No, Riabov," he said. "Do not call. You will get calls from us wherever you are, wherever you go. Wait for them. Wait." With that he hung up.

If I got no more of these mysterious calls during the next ten weeks, I think it may have been because I was doing so much traveling, and all by air. I made stops in Munich, Zurich, Johannesburg, and Paris, and it was almost mid-March before I was back in Vienna once more.

Another stranger called then—on March 10. All he said was, "We will meet—some place—in—"

"When? Where?"

"In the near future." With that he hung up.

I was beginning to think that perhaps the time had arrived for me to go home for good, and by home I don't mean Moscow. Less than two weeks after this there was a call from still another voice strange to me.

"Why not go to Moscow, Djon?" this man said. "People all over the world are there. Many of your friends are there, a great many. Would you not like to see your friends there?"

"I would like to talk to you about it personally," I said.

"That can be arranged," he said.

"Soon?"

"Yes," he agreed, "very soon."

But I never heard from him again.

The next person who called had a voice not entirely strange to me, but I could not quite place it. "We have an assignment for you," he said. "We want you to find out something for us. It is work you are suited for. You will get your orders soon."

On that same day, April 1, I got a letter from Jack Soble, who had got my Vienna address from my son. He was writing to announce that they had decided to settle in New York permanently, come what may. He was looking forward to seeing me. "There are things to talk over, many things."

Eager as I was to return to New York to see him, I waited a month in Vienna for the promised assignment.

It never came. There were no more provocative and mysterious phone calls, either.

I was back in New York late in May, and Jack

visited me at the Savoy-Plaza. But, as always, he refused to stay there, and we took a walk in Central Park. If he had looked bad before, he now looked like a man completely whipped.

"You once expressed interest in the Trotskyites and Mensheviks, didn't you?" he asked.

I nodded, and listened as I had never listened to anyone else in my life. Was the long ten-year wait over at last?

He took a long time to tell his story, but here is the gist of it. Years before, he had worked with a man named Mark Zborowski. This was at the time Zubilin was still running the underground network in the United States. Zborowski had been sent here to check on the Trotskyites and managed to become a member of their organization.

What terrified Jack now was that Zborowski had recently been questioned by the FBI, which Jack suspected had been following the other man for a long time. He felt that the FBI might have been put on Zborowski's trail by a former Soviet diplomatic attaché named Barmin or Bramin, who had come to the United States after defecting from the Party. This second man, Jack believed, was now working "completely for the Americans" and knew much about Zborowski, and hence probably much about him, as they had exchanged "tons of messages" and had frequent meetings down through the years.

Lately Jack had been waking up each morning dreading a call from the "three-letter organization." It had not come, so now he felt that Zborowski had not told very much to the FBI. But he wished me to urge Moscow to get Zborowski out of this country before he had a chance to tell all that he knew. He pressed me to urge the Communists to lose no time about it.

So far as Jack himself was concerned, getting back his American passport had become the important thing in his life. He had written about it to the State Department twice during the past month, but had got no satisfactory answer. In view of this, he was willing to accept the fake Soviet passport I had said I could get for him when he was living up in Canada. His talk was getting wilder and wilder. He next said that Moscow should send him the fake passport, and also $5000 for expenses. He thought he would have a group picture made of Myra, Larry, and himself so they could all travel on the one document.

He had been so hard up that recently he had humiliated himself by asking Alfred K. Stern for a loan. Stern, he explained, was living with Martha in Mexico City. They were making a fortune there by loaning out money at high interest rates. And they were afraid to come back to the United States. "After I humiliated myself that way, he refused me the money. He refused politely, I must say. Now, don't you see that Moscow is my last hope?"

He had been studying Spanish, he said, and was now willing to go anywhere Home wanted. He was ready to do anything, to tell anything they wanted to know. Knowledge of Spanish would make him a useful secret agent in the Argentine or any other South American country.

"What can I do" I said. "You've never told me a story that made any sense. Or one I could pass on to them that they believed. Give me that story now." To get him started, I informed him that I had learned he had sold his factory in France to a Frenchman. And now Jacques Ajer was the plant's general manager.

Jack was not so distracted that he could not give me some more of the old double-talk he had been feeding me for years. The money he got for the factory, he said, had all gone into the Montreal brush company. The one thing new he told me was that Ajer was sore at him. "That is because when I left," he said, "I took with me all of the factory's correspondence with our German customers, also their addresses."

A few days later Jack came to my room at the Savoy-Plaza at six p.m., and wrote six more letters for me to take to Vienna for him. He used the hotel's stationery.

There was little new in them. The first, nine pages long, described his passport troubles, starting in 1952 when he left France. His alibi was that he had done nothing only because he could get no instructions from Moscow. He had figured out how to get to South America without a passport. He would go to Mexico or Cuba, where none was required, report to one of the Russian diplomats in Havana or Mexico City, and proceed to wherever he was ordered to go.

The second letter, thirteen pages long, summed up his financial troubles. In this he insisted that he had been sent no money from Moscow since 1947, despite being told during that same year that his salary was being raised to $900 a month. He did admit that he had been given money to pay the other Comrades who worked with and for him and also to build his factory. This he had sold for $20,000, but all this money had been lost in the Montreal brush business because the United States ban on Chinese and Russian bristles stopped even the disguised ones from getting in.

The third letter, two pages, explained that he had not paid his Party dues because Korotkov had promised they would be paid for him.

The fourth letter, nine pages, gave reasons why

Moscow must take action to get Zborowski out of the country. In this he said there was a chance that Zborowski, whom he referred to as "the Polack," had a wife and a baby, and might be working for the FBI. Yet he was convinced, not having been picked up himself, that Zborowski had not told the FBI everything and would be glad to leave the country.

The fifth letter, eight pages, named all the collaborators who had worked for him in the past, including the insane Slava and the Sterns, and said some of them were awaiting instructions.

The sixth letter, two pages, reminded Moscow that he had a good oral and written command of Russian, German, French, and Spanish which would make him valuable to the Party anywhere in South America.

Each letter was signed "Peter."

Before leaving, Jack had made me promise that the moment I was given the money he wanted I would deposit it in his name at the Crédit Suisse in Geneva. When I asked him for the family group photo he wanted pasted in his fake passport, he said he would not need it until he got to Cuba or Mexico.

In Vienna I was met with the same chilly reception that I had had the last time. On June 10 a call came to me in Vienna. The man on the phone said, "When will you be ready?" On finding me evasive he said he would wait until October to get together with me. When I pressed for an immediate meeting because of Abram's letters, the caller said these were of no interest to him whatever, and hung up.

I flew to London and back. On June 22, there was another call from another stranger. "Are you ready to go?" Again I spoke of the papers in my possession and said, "I have explained about them to the man who called before."

"I have nothing further to say to you until October," he replied, and hung up.

I kept trying through June and most of July. But there was no answer to phone calls. On July 23 I got a desperate letter from Jack, asking me to take immediate action. There was a P.S. from Myra; she hoped I was all right and asked that I give them a decision soon.

Back in New York in August I did not have the heart to tell Jack that I had been unable to get anyone in the underground to accept his letters and had put them in a safety-deposit box in the Zurich branch of the Crédit Suisse.

When I saw him the first thing he asked was, "Who did you give my letters to? Was it the right man, Boris, are you sure it was the right man?"

"A minor individual," I said, with a shrug.

That drove him frantic. "My life story," he cried, "and you give it to a minor individual! What did he look like, this fellow? How do you know he was a responsible person—"

I cut him short by pointing out how often he had entrusted important documents to mailmen and others when unable to get in touch with higher-ups. That quieted him down a little. He said that he understood I would not betray him; it was only that the letters were such dynamite.

Then he sat down and sadly reviewed his prospects. Again he said he doubted that Zborowski could have told the FBI too much. "If he had, I would have been questioned by them by now, wouldn't I?" he asked.

But he still had plans if everything failed, he said; he could always go to Mexico and get in to see the Russian ambassador there. "I'd tell him *everything*, and he would arrange to send me to Moscow. After all, my services are still valuable to Home. After hearing my story they might even give me diplomatic papers and I could fulfill my lifelong ambition of living in Buenos Aires as a member of the diplomatic staff there."

As I looked at him I marveled that the instinct for survival in this battered, bruised, doomed man was still so strong. He just would not admit he was a goner. He was a fighter who could not quit. I had to respect that, if nothing else, in Jack.

"This country has become hell to live in," he told me that day. "Oh, *they* will take me back, Boris, they must, they will," he said, near to tears. "I am, after all, a true revolutionary. No man can deny that."

I told him I would be back in Europe by the end of the following week. Before I left New York, Jack wrote more letters which he asked me to deliver for him, one of them twenty-six pages long. Not one said anything new.

I put these letters with the others in my safety-deposit box in the Zurich bank. At the moment I was planning a new business project that fascinated me— a film series about the achievements of twenty-one European scientists who had won the Nobel Prize. I spent five weeks visiting some of these distinguished men, who are among the world's most adventurous thinkers and doers. They proved to be gentle people, all of them, the *crème de la crème* of humanity. Talking to them was like breathing fresh air after living for years in the sewer of the espionage underground.

Not until October 8 did I get back to Vienna. Nobody answered my repeated calls to the old number, so I wrote a postcard to Jack, who had been cabling me almost every other day. All I could think of to say was, "No luck yet, but will keep on trying."

After air-mailing this I went to the Soviet consulate at Argentinerstrasse 27. I managed to get in to see the consul but I could not even make him understand what I was talking about. Next I did something rash and dangerous. The Communists had warned me almost from the beginning against approaching any Soviet embassy. Also I had not forgotten the scathing abuse showered on me by Zubilin when I sought him back in the forties at the embassy in Washington.

Nevertheless, I just barged into the Russian embassy in Vienna and demanded an audience with the ambassador. I spoke like a man who was entitled to one. I gave my name as Riabov and said I had an important message for His Excellency. I was taken to a large room and locked in there. As the attendant locked the door, I could hear him rattling the knob to make sure I could not get out.

I was just beginning to regret my impulsiveness when a key turned in the lock. The doorman came back and said, "Someone will be here to see you in just a few moments."

The man who appeared was blond and slightly bald, with very pale blue eyes. He had the sort of cynical smile that turns one's heart to ice. "Comrade Riabov," he said, "come this way, if you please."

He led me into another, larger room, and closed the door behind me. "Give me the message," he said.

"Are you the ambassador?"

That seemed to amuse him. As he shook his head he smiled again, but there was no more warmth in the smile this time than before.

"I wish to give these to His Excellency personally," I said.

"He will get them," he promised.

I then produced a large brown envelope containing the letters. I took out each letter and showed him the names I'd written on each one—Korotkov and Mikhail Petrovich.

"The right persons will get these!" he said. "Come back on November eleventh for the answer."

From Vienna I continued my visits to other Nobel scientists—in London, Paris, Berlin, and Munich. I wrote Jack from London that my stay in Europe would last longer than I had anticipated. This would, he knew, mean that I had given his letters to the Russians, and was awaiting a reply.

I tried to get back to Vienna on November 11, but was a day late. After failing to get an answer from a telephone call to the old number, I went to the Russian embassy by taxi, arriving there at eleven o'clock in the morning.

This time another man saw me, a black-haired fellow in his late thirties. He introduced himself as Vadim and said he was sorry he could give me no answer. He explained that the trouble the Soviet Union was having with the Hungarian counter-revolutionaries had upset all routine.

"Could you return tomorrow at the same time, Riabov?" he asked.

I could and I did. "You are not to meet Peter again, Riabov," Vadim said, quietly. "Not under any circumstances."

So this was it. All that letter-writing, all that agonizing weighing of words, all those conferences with Myra and myself, all that scrambling and shifting and pleading had got Jack Soble nowhere. And, with his usefulness to Moscow over, so perhaps was my usefulness to the United States over. But I thought it best to ask Vadim, "What about me?"

"You are to hold yourself in readiness for another assignment during the last week in January. Show yourself by appearing in front of the Opera House. If no one contacts you, go to the rear of the Opera House and stand there near the Sacher Hotel."

Mikhail Petrovich had sent me greetings, he said, and he suggested that I not tell anyone that I was in Vienna or had been in the embassy. He advised me to leave Vienna at once, if possible.

I left next day, stopped over in Paris, and spent almost a week vainly trying to get in touch with Jane Foster Zlatovski. I reached New York in late November, but then had to hurry off to California on urgent business. It was not until December 6 that I was in New York again and telephoned Soble. He came to my room in the Hotel Savoy-Plaza. I told him that I had been instructed not to communicate with him. The Soviets would do that when they saw fit.

This seemed to satisfy him, which surprised me, though by now he was reduced to clutching at even the shadow of any straw of hope. He said that the same thing had happened to him in Paris in 1947. He had lost his contact and had asked Albam to establish a new one for him. Albam had reported orders not to talk to him again, and "they" had got in touch with him when they knew it was discreet.

He did ask if the Soviets had hinted that they would grant him any financial assistance, and I had to say no. He spoke again of going to Mexico City and forcing matters at the embassy there. His boy was seventeen now, and eligible for the draft. "I do not want him to serve in the United States Army!" he said.

I carried a final letter from Jack Soble for the Center when I went back to Europe on December 14, 1956, to try to complete my plans for the Nobel Prize scientists' film. On New Year's Eve I was invited with some other theatrical men to a screening of a picture starring a remarkable new performer, a comedian named Brockman.

After the screening, which took place in East Berlin, I met a cameraman I had known in Paris. He was Vladimir Povsner, who was then running all film activities in East Berlin. He suggested we have dinner and promised to call me. When he did phone he said another man, whom he had introduced to me after the screening, wished to come along.

I said I would be delighted if he joined us. But the next day Povsner's secretary telephoned. "Povsner will not have dinner with you!" she said. Before I could reply she slammed down the receiver.

This was a warning if I ever heard one. I could only assume that Povsner had been tipped off that I was poison as far as the Communists were concerned, and that he would be crazy to be seen having dinner with me.

But this posed the question of how safe it was for me to keep the rendezvous arranged for me in Vienna during the following week, the last week in January. Were my suspicions that I had become a marked man justified? I could not be sure, but I was careful to keep out of the East Zone during the four days it took me to complete my business in Berlin.

The more I thought of it the more frightened I became. In the end I fled to Munich. I waited there, trying to decide what to do. At seven a.m. on the day before the rendezvous, I was awakened by footsteps in the corridor. My heart started pounding like mad.

The feet stopped outside my door.

Was this where I would meet my end? In a room at the Hotel Bayerisherhof in Munich? Someone banged on the door. I tried to stop breathing. The banging resumed. Then it abruptly stopped. As I held my breath I saw the knob slowly turn—and thanked my stars I had not neglected to lock the door.

Next I saw a long, thin envelope thrust under the door. I got out of bed and tiptoed over. I held my breath again as I bent over and picked it up. It was a cablegram. I listened at the door, not having heard anyone leave. Was it a trick?

Trembling like a man with the ague, I walked to the bathroom to open the envelope. I did not care to risk making a noise even by ripping open the envelope in the hotel bedroom.

There was only one word in the cable, which was from "my secretary" in New York: CINERAMA. It was the code word by which the FBI had promised to warn me of danger!

That same day I was on a Pan-American plane bound for New York. My two FBI agents were at La Guardia Airport to greet me.

As I stepped off the plane and joined them, the older one said, "Thank you, Mr. Morros! And now you can go back to your old trade of making movies. We are arresting Jake Albam and Jack and Myra Soble today. So we will not need you any more, except as a witness at the trial."

What they had neglected to mention was that I was the government's only witness against the members of the Soble spy ring. However, the evidence I had amassed under the FBI's direction was so damning that none of the three cared to risk standing trial after being indicted by a Federal Grand Jury. Of the six counts in the charge, one—conspiring to transmit secret United States defense information to Soviet Russia—carries the death penalty. After the guilty pleas were accepted by Federal Judge Richard H. Levet, the Sobles' attorney, George Wolf, explained that Jack and Myra had insisted on throwing themselves on the mercy of the court because "they had a burden they wanted to get rid of."

In May 1957, Jacob Albam and Myra Soble were sentenced to five and a half years each. Sentence on Jack Soble was postponed until September.

Jane Foster Zlatovski and George Zlatovski were also indicted on July 8 for conspiring with Russia against the United States. But, though they expressed great indignation in Paris at "the absurdity and injustice" of this, they refused to come back to New York to clear their names. And United States Attorney Paul W. Williams and his chief assistant, Thomas B. Gilchrist, Jr., were unable to extradite them because French law treats espionage as a political instead of a criminal offense.

On September 8, similar charges against Alfred K. Stern and Martha Dodd Stern resulted in their indictment by the Grand Jury. The Sterns had been living in Mexico City shortly before that. When subpoenaed to appear before the Grand Jury in New York, Alfred and Martha agreed, and even accepted $967 for transportation expenses from the Federal authorities. Instead of coming to New York they vanished. It was rumored that they had paid $10,000 for Paraguayan passports for themselves and their twelve-year-old-adopted son, Robert. In the interim between the subpoena and the indictment, they had been able to transfer over a half million dollars' worth of securities from the United States.

As it turned out, the Sterns had flown to Amsterdam, and from there to Prague. "Our hope of bringing them face to face with a court now seems to have vanished," said Mr. Williams on hearing this news.

That same month Jack Soble was sentenced to

seven years in federal prison. Judge Levet, in impos-
ing this sentence, announced that he was reducing
the sentence of Myra Soble to four years and of Jacob
Albam to five, as a reward for their cooperation with
the federal authorities.

Some time earlier, the New York *Herald Tribune*
had published an editorial under the heading, "Mr.
Morros Turns the Tables." This said that my story
"has all the authentic E. Phillips Oppenheim touches
—code messages; contacts with agents in New York,
Munich, Vienna; secret discussions in Moscow itself;
bodyguards and narrow escapes. And it also has con-
crete results in the conviction of Soviet spies in this
country and an intimate view of Soviet operations
everywhere. . . . Mr. Morros has given some high
spots of his exciting story to the press with a gusto
that makes light of the shadow under which he has
lived. . . . But on the record he has served his country well, by turning the tables on a shrewd and dangerous band of conspirators."

But Alfred K. Stern, turning up in Prague suddenly, begged to differ. He declared I was merely a
publicity hound, and added, "What a reflection on
the government of the United States that it is building up such a sordid character, trying to make him
a hero to the American people!" I, of course, was
"the sordid character." And Alfred added, "When we
have an opportunity to examine the recent statements
and charges, we may issue a longer statement and
further explain the motives behind these fantastic
accusations. In the meantime, we are visiting this
peace-loving country and enjoying an interesting and
restful trip."

By that time Congressman Francis E. Walter, chairman of the House Committee on Un-American Affairs, had identified the "atomic couple" as Dr. and

Mrs. Henry Spitz. The Spitzes also declined to return to the United States. Dr. Spitz gave out a statement that the charges against him and his wife were ridiculous.

During 1958, a series of newspaper stories about Martha Dodd Stern appeared. In these she described herself as a victim, along with Alfred, of a United States campaign of "vilification and slander." In Moscow, on January 2, she wrote an article praising the Central Committee under Khrushchev for "easing tensions and establishing an atmosphere of trust" in the Soviet Union. She also praised Moscow's boulevards, its low prices, its cars, and even its weather.

Two months later she went back to Prague and apparently was preparing to make a new literary career for herself there. This daughter of an American ambassador said she had left the United States because she had lived there "in an atmosphere of fear of persecution." When asked how she liked the Communist-dominated Czech capital, Martha said it filled her with enchantment and a feeling of relaxation.

I must say that I'm glad somebody likes it.

I too can relax now. For with my help the Soble spy ring has been destroyed.

And while this book was being written two events occurred which may prove significant in the FBI's continuing fight against the entire Soviet espionage apparatus in this country. One was the grotesque attempt of Jack Soble to commit suicide by eating a large quantity of nuts and bolts in the machine shop of Lewisburg Penitentiary. As he knew at the time he was about to be taken back to New York to appear before a Federal Grand Jury there I can only assume he was trying to escape giving testimony against former Comrades. I strongly suspect that these are members of other Russian spy rings here whose existence he never revealed to me.

The other was the arrest and indictment for perjury of Mark Zborowski, the man Soble had asked Moscow to get out of the country before he "tells all he knows." A fifty-year-old research assistant in anthropology at Harvard, Zborowski was accused by the government of lying when he denied before a Federal Grand Jury in New York that he had met Soble between 1944 and 1947. During those three years the Justice Department charged that the pair had more than fifty meetings. As this book was going to press, Zborowski's bail, originally set at $20,000, had been reduced to $2500 and his trial was indefinitely postponed. Not long afterward Ilya Wolston, Jack Soble's mysterious "Slava," was given a one-year suspended sentence for contempt of court. He had failed to respond to six subpoenas issued by a Federal Grand Jury in New York. Wolston pleaded guilty but gave mental illness as his excuse.

I know nothing of the activities of these two men except what Soble, a confirmed liar, told me. But I do know that the crushing, expulsion, and imprisonment of all Russian secret agents in the entire Soviet espionage system in this country continues. The FBI can be counted on to keep its great work up until none is left.

As for me, the words "Thank you, Mr. Morros!" from one of the Bureau agents, remain the most exciting words I have ever heard on stage, on screen, or in real life, and all the reward I ask for my ten years' work with the FBI.